FAMOUS
SCOTTISH LIVES

FAMOUS
SCOTTISH LIVES

IAN FELLOWES-GORDON

ODHAMS BOOKS

First published: October, 1967
Reprinted: April, 1968
Reprinted: November, 1968

Published for Odhams Books by
The Hamlyn Publishing Group Ltd., Hamlyn House,
42 The Centre, Feltham, Middx.

© Ian Fellowes-Gordon, 1967

MADE AND PRINTED IN GREAT BRITAIN BY
ODHAMS (WATFORD) LTD., WATFORD, HERTS.
T.1268.R2.N.

CONTENTS

CONTENTS

Illustrations

PREFACE

The first book about Scotland was *The Life of Julius Agricola*, written by Tacitus, his dutiful son-in-law. It tells of the days in our first century A.D. when the Romans invaded North Britain. They hacked their way northward, and after two long years their large, well-trained, well-armed, army had got as far as the Firths of Forth and Clyde.

Not exactly a *blitzkrieg*. Indeed, from what Tacitus tells us of his father-in-law's campaign, it was painfully slow and horribly expensive in manpower. Much of Britain in those days was a forest broken up by squelching bog and sudden, unexpected, loch or stream. And it was always as the Roman army cursed its way through bog or stream that the North Britons descended and cut them to shreds.

So after two years of campaigning, Julius Agricola had made it only as far as the south banks of Clyde and Forth. And Tacitus points out, a trifle unkindly, that had he been fighting a unified people instead of a great many mutually quarrelsome tribes, he might never have got there at all.

But if Agricola thought his troubles were over, he was mistaken. The land of high hills beyond Forth and Clyde was inhabited by a tall and terrifying people with hair of a magic redness which to this day can be found only in Scotland. (There are red-headed descendants in plenty of these early Caledonians all over the world from Montreal to Malawi, but the startling hue has faded.) And these red-headed warriors from the mountains were not only the toughest nut Agricola had to crack—fierce, brave and immensely strong—but they had the disconcerting habit of sweeping southward into the lands Agricola had already subdued and starting things up again. He hastily built a line of forts, right across the waist of the country, to stop them.

The Roman legions, and the forts, had a deterrent effect. Indeed, the Highlanders received a salutary lesson at the battle of what Tacitus calls *Mons Graupius*. The name has metamorphosed into "Grampian", and now those rugged hills are about all we have to remind us of the first recorded battle on Scottish ground.

But when Julius Agricola was recalled to Rome the Highlanders broke through his line of forts and entered the lands to the south.

This they have continued to do.

The strange, complex, amalgam of Pict and Scot and Briton and Saxon—and just plain Sassenach—has trickled, surged, and at time exploded over the Border ever since, civilizing the lesser breeds below—or perhaps just adding a little stiffening to a nation of shopkeepers. For although the Scotsmen of today number but a tenth of the United Kingdom population, they comprise more than a fifth of its professional people.

Indeed it has been said that the best thing for our twentieth-century world, and in particular for Scotland, would be for this exodus to speed up. If all these complex people could get away from their homeland and move outwards in some Celtic *Diaspora*, think what might happen: if Baird and Fleming and Reith and Adam and Mary Garden had to get out to perform their wonders, think what five million more might do, sweeping across the globe. The mind boggles.

And then uncomplicated English shopkeepers, bucket-and-spade in hand, trousers rolled to the knee, fishing-rods at the ready, could move in and enjoy themselves—in the process commercializing the place to everyone's advantage, as a vast and splendid holiday camp.

But the Scots would never let them. For they are, as any English government from the time of Edward I can testify, a perverse people. They make, as everyone knows, the finest whisky in the world, and jealously guard the secret. They make a point of demanding so-and-so's brand of it in the pubs and shops and, unlike people in other climes who do the same, they know whether they get it or not.

But only in Scotland is it drunk with fizzy lemonade to drown the taste.

Not, of course, that even a sizable minority would admit to the sacrilege.

Perhaps I just have the wrong friends. But I suppose I have, in Scotland, drunk as many gallons, sweet and fizzy, of our national drink, as in the generally accepted manner. We have loudly demanded so-and-so's brand—not always the same brand, but any of a number of rare and expensive ones found only in Scotland: and then, making sure that we have not been fooled or defrauded, we have mixed it reverently with fizzy lemonade from a screw-top bottle and gulped the lot.

And I have sat with a Scots copy-writer, dedicated to the proposition that cool, un-iced, spring water is the only permitted diluent of the national drink. And as he wrote his deathless prose he drank his Scotch by the tumbler. In pasteurized, homogenized, milk, with a lump of ice floating on top.

But all this is only a prelude—a warning, if you like—against what follows. You must judge for yourself, unless you already know, what the Scots are really like. There is no theme or moral to this collection of them: it is merely the lives set out, sometimes with love, sometimes a little malice, of rather more than thirty entertaining men and women. Not all of them were good, not all were very clever; but I hope you may find their lives as fascinating as I have.

You may feel, reading of Scotland's past and her present, that the Scots are now, more than at any time since the union of the crowns, a separate entity, divorced from the "Swinging Britain" of the south. That, far from being assimilated and "British", an increasing number of them are starting to think of themselves as Scotsmen first. There has always been a strong emotional undertow dragging Scotland back to the past. You may feel that this is not such a bad thing. To many intelligent people of a few years ago, the idea of an aggressive Scottish Nationalism was simply ludicrous: a lot of kilted crackpots, a tenth of the United Kingdom population, expecting to have their own mini-

Army, Navy and Air Force and a seat at the U.N. among the Newly Emergent Nations. And, of course, a prestige international airline of their own, just like the rest. Myself, I found this idea foolish and humiliating. The Scots have contributed greatly to Britain—but it would be nonsense to pretend they got nothing back, that they were not dependent, in a thousand different ways, on the other inhabitants of this island.

But perhaps, taking a look at these thirty-odd men and women—and there will be plenty to disagree with my choice and protest that others greater have been left out and several unworthy put in—you may wonder whether Scotland might not, after all, make a go of it.

That is not my concern. James Watt, Mary Queen of Scots, Sir Henry Raeburn—and the rest—are here because they are remarkable, and entertaining, people in their own right.

I am indebted to many fellow Scots, in particular to my father and my friend Robin Richardson, for their suggestions. And I would like to express my indebtedness, too, to the following publishers who have allowed me to quote from books published by them: Hutchinson Ltd., *Roamin' in the Gloamin'* by Sir Harry Lauder; and *James Lithgow, M ter of Work* by J. M. Reid; Michael Joseph Ltd., *Mary C en's Story* by Mary Garden and L. Biancolli; Duck-w h Ltd., *Keir Hardie* by H. H. Fyfe; and Drummond L ., *Lady Nithsdale and her Family* by H. Tayler.

IAN FELLOWES-GORDON
July, 1967

QUEEN MARGARET
OF SCOTLAND

November in Scotland brings two big Saints' Days. One of them, St. Andrew's, is a feast all over the world in Scottish communities, rivalling, in places, that of the uncanonized Scot we revere at the end of January.

The other belongs to Margaret of Scotland.

It has been said, unkindly, that Margaret was only canonized because there was no competition: Scotland is a land not noted for saintliness. Just as far-flung lands, and those nearer at home, may be rewarded by the elevation of some uninspiring character to a peerage in Her Majesty's Birthday Honours, simply in order that North Mgloppo-land or Little Fiddling be represented, so they hit upon Margaret, the best of a bad lot at a particularly bloody time in Scots history.

And certainly the tale of her life and death is very different from that of other saints who Christianized whole communities and often died for their beliefs. Margaret died in bed, and it is not on record that she really converted anyone to Christianity. She was never persecuted, so far as we know, never vilified. Throughout her life she seems to have been loved, admired, emulated.

Thereby hangs our tale. Queen Margaret of Scotland, Saint Margaret, civilized a country by her example.

Which is considerably more than can be said of the rest of us.

She was a woman whose influence was enormous. And all of it was good.

The story is set in the blood-stained eleventh century, a century roughly bisected in Britain by the arrival of the Conqueror from Normandy. Margaret puts in her first notable appearance immediately after this event, but to get some idea of the person she was, what made her tick, we must go back to well before William's descent on the English coast.

King Edmund II of England—Edmund Ironside—had shared a brief rule with the Dane, Canute, at the start of the century. He died, or was murdered, in 1016, and Canute took over the whole of England. He was determined to hang on to it, to resist any return of an Anglo-Saxon ruling house. Edmund's sons were an obvious threat to this dream, and their guardians decided to get them out of the country for their own safety.

Via Scandinavia and central Europe, they were smuggled to Hungary, a country with a monarchy already famous for its enlightenment: King Stephen was a Christian, and a real one, beside whom the blood-drenched rulers of England and Scotland were savages.

The elder of the two English refugees, Prince Edward, grew up and married Agatha, King Stephen's daughter. Here, in the warmth and civilization of southern Europe, their son and two daughters were born and brought up. They were destined for fame: Edgar would briefly become King of England; Christina, the Abbess of Romsey;

Margaret, with whom we are concerned, Queen of Scotland and a saint.

They were all brought up in the Hungarian castle of Reka, and here they were steeped in the Christian faith. Perhaps the absence of war, of any kind of bloodshed, in this sunny land, made it easier to grow up with one's Christianity intact.

It was in 1056, with King Canute dead and a Saxon king back on the throne of England, that little Margaret was invited to an England she had never known, with parents, brother, sister. The family made their way to the French coast, sailed for London. Soon they were moving up the Thames, noticing the great new church, the Westminster Abbey, which was rising from the marshy ground.

They disembarked, were made welcome. With Canute dead they had nothing to fear, the future could hold nothing but good. They met the Scottish prince, Malcolm, who was ending a long exile in England and would return within the year to be crowned King of Scotland. He was considerably older than Margaret, who was still a child; but when he left London she remembered him.

(His coronation in 1057 is the first Scottish one of which we have record: our knowledge of the Scone Stone dates from that year.)

Time moved on: there was briefly a king called Harold on the English throne, but he, as we know, died at Hastings. Margaret's brother Edgar—Edgar Atheling—was next in line and he was hastily elected. But it was a futile gesture of defiance, with the Norman William consolidating his position; soon Edgar surrendered to him. A return with him to Normandy, then a sudden decision to break completely, dash back to England.

He was a refugee now, a marked man. With his sisters and his now-widowed mother, Agatha, he boarded a ship.

Perhaps they wanted to get to Scandinavia. Whatever their intended destination, they were battered by terrible storms and eventually found themselves still in Britain: wrecked on the shore of the Firth of Forth.

Malcolm—the Malcolm they had met and remembered

nine years before, in England—was king of this strange
northern land: King Malcolm III of Scotland, Malcolm
Canmore—more prosaically, Malcolm Bighead, a straightforward name not covering any abnormality, just a fine and
manly head. He was in his castle at Dunfermline, north of
the Firth, when he learnt that the little party had been
shipwrecked. He made haste to reach them, bringing as
many royal attendants as could be assembled in time: he
also brought their wives, to minister to the ladies.

And so Malcolm and Margaret met again, and, tradition
has it, at St. Margaret's Stone. The courtiers who had
galloped with Malcolm, who knew him as a rough, Gaelic-
speaking chieftain, were surprised to find he spoke English,
too. He spoke it now to these bedraggled victims of the
wreck, huddled round their driftwood fire. He behaved,
too, in a courtly, gracious way they had never seen.

He had been a decade away from the English court. The
child he remembered had grown into this beautiful woman
(never mind that her clothes were soaking, her hair awry:
she was the most beautiful woman Malcolm had seen).

And so they reached Dunfermline. To the Hungarian
Agatha this northern fortress must have seemed the end
of the world, or beyond. Yet her son was safe from the wrath
of William: that was all that mattered.

To Margaret, "Fair Margaret" as the Scots now began to
call her, this was exciting, a challenge. She liked these
rough-hewn men and women straight away, liked their
kindness, their generosity, though she understood not a
word they spoke, and they not a word of hers, whether she
spoke in English, Hungarian or French.

The family was made welcome at the castle. It was little
more than a tower; in fact, it was known as "Malcolm's
Tower"—but whether or not they all lived inside, they
were safe and well cared for. Summer went through
autumn into winter, and soon there was snow piled high
round their tower: Margaret loved it all. In a few years
time she would be a nun. She had planned this from childhood; she wondered where she would take her vows.

King Malcolm had a different idea. He was widowed and

lonely. And now, washed up on the shore of Scotland as if by Divine providence, had come the most beautiful girl he had ever seen; a girl, too, from a royal house. She was from two royal houses, Hungarian and English, and she had a regal grace—and an education—at which he could but wonder. He asked her to marry him. She was shocked. She was delighted. She prayed for guidance.

In 1070, Malcolm III, King of Scotland, married at Dunfermline Margaret, great niece of Edward the Confessor, granddaughter of King Stephen of Hungary, and sister of the rightful heir to the English throne, Edgar Atheling.

A little later Margaret founded the great Dunfermline Abbey which was to play so large a part in Scottish ecclesiastical history. Sadly, nothing remains of the one she built, which must have been completed a year or so before her death in 1093: what remains at Dunfermline was begun a hundred years later. In this church, which she insisted on making supremely beautiful with her own gold, silver and jewels, she placed the Holy Rood she had been given by Saxon forebears. One of these had received it from the Pope two hundred years before. The black case, with its gold and ivory ornamentation, was believed to contain a relic of the true Cross. It later gave its name not only to an abbey at Edinburgh, but to a palace where, hundreds of years later, her descendants would rule over Scotland.

Margaret's Dunfermline Abbey was gutted at the start of the fourteenth century by the English Edward I. He was fighting against both Wallace and Bruce at the time, determined to do all the damage within his power, to bring Scotland to her knees. There were other assaults upon the Abbey: then finally the religious reformers of the sixteenth century destroyed it for ever.

It is hard not to have some feeling of sorrow over the destruction of so much of Scotland's architectural beauty during the sixteenth century.

And certainly Margaret brought beauty to Scotland. She seems never to have rested; to have rushed about her new kingdom, not only building fine churches but organizing what today we would call Welfare. It was an example that startled and impressed the rude Scots of her eleventh century. Not only did this woman insist on beauty everywhere, wherever it was humanly or divinely possible of achievement—but she washed the feet of beggars.

The church to which Margaret gave her life was the old Celtic church, to which she brought ideas and observances from the greater church outside. Scottish Episcopalians tend to see Margaret as invincibly on *their* side against the drabness of the puritans, the sternness of the kirk. But John Knox lived five hundred years after Margaret; circumstances were entirely different; and we can only conjecture what Margaret's feelings about the church of his time would have been. For though she loved beauty and brought it in abundance to her adopted land, she was, above all, a Christian. She would have clung to her beliefs, however bleak the surroundings.

There is a story, accepted as true, that Malcolm saw her disappear each day into the forest and at last grew suspicious. She never seemed to be carrying a basket or anything in which she might put the fruit or flowers or herbs she picked: could she have a lover whom she met there?

Sick with apprehension, at the same time sick with shame at himself for being in its grip, he followed her. The forest path wound here and there and he had difficulty keeping up, without being seen.

At last he reached her. She had stopped; he could tell, because her cloak had been laid aside, on a bush. Tiptoeing, he found the mouth of a small cave, saw her footprints.

He crept in, dog at his side. Then the dog moved ahead, he couldn't call it back. The next thing was his wife's voice talking to it. "Foolish old dog, why have you followed?"

He crept up farther. In the near-darkness he made her out, kneeling at an altar in the rock, a natural ledge.

He stood up. "Why are you here?" he asked. "What do you do in this dank, dark cave?" And yet he knew, and his shame came back.

"I pray, my lord. For Scotland. This is the only place where I can be alone to pray."

But it was not only religion and beautiful churches that interested her. Margaret worked frantically hard to spread craftsmanship over Scotland. She brought in glass-blowers, illuminators of books, makers of fine cloth. She employed teachers to teach reading and writing in the Court circle, ran classes herself for children. She loved children, and her own eight—two girls, six boys—were almost unique in that eleventh century: all reached maturity. Her work for Scottish education, starting with her own children and embracing the whole nation, was great. To this day the Scottish zeal for learning, the widespread facilities for obtaining it, owe much to Queen Margaret. She made her illiterate, well-meaning husband import teachers, not only of reading and writing. arts and crafts, but of foreign tongues. As for embroidery, at which she was expert, she trained girls herself to go out and spread the knowledge. A whole generation of girls learnt these undreamt-of refinements either directly or indirectly from their queen. She taught them to cook, to sew, to look after their children.

She taught Scotland how to bathe.

She was a missionary. And though she was Scottish only by adoption, perhaps the Scottish excellence in that field has descended from her. She was a missionary who tried to spread not only the beauty which she was convinced went with spiritual enlightenment, but also an earthly civilization of well-fitting—even pretty—clothes; decent, well-cooked food; clean skins—to a rude northern race which knew nothing of the refinements of life as lived in other European capitals.

The King moved his own capital from the crude Tower at Dunfermline, across the Forth to Edinburgh, to the mount that overlooked that town.

In addition to her work of teaching, Queen Margaret was one of her country's more able diplomats, and the Kingdom of Scotland basked in unfamiliar peace for years during her reign. But in the summer of 1093 her husband, now over sixty, was invited south to parley with the English king. He agreed, set off.

On the way south he saw a foundation being laid for Durham Cathedral.

When he reached Gloucester, the rendezvous, it was to find to his horror that William Rufus, the English king, had lured him south to make hostage of him: Malcolm turned about, escaped. It was only when he got back home to Edinburgh, was united with his wife, that he realized he must, for Scotland's honour, go back and avenge the insult. He raised a force which included his sons Edward and Edgar, and marched south.

Margaret watched them go. Her own health had failed sadly in the past few weeks, and though the others had little suspicion she was anything more than tired from years of overwork—after all, she was years younger than Malcolm her husband—she sensed she would never see him again.

Malcolm marched south, till he came to Alnwick. Here the castle presented a major obstacle. It was one of the great fortresses of the day and its site, in fact, had been chosen by the Romans. Now it was occupied by the Earl of Northumbria, under orders to stop any northern invader.

Treachery, which was so often the Achilles heel of Scotland, cost Malcolm his life. He might have taken the castle at Alnwick: but one of his own nobles literally stabbed him in the back as they rode towards it.

The dying king was lost in a thicket, as he fell from his horse.

Despite this disaster—which only a few Scots knew of—the battle seemed to be turning in Scotland's favour. Then, English treachery was added to Scottish. The Alnwick garrison sent out a party with a white flag: Malcolm's son Edward advanced to meet them, and a hail of arrows mowed him down.

The battle was lost now, irrevocably, and Malcolm's other son headed home with the news. He rode fast but the journey took four days and when he got to Edinburgh it was to learn his mother was dying.

Already dead Malcolm's brother, Donald Ban, knew the truth, was preparing to march on Edinburgh himself and demand the throne.

Margaret was told the news of her husband's death, the death of her eldest son with him. Then with a last prayer she died.

In no time Donald Ban was besieging Edinburgh Castle. It fell to his forces, and as the invaders marched in Edgar brought his mother's body down the precipitous north face, to safety. He was helped by his younger brothers in an astonishing feat of mountaineering, and Margaret's body was taken in secret to the Forth, to Queen's Ferry. There she was rowed, on her last journey, to Dunfermline, where she was buried.

For her sons and daughters the enemy was no longer an English king, though that one had been responsible for their father's death: it was their own uncle, Donald Ban. In fact, the boys found their way to England and were protected and looked after by William Rufus; the girls went to their aunt, Christina, now Abbess of Romsey.

Years later, Malcolm's remains were brought north and buried beside his wife at Dunfermline. Years after that— a hundred and fifty years after her death—she was canonized.

A complicated, bloody story—with many of the details in doubt, and all of the dates—but typical of its time. And the only beam of light in a sordid century must have been the good and beautiful Margaret of Scotland.

SIR WILLIAM WALLACE

"He was hung in a noose and afterwards let down half-living; next his genitals were cut off and his bowels torn out and burnt in a fire; then and not till then, his head was cut off and his trunk cut into four pieces."

Many things have contributed to the still "half-living" enmity between Scotland and England—perhaps nothing more than this futile sadism on the part of England's Edward I, as described with relish by the contemporary English writer, Matthew of Westminster.

Wallace's head was then stuck on a spear and fastened to London Bridge: it would be joined by those of other Scottish patriots. The quarters of the body were distributed, like the laird's haunches of venison, to three Scottish towns and one in northern England, "for terror and rebuke to all who should pass by and behold them."

This savagery on the part of an English king who boasted his title, "Hammer of the Scots", is remembered to this day. To some Scots, the sightless eyes of William Wallace, Scotland's greatest hero, still look down upon the Thames. They remind them of death to the English, hatred for the English, for all things English. And a devotion to all things Scottish, right or wrong, which perhaps has done as much harm as Edward.

But to start at the beginning.

Scotland's national hero was born in about 1270, possibly in 1274, which would make him an exact contemporary of Robert Bruce. He was the second son of Sir Malcolm Wallace of Renfrewshire, whom today we would call a small laird, a country gentleman. Like many Scottish and English names, his had undergone considerable adjustment. There are over twenty recorded spellings of it, including Wallensis and le Waleys, suggesting that the family was originally Welsh, or had at least lived there. Sir Malcolm and his immediate forebears came from a class somewhat below the nobility, a class who have always exercised a great influence on Scottish thought and Scottish development right from the time of Wallace, through the Reformation (which they mostly accepted, even helped to push through), to the present day.

Almost all of what we know—or think we know—of William Wallace's youth comes from the remembered utterance of old Blind Harry, a sightless minstrel who lived two centuries after the London butchery. He was able, while incessantly contradicting himself over dates and names and places, to build up a repertoire of Wallace Deeds and Wallace History. He travelled everywhere, Blind Harry did, and when he told his tales of heroism, people listened, people remembered.

But we are little concerned with Harry's tales of the Wallace childhood. He was a second son from Renfrewshire, and whether he was twenty-three or twenty-seven in that year he bursts into history in 1297.

As John of Fordun put it buntly in his *Annals*, when those annals reached the year 1297: "In that same year,

William Wallace lifted up his head." There had been no previous mention of the name.

So we may skip his youth and leap to 1296. It is the year before he enters history, but its events must be glanced at in order to place him.

On 28 March, 1296, King Edward, having decided he would deal with the Scots as he had the Welsh, crossed the Tweed. He would show the flag and give them a good lesson. He would start with the town of Berwick.

Now in those days this attractive town was far more than that: it was the greatest seaport in the whole of Britain, with the huge Scots wool trade centred on it, and the riches of Europe pouring back. It had a well-defended castle, but the town itself was unfortified. So, naturally, it was the town that Edward attacked, and utterly destroyed. The resistance was gallant and long, but it had to end. When it did, the butchery that took place was reminiscent of Genghis Khan (whose exploits had taken place but a few years previously). There were soon some sixty thousand corpses rotting in the streets of Berwick, many of them women and children.

Perhaps it was *not* the butchery of Wallace, but simply this behaviour at Berwick, which we may call the most inept piece of Anglo-Scottish relationship in history. If King Edward I had not sacked Berwick on Good Friday, 30 March, 1296, relations between the two countries might well have been different.

And, of course, there might never, at least, in recorded history, have been a William Wallace. So we must count our blessings.

William Wallace now lifts up his head: and he does so by killing the sheriff of Lanark. It seems to have been a Scottish raid under Wallace's command, on one of the hated English garrisons, but the incident has been so garnished over the intervening years that details are hard to assess. Some have claimed it as an affair of the heart, with Englishmen mocking a young woman and Wallace revenging her. Some have asserted that the English sheriff, Sir William Hazelrigg, had burnt down Wallace's house and killed his wife (but Wallace never had one) and Wallace rushed to Hazelrigg's and killed him there.

There is no doubt about what followed. Men from all over Scotland flocked to join the young patriot. By June, 1297, his force was large and growing fast.

What was he like, this young man in his twenties who was soon to embody the spirit of Scotland? According to Blind Harry he was very tall and very strong (though we might not think him tall today). He had piercing blue eyes and fair hair, with the mark of a wound on the left side of his chin. He always looked serious, often looked sad.

The nobles of Scotland, most of whom come pretty badly out of this period of history, made no effort to join Wallace's guerrilla army. The campaign began and was continued under the leadership of country gentry, like Wallace himself and Andrew de Moray, who seized the imagination of ordinary men.

Scotland at the time was without a king, the puppet John Balliol having been taken to England by Edward for what in this age we might call rehabilitation or even brainwashing. Much of Scottish resistance was in favour of John, though the people were divided among themselves. Slowly a few nobles were banding together, inspired by tales of Wallace's example: but resolute action by English forces was making any action by a "Scottish Army" an impossibility. The nobles refused to put up a common front, and as the historian Palgrave describes them, "All the leaders were independent, all intractable. They would neither fight, retire, nor treat by common consent."

On 7 July, 1297, the only well-armed body which could reasonably have been called a Scottish Army capitulated to the English. One of its leaders who surrendered was the Earl of Carrick, soon to be King Robert Bruce, but what was demanded of him was his infant daughter Marjorie, though we have no record that she was ever handed over. Other nobles were imprisoned: the Scottish Army was non-existent.

But Scotland was far from dead. Wallace's guerrilla force had caught the imagination of the people and the country was aflame with patriotism. Thousands, armed with cudgels and staves, and whatever more effective arms they could lay hands on, rushed to join him.

The guerrilla force, Wallace's force, began to attack and destroy English garrisons: one by one they were mopped up: Brechin, Forfar, Montrose, Urquhart, Aberdeen, Inverness; till there remained but one north of the River Forth, the castle of Dundee.

Wallace planned to take this.

He had begun a siege which, without the heavy equipment, the siege engines, which medieval armies required, would be long and slow, when news was received that English reinforcements were on the way. It was a large English force under two of the men Edward had appointed to the highest offices in Scotland, Hugo de Cressingham as Treasurer, and the Earl of Surrey, Governor. It was now marching as fast as it could go, moving north to avenge the recent defeats. As Edward had remarked after the sack of Berwick: "He does good business who rids himself of dirt"; this, again, was the plan: wipe out, obliterate.

Wallace left the siege of Dundee Castle to the citizens of the town. They might not be able to invest the place, but at least they could deny it victuals. He rushed off south at the head of his guerrillas, rushed to head the English off at Stirling.

That town, a gateway to the north of Scotland, had one bridge across its river, the Forth. Wallace rightly concluded that upon this solitary crossing point would depend not only Stirling but perhaps the whole of northern Scotland. If the English took Stirling, Scottish morale, which had soared higher with each success, would plunge. At all costs, he had to hold Stirling.

The odds against him were enormous. The English army was far greater than his own: it was a professional army of Welsh and English, with heavy cavalry. Much of it had seen battle in France, in Palestine, and elsewhere. Against this, Wallace now proposed setting a half-trained, half-armed rabble, consisting almost entirely of foot-soldiers—or at least, men on foot—bearing only the twelve-foot spear.

They were baffled and uncomprehending about refinements like battle-lines, organized deployment, advance or retreat. It would be, as it always had been, every man for himself.

What they did have was a respect and love for their young general.

The bridge (which has been replaced in more modern times: hundreds of years ago) was entirely of wood. It spanned a river twenty-five yards across. The Scots took up position well to the north and waited.

On came the English army, marching from Berwick, marching fast under its commander, the Earl of Surrey. They got there and, as was the custom of the times, messengers were exchanged asking for a Scottish capitulation and forcefully rejecting it. Both sides lay low.

Early the next morning, 11 September, five thousand English infantry with a few Welshmen crossed the narrow wooden bridge. There was confusion at the start, for Surrey was asleep and the advance was ordered without his knowledge. Not a Scot could be seen: the entire five thousand turned round and filed back again.

At this point Surrey arose from his bed, paraded his force and gave the accolade of knighthood to some of his junior officers. He was uncertain and a little worried about what to do next.

As for the Scots, though we have no precise map reference for them, it seems likely they were grouped on hills a little to the west of the famous Abbey Craig, where Wallace's Monument now stands, and were thus separated by a wide green plain of a mile and more from the river and its wooden bridge. They were hidden from the English force. The messengers, who had approached their position to be rebuffed and sent back with a haughty refusal to discuss settlements, had made wild guesses about the Scottish strength. These guesses, hundreds of cavalry, tens of thousands of infantry, coupled with Wallace's message, "Let them come up when they like and they will find us ready to meet them to their beards——" sowed confusion, alarm, in English breasts.

England might still have won the day if the advice of a Scottish turncoat had been taken. Sir Richard de Lundin was serving under Surrey and he now suggested that a part of the English force ford the river at a place he knew, some distance away from the bridge. There, he assured his commander, they could cross "sixty at a time". For some reason—perhaps the general feeling about Scots integrity —this advice was disregarded. The English were ordered over the bridge, and for two long hours they filed over it, led by a gallant knight, Sir Marmaduke de Twenge.

Wallace and his force, up their hill, stood without moving, and watched. The timing of this was the most agonizing of decisions—and Wallace timed it correctly. His force was ludicrously outnumbered, and with each succeeding file of Englishmen north of the bridge, disparity grew. But if he attacked too soon, before enough of the English had crossed over, he would only cripple a part of a larger force. It would then come on, like a wounded tiger, to ravage Scotland.

But what was "enough" of the English force? How many of them were there?

Wallace watched, counted, estimated.

Exactly at the right moment he gave the signal. As Blind Harry relates it, no other man was allowed to blow a horn ("In all the host, should no man blow but he——") and when the electrifying call was heard the Scots force charged, as a man.

Down their hills they came, screaming, vicious spears at the ready. The English watched them. It was a frightening sight, this mass of armed peasantry hurtling towards one, but they would be outnumbered, outfought, just as soon as it was clear what the yelling horde proposed to do.

And before the English realized it, the Scots right wing had seized their bridge-head, cut them off from retreat and from reinforcement. They still outnumbered their attackers, but now there was panic and the Scots force ploughed on, making the most of it. While Englishmen debated which way to turn, whom to obey, men with vicious spears and knives hacked a way among them. Speared horses flung their heavily encased riders to the ground, where they lay twisting like upturned beetles before Scotsmen impaled them. The English infantry rushed in all directions but were slowly forced into a loop of the river just east of the bridge, as Wallace had planned. Here they were speared like pigs, their blood-soaked bodies toppling into the river, dyeing it crimson, toppling on to the fleeing forms of other Englishmen trying to wade and swim back to safety.

Hardly any made it, and yet, with the lightly clad infantry failing in the desperate attempt, one enormously over-dressed knight is reported to have staggered back, leaving his dying horse on the north bank.

England, for the moment, was defeated. The bridge had been severed and set on fire, but the Scots were already pouring over the ford the English themselves had been recommended, pouring over it in their hundreds to despatch the demoralized force on the south bank. Hacking, stabbing, spearing.

Most of the English leaders were killed, including the much-loathed Cressingham. It was an age of savagery, and we must bear this in mind when we consider what was later done to Wallace: he seems to have condoned the flaying of Cressingham's corpse and the distribution of strips of the skin among soldiers, "not as relics, but for hatred of him".

Scots losses were few, but a young man who might some day have become as famous and effective as Wallace himself perished in the battle. He was one of Scotland's bravest, Andrew de Moray.

There is a similarity between the conduct and tactics of this great Scots victory and another, as famous, seventeen years later: the victory of Bannockburn under Bruce.

This victory was the greatest thing in Wallace's life. The remnants of the English fled in panic. Yet we must make exceptions, for the gallant Marmaduke de Twenge refused to essay retreat. ("I drown myself for no man!") He kept a small force of men faithful to him on the north bank, killing all Scotsmen who came near, and somehow managed to escape the carnage which destroyed virtually every other English leader.

Within weeks, the whole of Scotland was free of Englishmen—a state of affairs which has never obtained since. Wallace rushed south, recaptured Berwick. The English garrison of Stirling Castle had surrendered right after the battle of the bridge; that at Dundee as soon as it heard the news. Wallace went over the border, began taking bitter revenge on north England, particularly Northumberland.

He returned, greatest man in Scotland, to be knighted by either the turncoat Earl of Lennox or Robert Bruce, the Earl of Carrick. There have been doubts as to whether he ever *did* receive the accolade, but it is referred to by his contemporaries; in a charter of 1298 he refers to himself as "Sir William Wallace, Guardian of the Kingdom of Scotland and General of the Army of the same——". As for being Guardian of Scotland, he may well have assumed the title for himself—but if William Wallace was not his country's guardian at this moment, there was no one else. Possibly the Earl of Carrick, soon to become Scotland's king: but at the time he had his father a hostage in English hands and would have feared to endanger him.

Once again the nobles of Scotland, perhaps through simple jealousy, refused to side with Wallace. Lord Hailes, the great eighteenth-century historian, tells us: "His elevation wounded their pride; his great services reproached their inactivity in the public cause".

While this was happening, Edward made haste to get back to England, from his campaigning on the Continent. He reached home on 14 March, 1298, having concluded a convenient truce with the King of France, and headed north. His army mobilized about him and the Scots who had dispersed to their homes rallied again to Wallace. But once again there were few Scottish nobles prepared to come out openly for their country's independence. In the next—disastrous—battle, there would be but one Scottish earl, Robert Bruce of Carrick. Wallace's force would once again be the little folk of Scotland: farmers, peasants, small lairds.

Edward's army, when it got to Coldstream and crossed the Tweed on 3 July, was much larger than Wallace's and divided fairly evenly into infantry and armoured cavalry, perhaps seven thousand of each. Wallace today had adopted a policy of strategic retreat, knowing there was already dissension between English and Welsh contingents, knowing, too, there had been trouble in getting provisions up from the south. Not only was there shortage of food for the invaders, but the wine which was an essential to morale had been delayed; the ships which were to bring it were somehow missing *en route*. If Wallace could keep out of sight and lead the English on, they would exhaust themselves in starvation and mutiny. At which point he would destroy them.

His scheme went agley, thanks to two Scottish turncoat nobles, the Earls of March and of Angus, who had sent out a small boy as spy for the English king. He came back to announce that Wallace was in ambush at Falkirk and might attack from behind the English force.

"God be praised!" Edward is supposed to have shouted, "God be praised who has brought me out of every strait! They shall have no need to follow me, for I shall go to meet them, and on this very day!"

And so he did. Controversy still rages over the conduct of the Battle of Falkirk: should Wallace not have gone on retreating, when he knew Edward had found out his disposition? Surely by this method he would have worn out his pursuers? Why did he stand and fight?

Should the Battle of Falkirk have been fought at all?

We have little space for the disaster of Falkirk. Wallace had placed his men in four schiltroms, circles facing outward, long spears at the ready, front rank kneeling to let a rear rank take aim over their shoulders. Between these four clumps were archers: behind them, Wallace's very few cavalry.

This Scots cavalry broke and galloped away as the huge, armoured, English horses charged them. Wallace himself was horsed, and he and a few others stood fast, but it is little exaggeration to say that the Scottish cavalry, outnumbered, out-armed, fled in sudden panic.

The infantry schiltroms held. Within minutes, one

hundred and ten great English horses were piled in heaps around them.

Now it was the turn of the English infantry. Many of these were armed with the new longbow, a weapon which could put an arrow through a suit of armour. Falkirk, like Hiroshima, was fated to be the testing ground of a new weapon, and, as at Hiroshima, the weapon was even more effective than had been expected. A thunder of arrows tore into the schiltroms, and though these held fast for a time, the bowmen took terrible toll. Soon the Scottish infantry was unable to close up because of the piles of dead on each side of each man. They were invaded by the English horses and their armoured knights. It was over.

For Wallace, the greatest hero Scotland had ever had, this was really the end. It has been said, not quite fairly, that he left on the field at Falkirk not only his army, but his reputation as a leader.

And yet this swift butchery was the only victory King Edward had in the whole campaign. It was a tactical victory: strategically, it was an English disaster. But it spelt the end of Wallace.

A few years later he was captured. Edward, desperate to have him in his power, had offered lavish rewards, mingled with dire threats, and eventually, some say, he was betrayed. As Professor Joad might have said, "It all depends what you mean by 'betrayed'", in a shifting, fluid war, with men changing sides. On 5 August, 1305, he was in English hands, near the border.

The trip to London took seventeen days. By the time prisoner and escort reached the English capital all the paraphernalia of a "trial" had been arranged. It was, of course, completely bogus: sentence had been decided and would be carried out: yet it would be necessary that the proceedings be made as public and unpleasant as possible. On Sunday, 22 August, Wallace arrived in London, and the trial began the next morning.

He was not allowed to plead. Indictment; sentence— that was all. The horrors of the sentence were lovingly

Brought up in the sunshine and warmth of southern Europe, Margaret (*left,* in the painting by Correggio), came to Scotland as a young girl by the accident of shipwreck. She had spent a few years in England and had met Scotland's King Malcolm III. Now, fleeing with her brother, her sister and her mother from the invading Normans, she was shipwrecked on the shore of the Firth of Forth. Malcolm came to their aid and soon asked her to marry him. She had planned to be a nun, but she accepted him and devoted the rest of her life to helping his people.

Much of what we know of Sir William Wallace, Scotland's greatest hero, is what has been passed down by the sightless minstrel Blind Harry, who lived two centuries after Wallace's death. This ancient painting, *right,* almost certainly done after the hero's death, does at least show the "piercing eye" his contemporaries noted. It is the face of a leader, a man prepared to give up his life for his country. We know that his hair was fair and that on the left side of his chin—hidden in this painting—there was a long, deep scar. Wallace must have looked like this in the last years of his short life, shortly before being captured by the English and taken south to London. There he was vengefully mutilated before being killed and having his four quarters sent as a warning to three towns in Scotland and one in northern England.

SIR WILLIAM WALLACE FROM AN ANCIENT PAINTING IN THE POSSESSION OF SIR JOHN MAXWELL "POLLOK"

As with William Wallace, we have no contemporary portrait of King Robert Bruce, but this one is probably accurate. It depicts a man—much older than Wallace when he came to fame—who was not only a tough and fearless warrior but a wise and good king. The scene below, almost as famous as the one in which he is supposed to have taken inspiration from a spider, shows him with the same battle-axe, rising in his stirrups at Bannockburn to smash with one tremendous blow the helmet and skull of an English knight.

detailed at the end of the "trial", with ponderous, pompous, reasons for each detail: disembowelling would be for "the immense wickedness which he did to God——" and so on.

Sentence was carried out as soon as the mockery of a trial was over and the condemned prisoner had been dragged through the streets of London on a hurdle to what is now Smithfield. There he was butchered.

A gallant life was over. Though many of Wallace's supporters left him towards the end, he had set fire to the hearts of the great mass of men in Scotland. That fire would never die out. Less than a year later, Robert Bruce, Earl of Carrick, began his own campaign against the English king. And he, being a noble, not a mere commoner like poor Wallace, was able to initiate that campaign by crowning himself King of Scotland.

But that is another story.

ROBERT BRUCE
(KING ROBERT I)

A little to the south of Cherbourg lies a village which once bore the name of Brus. Centuries of mangled spelling and mispronunciation, of the sort which was able to make Elephant and Castle out of Infanta de Castille, or Rotten Row from Route du Roi, has changed this to Brix. There was no French Academy in those days to regulate such things.

Yet this small, unprepossessing village deserves to be held by Scotsmen in as much reverence as many of our numerous national shrines and tourist traps. For from that border country between western Normandy and Brittany came the family of Scotland's greatest king, and perhaps her greatest son. Noble emigrants from Brus took as their name "de Brus".

As "Bruce" this would become the greatest name in Scottish history.

He was a brilliant general, a practised schemer, a murderer. And, set in the context of his time, he was a good man. "Good" is an epithet sparingly distributed among Scottish sovereigns—and half an hour with any book on Scots history should make this clear—but King Robert, criminal record and all, was a profoundly good one. Kingship seems to have made him so, for there is much, very much, with which we can find fault before his accession. But as King of Scotland, Robert Bruce established a complete understanding and sympathy with his subjects which no ruler of Scotland has achieved, before or since.

(Had Margaret, saintly Margaret, on another page, been a ruler, not a consort, we would have had to make exception for her. As it is, the only other monarch in these pages, Queen Mary, seems a more typical example of the relationship between the Scots and their rulers.)

History is made on the toss of a coin, the spin of a wheel, an accident of fate, and, had it not been for one of these, Robert Bruce would probably have remained unsung, as a lowland Scots nobleman, the Earl of Carrick. But in one of the more bizarre accidents of history, the last Scots king of the Canmore line died through a sudden after-dinner urge to visit his young French wife on the far side of the River Forth—and left the way open to others.

It was mid-March of 1286 when it happened. King Alexander III was finishing his meal in Edinburgh Castle, washed down with good French wine. Outside, the air was chill, a thin sprinkle of snow was moving across the battlements, and one of the worst evenings of the winter was just beginning.

No matter. A man—and a king to boot—does not let wind and weather keep him from the woman of his choice. Alexander leapt up from the table, mounted his horse, rode furiously to the ferry at Dalmeny. Here the ferry master implored him to get back to his castle, but the king brushed aside the entreaty and was rowed across two miles of icy, churning, water to Inverkeithing. Here, too, he was urged—nay, shouted at—to go back, for a storm had got up, the wind was screaming in from the sea, and there was no moon. In a king-and-subject dialogue which could scarcely have taken place outside Scotland, the Inverkeithing bailie roared at his monarch, "Get back, get back! How many times have I told ye, night travel will do ye no good?"

An English king would have promptly chopped off his head, but Alexander merely shrugged his shoulders and set off along the coast road towards the Manor of Kinghorn, where he had left his young French queen, Yolande.

Early the next day his body was found, broken-necked, at the foot of the cliff.

Yolande, only six months married, had been his second wife, after the death of the first, Margaret. Margaret had borne her husband three children, all of whom had died young, but one, another Margaret, had married the King of Norway and given birth to a female child before she died.

This three-year-old "Maid of Norway" was now, with the snapping of her grandfather's neck at the foot of a cliff, the Queen of Scotland. And immediately King Edward I of England decided he would like to marry her off to his own son, heir to the English throne. The governments of Scotland and Norway agreed; and the little girl was put on a ship.

She was taken ill, the vessel stopped in the Orkneys, and there she died.

Robert Bruce was just sixteen.

But there were several years to go before he would enter the pages of history. There were many contenders for the throne of Scotland. Of those who came forward, thirteen Scottish nobles, only three had a reasonable case, and only two need concern us. They were Robert Bruce the elder, a man of seventy-nine, and John Balliol. Edward was asked to arbitrate between their claims and he chose Balliol.

Seldom if ever has a country had a more helpless and unfortunate ruler. The fault was not really Balliol's, for there was little he could do against the might of the English king, and he had to agree to complete subservience. The day after his award of kingship he had to do homage to the King of England as his lord and master.

And it was the reluctance of this vassal-king's subjects to stump up money and men for the English monarch's adventures in France that brought about Balliol's downfall. He held a Council at Scone to ask his people's advice, and they told him to refuse. He did so. The next year his country openly signed a treaty with France—the start of the Auld Alliance—and thus thumbed its nose at Edward and his English. The impertinence resulted in the sack of Berwick in the following year on Good Friday, 30 March, 1296: a brutal and senseless slaughter which among other things triggered off the hostility of William Wallace and, as we can see on another page, resulted in the crashing defeat of an English army at Stirling.

But it also led to the banishment of poor Balliol. "Toom Tabard", his Scottish subjects called him, Old Empty Coat, and after Edward had butchered the inhabitants of Berwick and several other places in one of the greater blood-baths of the thirteenth century, he sent for him. Balliol stood in his shirt and drawers, like any offending vassal, and handed over a white wand to the Bishop of Durham as token of surrender. (Why the Bishop of Durham? Because he was Edward's representative, and the little transaction was too unimportant for Edward to be present.)

So much for Balliol. Three years' banishment to England, then permission to go to France. Edward meanwhile helped himself to the Stone of Destiny, on which Scots kings had been crowned since the days of Saint Margaret, also to Margaret's Holy Rood, the precious relic of the Holy Cross. Any other relics or documents which might show that Scotland had once been an independent kingdom were gathered up, taken south to England.

The history of the next ten years is largely that of William Wallace, and just as Wallace's campaign against England was triggered off by the sack of Berwick, so the trial and murder of Wallace were a spur to Robert Bruce. As he and Wallace had been much of an age (possibly exactly the same age; we are doubtful about Wallace's date of birth), we can see that these two great Scottish heroes performed their feats at quite different ages: Wallace was perhaps twenty-three at Stirling; Bruce was forty at Bannockburn.

He was thirty-one at Wallace's death and now he enters history. He had alternately supported and fought against the English king, like most of the Scottish nobles, but now he made up his mind to win the throne of Scotland for a Scotsman, and preferably himself. His family's claims had been only marginally less valid than Balliol's, and with his grandfather and father both dead and no longer a fear that Edward might do them harm, he set out to conquer the English king.

First of all, he got involved in the least savoury episode of his life, the murder of John Comyn, "The Red Comyn", within the sacred precincts of Greyfriars Church in Dumfries. Historians disagree as to the reason for the deed. Perhaps Comyn was about to betray a joint plan of revolt. Perhaps it was just rivalry over the throne of Scotland. Some say Bruce did not strike the fatal blow, that it was done by his companions. Others say Bruce had the dying man brought to him at the altar steps and there despatched him. It seems likely, though, that the killing was unpremeditated, the climax of a sudden quarrel.

Six weeks later, knowing he had set in motion half a dozen different chains of events—the Pope had excommunicated him, Edward thirsted for his blood, every man's hand was against him—and knowing it was too late to turn back, Bruce had himself crowned King of Scotland at Scone—even though, as we have seen, the Stone of Destiny was already south in England.

The correct person to crown a King of Scotland was the Earl of Fife, but he was enjoying for the moment the approbation of the King of England, basking in the fitful sunshine of that monarch's smile, and he understandably refused. His sister, the Countess of Buchan, bravely volunteered to do the deed, and in the presence of only four Scottish bishops and four Scottish earls placed a golden coronet on the head of the man who would become Scotland's greatest king.

(Why a golden coronet? How about the Crown of Scotland—or had Edward taken that too? No, John Balliol had taken it away with him.)

A little later the Countess of Buchan would be captured by the English and suspended in a cage from the walls of Berwick Castle—for four years—to atone for this crime. A similar fate would befall Bruce's sister. Both would survive.

From now on, though, King Robert of Scotland was constantly at war with England, though for long periods it was almost a personal war of one man against a nation. Early in his reign he and a few loyal supporters were harried through the highlands of Perthshire and had to escape from Scotland to hide on the island of Rathlin, near the coast of Ireland. They spent the winter of 1306 there, then came to Arran. From here Bruce got back to the mainland, though the exploit nearly cost him his life. It had been arranged that a signal fire be lit on the Ayrshire coast when it was safe to land. A fire duly sprang up and Bruce landed; but the fire was a mistake, it had been lit in another place by other men, and it meant nothing. Bruce decided not to sail back to Arran but to risk guerrilla warfare against a large English garrison.

This was the real beginning of his campaign. He came within inches and seconds of being killed or captured on half a dozen occasions, but escaped with his life and most of his men, and at Loudun Hill was able to inflict his first real defeat on the English. Edward I, wild with rage, now led a punitive expedition but got only as far as the border, at Burgh-on-Sands, before he died. The "Hammer of the Scots" was gone—aged sixty-eight.

And King Robert of Scotland found himself up against a lesser adversary, the weakling Edward II, whose child marriage to the Maid of Norway had been cheated by death. It was still 1307—only a few months had elapsed since King Robert's return to the mainland—but the tide had really begun to turn. One by one, while Edward II dithered and quarrelled with his subjects, the Scots captured the castles which had been in English hands.

By the summer of 1314 only one remained to the enemy: Stirling.

And so we come to Bannockburn. The dramatic story begins with an almost fairy-tale bargain. Sir Philip Mowbray was the English garrison commander at Stirling, and while it was being besieged—by Robert's brother, Edward Bruce—he had made the odd pact with Edward that if the English king didn't send an army within twelve months to relieve him, he would hand Stirling Castle back to the Scots.

In June of 1314 time was running out. Either King Edward II of England came and fought by Midsummer's Day, 24 June, or Sir Philip Mowbray and his garrison put down their arms.

On the long summer evening of 23 June—one of those really long evenings that the English never see (unless they invade Scotland), the largest force ever led by an English king drew near to Stirling.

There was, of course, no element of surprise. No four-teenth-century army could move from England, over the border and up into Scotland, without giving plenty of warning. Robert Bruce, with a force roughly half of Edward's hundred thousand men, was waiting north of the Bannock Burn, a few miles south of Stirling, and he had prepared his position with care.

The forces met briefly just before dusk, contact was broken off for a few hours during the semi-darkness of a northern night, and fighting began as the sun rose on Mid-summer's Day.

Bruce had worked hard throughout the night, completing his position, digging pits and covering them with grass and straw, putting razor-sharp "caltrops" into the ground to lame the English horse and break up a cavalry charge.

Dawn came and the Scots were awaiting their enemy in

tight circles of armed infantry, the schiltroms which Wallace had used, great hedgehogs of bristling spears. Between the schiltroms were the few Scots mounted soldiers, and the few—not very skilful—Scots archers.

The English knights on their great horses, a different breed from anything north of the border, rode at the schiltroms. At the same time the superb English archers poured a barrage of arrows into these tight-packed clumps of men.

Had this gone on for long, the disaster of Falkirk might have been repeated. But Bruce had thought this out very carefully. An order went out and suddenly all the Scots mounted men were flung at the English archers. Shrieking defiance, they galloped across the plain on their few small animals, and caught the archers unaware. Bows were useless in this sort of close combat and very soon the archers, as a force, were out of the battle.

Without the deadly rain of English arrows to pile up Scottish dead inside the schiltroms, as at Falkirk, the schiltroms held. The English knights, finding their lances useless against a solid mass of armour, a vast tank with a hundred legs, hurled maces and swords in despair before turning to flee.

But the battle was by no means lost or won. Casualties on both sides were heavy, yet, though men might flee or perish, there were others to take their place.

And then an event happened which really decided the matter. A whole new Scottish army seemed to appear as if by magic, thousands of men tearing down a hillside, whooping with joy and bloodlust, waving banners, coming in wholesale reinforcement of the Scottish force.

The English lost heart—and the Scots took it. Soon the survivors of an English army were fleeing in shameful defeat, some across the marshy land with its lethal caltrops lurking to impale man or horse, some plunging into the Bannock Burn, turning its waters blood-red. Soon that narrow stream was stuffed, piled high from bank to bank, with dead and dying Englishmen. Knights, chargers, filled it. An eye-witness reported:

"Bannockburn betwixt the braes,
Of horse and men so chargit was
That apon drownit horse and men
Man might pass dry atour it then——"

Edward II, a tattered fugitive, reached the castle he had come to relieve. Sir Philip Mowbray told him politely that he was about to capitulate, and the unhappy English king fled to Dunbar.

He was lucky. Most of his followers were struck down in their retreat—though King Robert Bruce was kinder-hearted than most medieval monarchs—and those that were captured were used to ransom Scots prisoners, including Bruce's wife and their daughter.

As for English prisoners taken on this great Mid-summer's Day, the ransom which the Scots were able to extract brought sudden wealth to the country.

Bruce's victory was not the end of the war, but it was decisive. The bloodshed that went on for another nine years served little purpose. The Scots captured Berwick in 1318 and were able to plunder northern England almost at will; the English came north again, looting the abbeys of Melrose and Holyrood, burning Dryburgh. At last, in 1323, Edward made a truce for thirteen years.

The truce was broken occasionally, but overall there was peace between the two countries. In 1328 a treaty was signed in Northampton, formally recognizing Robert Bruce as King of Scotland. A year after that Bruce was dead.

But during those last fifteen years of his life, from Bannockburn to its close, he was able to concentrate on being a king. And although Bannockburn is one of the great moments in Scottish history, and Bruce one of the greatest —probably the very greatest—of Scottish generals, he is remembered as a great and good peace-time ruler. Having thrashed his country's enemy he worked hard for a just peace, and succeeded. He then made sure there would be no disputed succession after his death, no bloodshed and intrigue as there had been after the Maid of Norway's death; he tied up the details with fairness and legality.

For a brilliant leader in time of war, he was amazingly wise in matters of peace. He was—once he reached his country's throne—utterly just and endlessly patient. When he died he was universally mourned among his people as "Robert the Good". He had chosen to live and to die in an ordinary dwelling house on the west coast at Cardross in Dumbartonshire; not a palace, not a castle, just a house.

His last request was in keeping with the man, but it had an unhappy outcome. He was a devout Christian (Bannockburn had begun with a celebration of the Mass) and he regretted that life had not allowed him to go on a Crusade; would his life-long friend, Sir James Douglas, have King Robert's heart removed from his body, embalmed, and taken on one?

Douglas did all this. He put his king's heart in a silver casket, hung it round his neck and went out to fight the Saracens. He was killed, and as he fell he is believed to have flung the casket in front of him, saying, "Pass first in fight, as though wert wont to do; Douglas will follow thee or die". The casket was later found under his body, taken home to Scotland and buried in Melrose Abbey. Douglas's body was brought home at the same time—but in the difficult years ahead, the wise counsel and strong arm of Robert Bruce's friend would be sorely needed.

How do we explain or condone Robert Bruce's shifts of allegiance before he came to the throne?

I think we should discount them: patriotism in 1300 was a different thing to that of six hundred years later. A man had to fight for the side his family wanted to win, preferably the one mostly likely to do so, or it meant extinction. And though the nobles of Scotland come badly out of all this period of history, one must in fairness to them remember that with their scattered properties and their marital alliances straddling international borders, loyalty must have been a complex and confusing thing.

Bruce combined in a unique and fascinating way the qualities of skilful knight-at-arms, brilliant general, and wise ruler. He was able to rally an army by a feat of individual bravery (as when he reined aside at Bannockburn and, rising in his stirrups, smashed the helmet and skull of the English knight who had charged him on an enormous, mail-clad, horse): he could devise strategy to confound his enemies on the field: and he could, as a king, rule wisely and leave his country ordered, prosperous and proud.

MARY, QUEEN OF SCOTS

"Lo! The potent hand of God from above sent unto us a wonderful and most joyous deliverance. For unhappy Francis, husband to our sovereign, suddenly perisheth of a rotten ear—that ear that never would hear the truth of God."

Thus the demagogue John Knox, graciously observing the death of Francis, King of France, after a painful infection of the ear, which left his eighteen-year-old wife Mary, Queen of Scots a widow. Poor Francis had been a Catholic and if he had done nothing in his short life but be one, he would still have been a candidate for the hell-fires of John Knox. In fact, he did little else, for he reigned a year and was succeeded by Charles X.

In the meantime, the death of Mary's own mother in Scotland, the staunch and unpopular widow of James V, left that country without a Head of Government, and the young Queen of Scots was summoned back to the land she had last seen at the age of one week. She arrived at the port of Leith on 19 August, 1561, and there is every reason to believe she was miserable. During her years of absence the country had gone Protestant with a truly Scottish fervour, and the arrival of this young Catholic queen was heralded by boos as well as cheers; to make her feel thoroughly at home a group of citizens set fire to the effigy of a priest as she rode by. It was a thoroughly nasty day, with low cloud and thick fog, and John Knox had scarce put down his pen from commenting on the death of her husband when duty called him to seize it again and write:

"The very face of heaven did manifestly speak what comfort was brought into this country with her; to wit, sorrow, dolour, darkness and all impiety; for in the memory of man, that day of the year was never seen a more dolorous face of the heaven, than was at her arrival, which two days after did so continue. For besides the surface wet, and the corruption of the air, the mist was so thick and dark that scarce might any man espy another the length of two pair of butts; the sun was not seen to shine two days before nor two days after. That forewarning God gave unto us. But alas, the most part were blind!"

One wonders how the Auld Alliance ever got off the ground, for the prejudice of Scotsman against the other half of it has so often been loud and bitter. In more recent times Andrew Carnegie went on record as deploring anything "Frenchy"; and Knox, having already clapped his hands over the painful death of France's king, now went on to be grudgingly gracious about his own new queen. Yes, she *was* a whore, he admitted, "We call her a hoor" (no one but Knox did), "but she was brought up in the company of the wildest hoor-mongers, yea, of such as no more regarded incest than honest men regard the company of their lawful wives".

So much for France. Perhaps we have no reason, hundreds of years later, to puzzle over a certain French reluctance to have Britain in the European Common Market.

Mary brought with her a sizeable French court, which did her no good at all in the eyes of her subjects—but her own charm and stunning beauty won the majority of these over. She was tall (very tall indeed: six feet) with large and shining eyes set in a pale face. White skin, in those days when the average Scots or English epidermis was dark from dirt and exposure to the elements, was more highly prized than it is now; it had already been noted that when the young widow mourned her husband in the white of mourning—*en deuil blanc*—her face was whiter than her veil.

Her nose was straight, her lips firm and full. Her long hair, though contemporaries described it as blonde, seems from her portraits to have been darker, with auburn streaks.

She had agreed to respect the Scots Protestant religion, on the understanding that she be left in peace with her own. For many people this just wasn't good enough, and her Catholicism was held up to scorn throughout her short and unhappy reign. John Knox argued with her for hour after hour, day after day, shouting abuse when she failed to respond to the God-given logic of his arguments. So great was his following in the country that she was virtually powerless to upbraid or punish him and he gleefully noted all this down. A few hours closeted with Knox and "scarce could Marnock, her secret chamber boy, get napkins to hold her eyes dry——"

But despite this, Mary's first four years in Scotland, from 1561 to 1565, were happy and peaceful, in comparison with what was to follow. She stuck by her bargain not to try and bring back Catholicism to the country; she firmly refused the offer of the Catholic Earl of Huntly to help her do so. She also refused the many offers of marriage which had besieged her since the death of her first husband.

She did, however, accept in marriage a distant cousin, Darnley, son of the Earl of Lennox, and, like herself, with a blood claim to the English throne. As the suggestion that she marry came from Queen Elizabeth of England (who was to worry about Mary's designs on her own throne until she succeeded in chopping the younger rival's head off)

47

this may seem surprising. Elizabeth seems to have known, however, that the marriage, for a multitude of reasons, including Darnley's Catholicism, would weaken Mary's position in Scotland.

They were married, a tall young couple, in the chapel of Holyrood House on 29 July, 1565. Darnley, as he had wanted, was proclaimed King of Scotland.

From now on it was tragedy all the way, Darnley was a womanizer, and Mary, far from being the "hoor" she was dubbed, or a lewd woman, seems to have been completely frigid. In no time at all Darnley was openly seeking his pleasures elsewhere, while at the same time professing jealousy over her Italian secretary Rizzio. Mary had not so far awarded Darnley the "Crown Matrimonial" which would ensure his accession to the Scottish throne in the event of her death; and as he believed—perhaps rightly—that Rizzio was behind this decision, he organized a gang of conspirators and succeeded in murdering him—in Mary's presence.

If the marriage had been in need of guidance, it was now effectively finished. Mary, however, was already with child by Darnley, and for the unborn child's sake, as well as for what she believed to be the good of her country, she professed reconciliation with him. The child who was soon to be James VI of Scotland and I of England was born on 19 June, 1566, in Edinburgh Castle and Queen Elizabeth consented to be his godmother.

Darnley, who was a poor husband and worthless father, now decided he would leave and settle in France. His father, the old Earl of Lennox, implored him to do nothing so foolish, and Mary, though she can hardly have wished to see much more of him, added her entreaty; it would be a grave blow to the honour of the Scottish crown.

Darnley, whose sole interest in Mary lay in the capture of that crown for himself, agreed not to leave the country. But there could no longer be any pretence that the marriage was a success. Mary even began to have grave suspicions that Darnley would murder her as he had murdered her secretary.

He never got the chance. On 10 February, 1567, the house in which he was staying blew up and his body was afterwards found in the garden. Unfortunately for Mary's reputation, it was proved that the Earl of Bothwell, her new favourite, was involved in the plot. He was tried, and he was acquitted; but the taint clung to the queen. Unjustly, because Mary was convinced the plot had been directed at herself as well as her husband, and as she wrote in a letter at the time, she proposed to "take a rigorous vengeance of that mischievous deed, which as it should remain unpunished, we had rather lose life and all. We hope to punish the same with such rigour as shall serve for an example of this cruelty to all ages to come."

Her real friendship with Bothwell not unnaturally ended at this point; it had in any case been only platonic, for Mary was incapable of more. She had little reason to regret the death of Darnley, but she was in genuine fear of Bothwell's real motive: there was no chance, in the confused Scotland of the time, that she or anyone else would bring Bothwell to justice. The "trial"—as futile as William Wallace's, though this time we must blame the Scots, not the English—was held on 12 April in Edinburgh, and the accused was permitted to bring with him two hundred arquebusiers and no less than four thousand gentlemen. His accuser, old Lennox, father of the murdered man, was not allowed to enter the town with more than six of his own. It goes without saying that Bothwell was acquitted.

Right after the trial he held a large party in Edinburgh's Ainslie Tavern, for the sole purpose of getting the lords who attended to sign a bond reiterating that they believed in his innocence, and that furthermore they wished to promote his marriage to the queen. Bothwell, like Darnley, had no real interest in the woman, only in the throne.

He certainly took a dramatic step towards getting it. On 24 April the queen was returning from a visit to Stirling, where the infant James had been sent for safe-keeping, when some four hundred horsemen and Bothwell appeared, and demanded her surrender.

Argument will go on till the end of time about that encounter. Many have thought that Mary acquiesced in the kidnapping and went cheerfully to Dunbar with her captor, fully intending to marry him. To me this is nonsense; she and her small band of retainers were hopelessly outnumbered and commonsense would have dictated that she surrender right smartly, as she did. Our old friend John Knox was largely responsible for the belief over much of Scotland that she had not only organized the murder of her husband but rushed to marriage with his murderer.

She was a prisoner—as she would remain for almost all that was left of her life. And it was as a prisoner, transferred under strong escort from Dunbar to Edinburgh, that she was forcibly married on 6 May. Bothwell had his "Ainslie Bond" to brandish, proving that many of the Scottish nobility wished him to marry their queen: and he had the queen herself.

He also had a wife; but this boring detail was dealt with by rapid divorce. Not only did the Earl of Bothwell suddenly discover that he was far too close a blood relative of Lady Jean Gordon to be her husband; he also remembered a regrettable misconduct with a serving-wench. In no time at all he was free, and had married Mary.

She was dressed in full mourning—mourning for Darnley and perhaps for herself—at the ceremony. Unless she were an astoundingly gifted actress—which she was not —she can hardly have been a willing participant in, of all things, a Protestant marriage. The French ambassador refused to attend the hateful ceremony, but did report that "The opinion of divers is that the queen is the most changed woman in fact that in so little time, without extremity of sickness, they have seen." He managed to see her himself the next day and reported her words to him that he must not be surprised that he saw her sorrowful, "for she could not rejoice, nor ever should again. All she desired was death."

As we have seen, a number of Scottish lords had signed the "Ainslie Bond" approving of this shot-gun marriage— but a great number had not. These mustered their forces to rescue her and on 15 June these met Bothwell's at Garberry. The encounter ended with Bothwell's flight and Mary's surrender to the confederate lords.

She discovered, to her shock and dismay, that many of those who had fought to rescue her believed her the real murderer of Darnley; she it was who organized the conspirators, arranged for the huge quantity of gunpowder to be piled up inside the house at Kirk o'Field; she in effect who had lit the fuse. She was taken to Edinburgh behind a garish banner representing the murdered Darnley and the orphaned prince, while citizens screamed "Burn her! Burn her!"

A brief spell as prisoner here and then, while John Knox thundered threats from his pulpit, urging his spellbound congregations to "Burn the hoor!", it was decided to imprison her in a safer place. At midnight she was roused from an exhausted sleep, wrapped, while still in her nightclothes, in a cloak of coarse brown cloth and dragged from her room by soldiers. They got her into the street, mounted her on a horse and took her to Leith. From here she was ferried across the Forth.

From the north shore she was taken on another horse to the shore of Loch Leven, pushed into a boat and rowed out to the castle which would be her prison for the next eleven months. It was on one of four small islands in a loch which in those days was fifteen miles in circumference. The castle was a Scottish royal one, but the governor in residence was Sir William Douglas, laird of Loch Leven and the surrounding country.

Sir William and his wife were soon won over by their prisoner, and had she not been grievously ill for much of the time, her stay in the castle might not have been unpleasant. But she had been roughly handled by her lords and their soldiery and the injuries she sustained were complicated by the fact that she was pregnant by Bothwell.

He, by the way, was heading north as fast as his horse would take him. He would eventually get to Norway and settle there, without further thought for his bride. Probably he never knew Mary was with child by him: in any case, she lost the child by miscarriage shortly after her arrival at Loch Leven Castle.

At this point a delegation of Scottish lords arrived and forced her on pain of death to abdicate. Weeping, in great distress, she signed the instrument of abdication and the noble lords clumped out again and got into their boat. The infant James was King of Scotland.

Mary's health slowly recovered, and the Douglas family were kind to her. The laird's younger brother, George Douglas, became helplessly infatuated with the beautiful prisoner, so much so that he had to be banished to the mainland.

Someone equally infatuated was young Willie Douglas, a page in the household, who was probably an illegitimate son of the laird. He spent a great deal of time with her, trying to cheer her, and he often succeeded in making her laugh. She called him "my little friend".

One day—it was the 2 May of 1568 and she had been a prisoner in the castle for eleven months—Willie came in and bluntly said:

"Make ready to leave, Ma'am. Today."

"Today, Willie? But how can a poor prisoner escape from this island?"

"I will take you, Ma'am. At eight of the clock tonight."

And at eight he was back. With him was the queen's ten-year-old serving maid, dressed as a peasant child. She handed her royal mistress a cloak and, silently, Mary put it on.

Down the long stone passage, out into the evening twilight, and round the long way to the gate, lest the laird and his wife see them from the dining room. They reached the gate and Willie whipped out a key and opened it. A minute later they were in a boat and Willie was rowing as fast as his short arms would move.

At last Mary felt she could speak. "But how did you get the key, Willie?"

"Dropped the napkin on it at table, Ma'am. Always has it by him at meals, Ma'am——"

They got to the shore and there was George Douglas;

he lifted his queen from the boat, helped her on a horse and the party galloped off into the night.

They got to the Forth, crossed to the south shore in a fishing boat and made for the loyal Lord Seton's castle at Long Niddry. A few hours' rest there and the party galloped on to Hamilton Palace.

And here, for a short—all too short—period, it must have seemed if Mary were to get back her throne. There were cheering loyalists all round her, and the good news that a loyal army under the Earl of Huntly was heading down from the north to her defence.

But that same morning, Monday, 3 May, a messenger had ridden up to Moray, Regent of Scotland, who was to rule during the minority of the child James VI, and told him of the queen's escape from Loch Leven. Moray rushed to assemble his own army.

The two forces met at the village of Langside, in Renfrewshire. The loyalists, Mary's army, were ambushed, with Huntly's reinforcements not yet arrived, and they fled in ignominious panic.

So too did Mary—though her panic can hardly be dismissed as ignominious. With a tiny party consisting of little more than the faithful George and Willie Douglas, she rode as fast as she could to the shore of the Solway Firth and once again cast off in a small boat.

She had left Scotland for ever. On 16 May, 1568, she landed in the north of England. Nineteen more years of imprisonment lay ahead of her—and then, death on the block.

During these nineteen years she passed from prison to prison in England. She had hoped to be greeted hospitably by her cousin Elizabeth, but at her first halt, in Carlisle, she learnt that Elizabeth would have none of her until she had been cleared of complicity in the murder of Darnley. Surprisingly, she was. Surprisingly—because the most damning evidence was now suddenly "discovered": letters she was alleged to have written to Bothwell and which a noble earl now claimed he had found in Edinburgh after Boswell's flight, in a silver casket. These "casket letters" seem to have been a cleverly executed forgery, in which Mary is made to draw up plans with Bothwell, in French, for the murder of Darnley. Many people believed them to be genuine, but apparently the conference which investigated Mary's alleged guilt of the murder did not, for she was acquitted.

Her name, however, was effectively blackened by their "disclosures", so it was an easy matter for Elizabeth to justify keeping her in some sort of custody. As for the letters, Mary was never allowed to see them (when she might probably have picked out their author; for she maintained, while hotly denying having written or even thought any of the "letters", that many friends and enemies could imitate her hand). Nor are we; they disappeared from view three hundred years ago and all we now have are copies.

During Mary's years of captivity she was a constant source of worry to Elizabeth, and frequently of alarm. Several times she seemed about to be carried away by a rescue force, several times she was about to be betrothed to a foreign ruler who would invade England and place her —and himself—on its throne.

The last straw was the Babington Plot. It was intended to free Mary, murder Elizabeth and foment a Catholic rising. There is no doubt whatever that Mary, after her years of imprisonment, was pleased with the idea when news of it was smuggled into her by young Babington himself.

The plot was discovered and Mary, on 25 September, 1586, was led off to Fotheringay Castle in Northamptonshire to be tried for her part in it.

She had had no part in it; she had simply wished it well. Hardly surprising, then, that she was sentenced to death.

For her execution, inside the great hall of the castle, she wore a long-sleeved black satin gown over a petticoat which was of crimson satin above, crimson velvet below. The hall was packed with spectators who sat in eager silence while the warrant of execution was read and followed by a long sermon from the Dean of Peterborough.

The black satin gown was undone, taken away by a

serving woman. The queen, now all in crimson, placed her head on the block.

And so to the pious intoning of the Dean of Peterborough on 8 February, 1587—"So perish all the queen's enemies"—the life of Mary, Queen of Scots was ended. It had been a sad life, a tragic life—and a lonely one. She left behind her only son, who would grow up to be king, not only of Scotland, but of England as well. He was a rotten king, and nobody thanked her.

But to us, Mary—beautiful, complex, tragic Mary—has left a legend.

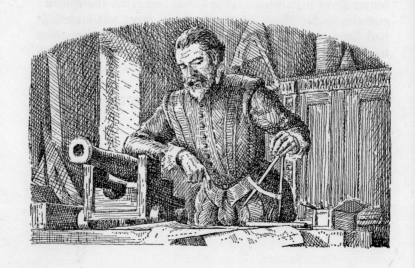

JOHN NAPIER

"He was born in the year 1550, at Merchiston, the seat of
his forefathers, near Edinburgh; four years after the birth
of Tycho, fourteen before Galileo, and twenty-one before
Kepler. But the youngest of these contemporaries reached
the summit of fame at an earlier period than he did. They
encouraged and emulated each other in their brilliant
careers. He was distant and isolated from the great arena of
letters; cooped up within the narrow limits of desolate
Scotland, and encircled with savage sights and sounds of
civil discord, above which the name of God was howled
by those whose hands were red with murder——"

And so, many years after John Napier's death, his
descendant Mark Napier paints a background to this extraordinary man's life. "When we regard his times and observe
the influence that, for so long a period of his life, the war of

religion exercised over his intellectual exertions, the wonder is, not that his great contemporaries of the continent became distinguished before him, but that after all he should have extricated his mind from so many toils, and have placed himself by a single effort—though one like the spring of a roused lion—at the side of the astonished demi-gods of science, who had been unconscious of their rival."

We may disagree with this biographer, for John Napier did so many things, so well, that his seat "at the side of the astonished demi-gods of science" owes a little bit to all of them.

But Napier was not only a scientist and what today we would call a technologist:

"The Church of Scotland was planted by such noblemen as Argyle and Glencairn; such barons as Tullibardine and Grange. It was rendered popular, and thus greatly aided, by such preachers as Knox and Goodman; and it became dignified in the eyes of Protestant Europe by its first and greatest theologian, John Napier."

Inventor of logarithms. Great theologian. Laird of Merchiston Castle. Surely, this is sufficient obituary for any man?

Not a bit of it. He invented the first pump for keeping mines free of water. In order to defend his country, he invented a burning-mirror, to set fire to an enemy's position; he invented a vastly improved cannon.

He invented, almost four centuries before credit for the invention was given to someone else, the tank. We must admit that it lacked the refinements of the 1916 model, but in Napier's own words, confirmed by others who saw it, the machine was "a chariot of metal, double musket proof, the motion of which was controlled by those within, and from which shot was discharged through small holes: the enemy meantime being abased, and altogether uncertain what defence or pursuit to use against a moving mouth of metal".

He was born, as Mark Napier told us, in 1550—shortly before his father's sixteenth birthday. It must have been an oddly pleasing life, growing up with virtually a teenage father and mother and a younger brother and sister, all sharing their youth together in a castle which echoed with laughter and the sound of games.

So perhaps it isn't surprising that the Bishop of Orkney, who happened to be his mother's brother, should have written to John's young father: "I pray you to send John to the schools either of France or Flanders, for he can learn no good at home."

The advice was taken: but in the meantime young John was sent to St. Andrews University, the College of St. Salvator. As was sometimes the custom, he boarded with the principal of that College, and we know that the bill for his board between October, 1563, when he went, aged thirteen, and July of the next year, came to £18. Quite possibly he went to the Continent immediately after this year: the only date we can be sure of after 1564 is 1571, the year he returned home from abroad. He married Elisabeth Stirling the year after that, and settled in a house near his parents, where he lived until his father's death in 1608 and then moved into Merchiston Castle. By this time his father had become a widower and re-married; there was bitter quarrelling between John and his half-brother and half-sisters over the inheritance.

Eventually this was peacefully—or almost peacefully—resolved, and John Napier settled down to becoming a model laird for the remaining years of his life: in the course of which he made remarkable discoveries about fertilisers. But let us go back a few years and see what else he was doing before he inherited the castle.

His hobby, throughout life, was mathematics. As we will see in these pages, some of the greatest achievements of Scotsmen have been the result of a hobby, a pastime: Scott and Buchan hated to be thought of as writers. Napier, whom we revere as the inventor of "logs", did it all in his spare time between running an estate, writing works on theology (and speaking fiercely on the subject), and inventing weapons of war.

His interest in mathematics began about the time of his

first marriage. (John, like his father, was widowed, and married again.) His interest lay in making it easier; and for the fact that he did, generations of scientists and mathematicians—to say nothing of schoolboys—owe him an unpayable debt. Not only were there no non-human computers (though Napier invented one, late in life), but there was no Differential or Integral Calculus; a multiplication like, say, $7653821 \times 4651 \times 9538807$ had to be multiplied out in full, digit by digit. Calculations of great complexity (and the one above is childishly simple compared with many) had to be worked out, hour after hour, multiplying, dividing.

Napier worked out a system of what he at first called "Artificial Numbers". Later he was to christen these "Logarithms", from the Greek word *logos,* in the sense of calculation, and *arithmos,* a number. Without plunging into the depths of mathematical theory (where I am the weakest of swimmers) we can sum up by saying that an artificial number, or logarithm, of any real number may be looked up in a table. To multiply two real numbers, however cumbersome, we merely look up their logarithms and add them together. A glance at the anti-logarithm table, which converts an artificial number back to a real one, gives us the answer, and a multiplication which might have taken ten minutes is done in a few seconds.

To divide one real number into another we simply look up their logarithms, and this time *subtract* one from the other. Glance at the table to convert this result back into a real number, and we have our answer.

(In the course of these experiments with artificial numbers, Napier invented the decimal point, which in itself revolutionised calculation.)

In 1614 he published his system under the awesome Latin title *Mirifici Logarithmorum Canonis Descriptio*; a description explaining the use of his new logarithms in calculations and particularly in trigonometry. The *Descriptio* also contained the all-important tables for converting into and out of logarithms. The work immediately took the world of science by storm. He had in fact already written a *Constructio* showing exactly how the logarithm tables were made, but for some reason this never saw the light of publication till some years after his death.

Shortly before Napier's death he published his *Rabdologiae* or "Numeration by Little Rods". These remarkable, finger-length, pieces of wood or bone, with figures on them, could do all manner of multiplication and division sums in a way which seems a bit cumbersome in the twentieth century, but which was a great step forward in the early seventeenth. With a pair of rather larger rods —and Napier described, much as he had described his tank and his burning glass, just how to make these—one could easily extract square roots, cube roots.

And in an appendix to this work he describes the manufacture of a first calculating machine, or computer. A simple thing of metal plates in a wooden box, but effective.

Not content with this, he added information about performing abstruse calculations on a chess-board, by moving counters.

All these works were translated from the Latin Napier liked to use, into other European tongues—including English. Perhaps the Latin sounded better than "The Art of Numbering by Speaking Rods, Vulgarly termed Napier's Bones".

But in John Napier's eyes, and those of many others, he was primarily a fighter for the reformed, Protestant, religion in Scotland. Many things combined to make him an enemy of the Papacy, from his admiration for John Knox to his shock at the Spanish Armada: it failed, and miserably —but Napier was quite aware that if it had *not* failed, Catholicism would have been enforced all over England and Scotland. Somehow he managed to find no less than five years to write his *Revelation,* refuting many Catholic beliefs and observances. This work, unlike the mathematical ones, he wrote in English, under the full title of *A Plain Discovery of the whole Revelation of St. John.* His reason for not writing in Latin was simple: "The insolency of Papists determined me to haste it out in English".

The book came out in 1594, and was dedicated to King James VI of Scotland (who was still a decade short of becoming King of England as well). The dedication implored James to see "that justice be done against the enemies of God's church". In case James was in any doubt about this, Napier sailed into his next sentence, counselling the king to "reform the universal enormities of his country and first to begin at his own house, family and court".

Interesting, this: the way Scottish monarchs have always been taken rudely to task by their subjects. Napier minced no words with James; Malcolm III was in the habit of being dressed down by bailiffs; poor Mary was brought to the verge of tears, time and again, by both John Knox and her own nobles. It doesn't take much imagination to prophesy what would have happened to a subject taking similar liberty with Henry VIII or Elizabeth.

Napier's *Revelation* was as enthusiastically received as his works on mathematics, and as often translated. Despite his hatred of Papacy he felt, like all educated men of the period, that his work should appear in Latin, and he resolved to publish an edition in that language. He kept waiting, however, for the devastating papal reply, which he would take note of before so doing—and it never came, though it was constantly "advertised that our papistical adversaries are to write largely against the editions already set out".

Napier's fame today rests entirely on the mathematical discoveries. His theology has been, if not superseded, at least arrived at by other independent brains; his tank and his huge burning glass and his water-pumps have been improved or discarded; but his logarithms, his decimal point, and his research into the fundamentals of arithmetic, algebra and trigonometry are still vital to our life today. Probably, when he first published his laboriously worked-out artificial numbers, he gave all the exact sciences as big a push forward as they had received in centuries. Astronomy and navigation, to name only two, were helped enormously.

But although using logs makes many calculations a great deal easier, somebody had to work out the logs in the first place—and this Napier did over many, many years: eventually he killed himself, like Scott, by overwork. The computations, he wrote, "ought to have been accomplished by the labour and assistance of many computers, but were completed by the strength of myself alone". We have avoided, so far, the spelling of the period, but perhaps we may set John Napier more firmly in it with these last words, in his will, made three days before he died:

"Johne Naipper of Merchistoun, being sick in body at the plesour of God, but haill in mynd and spereit. With my hand at the pen led be the nottars underwrittine at my command in respect I dow not writ myself for my present infirmitie and sickness."

The infirmity and sickness brought him to the grave three days later on 4 April, 1617. He was sixty-seven, and left behind him the son and daughter of his first marriage, and five of each from the second.

He left behind, too, his beloved Merchiston Castle (now a famous school), and seldom can a laird have been so involved in litigation and dispute about his property. Not only did his step-brother and step-sisters argue with him about his inheritance, but most of his neighbours, in particular the McGregors and the Grahams, seem to have been in a state of undeclared war against the laird of Merchiston. It is hard to assess the rights and wrongs of the various cases, but it seems reasonable to assume that a man with as precise a mind as Napier would be meticulously just in his dealings with his neighbours and demand the same treatment from them. He was certainly not the man to suffer either fools or knaves gladly.

The whole idea of logarithms—imaginary numbers of no real meaning in themselves but enormously simplifying work with real numbers—came on the world as a bolt from the blue. Nothing had foreshadowed it, no work by anyone else seems to have led up to it. It has been described in our own day as a momentous discovery, which "stands isolated, breaking in upon human thought abruptly, without borrowing from the work of other intellects or following known lines of mathematical thought".

It is "an island in the ocean which rises up suddenly from a great depth, to stand solitary, with deep water close around its shore".

And many wise men have wondered: did this all come as a Divine Revelation, to a wise and devout man?

If it did—and perhaps it really did—Napier's Divine Revelation was far from the sudden blinding flash of light we tend to associate with such occurrences. He worked, had to work, rather more than twenty years, before he was able to perfect his logarithms and to write about them.

Television, radar, penicillin: all these are brilliant discoveries; yet no one of them is beyond the ingenuity of an ordinary man to understand.

But artificial numbers? How does one arrive at such a concept?

Could it have been anything *but* some sort of Revelation?

LADY NITHSDALE

Winifred Nithsdale (she spelt her Christian name in six different ways, but we will stick to this as the easiest) is a border-line case in this book, for she was of English birth, and Scottish only by adoption—and, of course, marriage. But her life is so bound up with Scotland and the Stuart kings that she merits inclusion, I think, as much as anyone else in these pages.

After all, what is a Scotsman? Robert Bruce's family came from France, Wallace's from Wales; and most of us, with the minimum of ingenuity, can find ancestors of a very untartaned sort. Home is where the heart lies—and Winifred Nithsdale's heart was in Scotland.

Not that she owed it very much. William Maxwell, 5th Earl of Nithsdale, was one of the stupidest men in Scottish history: it is against this noble backdrop of boneheaded-

One of the most famous, most controversial characters in history, Mary Queen of Scots was nothing if not beautiful. This portrait, *left*, which hung for many years in the home of her good and powerful friends, the Hamiltons, is perhaps the finest. It shows the womanly beauty of full lips and straight nose—though not the six feet of height—which her contemporaries remarked. It also shows a little of the brooding, complex, fascination of a woman who has too often been shown as simply dignity incarnate.

n 8 February, 1587, Mary Queen of Scots was beheaded in the Great Hall of Fotheringay Castle in Northamptonshire. She wore a long-sleeved black satin gown over a petticoat which was crimson satin above, crimson velvet below—in order that her blood would not stain it. She was forced to listen to her Warrant of Execution and then a long sermon from the Dean of Peterborough. A moment after the scene depicted here, the black satin gown was undone and taken away by a woman. Mary placed her head on the block.

In this illustration, aft[er] a well-known painti[ng] by E. M. Osborn, t[he] Earl of Nithsdale h[as] just been laborious[ly] changed into woman['s] clothing by his wi[fe] Winifred. There h[as] been no time to shav[e] so, with paint to lighte[n] his beard and a ke[r]chief held to it, he [is] being smuggled fro[m] his condemned cell [in] the Tower. The who[le] master plan was t[he] work of a devoted wi[fe] — and Nithsdale d[id] little to further it. B[ut] though it worke[d] superbly well a[nd] Nithsdale got safe [to] the Continent, the[re] were many years [of] poverty and distre[ss] ahead for both of the[m] —years in which Win[i]fred Nithsdale remain[ed] a devoted helpmeet [to] her weaker husband.

The great Scottish mathematician, John Napier, *right,* who was born in 1550. We know that he refused to suffer fools gladly, or at all, and this portrait of him seems to suggest the fact. We must judge for ourselves whether it reflects any of the other extraordinary facets of this genius of many parts, who was not only mathematician, but theologian, writer, inventor and military strategist. In his own eyes, he was, above all, the Laird of his family property, Merchiston.

ness that Winifred, his brave and resourceful wife, shines like a diamond in a dust heap.

She was born Winifred Herbert, daughter of Lord Powys, an ardent Royalist—and, if we follow her family to the present day, she was an ancestor of the Duke of Norfolk. She married the Earl of Nithsdale and their life was uneventful until the first of the two great Jacobite rebellions, 1715. In that year the Old Pretender came over from France in an ill-starred attempt to gain the throne of England and Scotland in succession to Queen Anne, who had just died without surviving issue. As we all know, he failed, and the throne remained firmly in the pudgy hand of the German monarch who had been invited to succeed Queen Anne. The rising was squashed at the Battle of Preston and from there the Royalist prisoners, Scots and English, were rushed south to London. The lords among them were lodged in the Tower, awaiting their sovereign's pleasure—though not a one of them had any doubt as to what form of pleasure His Majesty would desire.

Six lords were tried together: Kenmure, Widdrington, Carnwath, Derwentwater, Nairn and Nithsdale. The Earl of Wintoun is always considered to have been dealt with at the same time, but a print of the six lords awaiting the verdict, all in a row, has somehow left him out. Nithsdale cut a sorry picture at that trial, protesting that he had only joined the Jacobite rising against his will. In fact, as it were, he had not risen—and most certainly he had not fought. He had been persuaded to go along with the others, and ride to Preston.

He went along for the ride.

The court would have none of this, and he was convicted of treason.

It was on 8 December that Winifred heard the news that her husband was a prisoner and on his way to London. Instantly she set off from the family home near Dumfries, on horseback. With her she brought her Welsh maid, Cecilia Evans; and the two gallant young women rode off into the snow.

An exhausting business at the best of times, for a man. But for two unaccompanied women in the depths of winter, the ride from Dumfries must have seemed terrifying.

Winifred was warned she stood no chance of getting south along the usual route through Cumberland and Lancashire, so she began her journey by going almost due east, right across Scotland, to Newcastle, where she hoped to get two places on the stage-coach. From there, on 15 December, she wrote to her sister-in-law, Nithsdale's sister, the remarkable Lady Traquair, who would go on getting her brother and his wife out of trouble for the next thirty years. On this all-important occasion, however, she had been able to do no more than take Winifred's small daughter, Anne, into her house. To Lady Traquair, Winifred wrote that: "I am safe thus far, but have got no places, so am forced to go on horseback to York, where I have as little hopes to get any, but met a gentleman that will be there a night sooner than I can, and will secure any that is to be had, if not, hire horses for me to London, which long journey on horseback I wish I may be able to undergo without stopping."

From Stamford, she wrote on Christmas Day (without mention of that date) that she had managed to get one place only in the stage-coach from York and had hired a horse for Cecilia Evans. But the coach got stuck at Grantham and soon she was again riding horseback through the snow with Cecilia and a new pair of horses. By Stamford they were forced to halt, for "the snow is so deep that our horses yesterday were in several places almost buried in the snow".

She adds, "I must confess that such a journey I believe was scarce ever made, considering the weather, by a woman. . . . However, if I meet my dear lord well, and am so happy as to be able to serve him, I shall think all my trouble well repaid. I think myself most fortunate in having complied with your kind desire of leaving my little girl with you. Had I her with me she would have been in her grave by this time with the excessive cold."

She arrived in London some time in January. We do not know the day, because she arrived so weak and ill that she was unable to write for several weeks—until 4 February of 1716.

> "I hope you will excuse, dear sister, my having been so long without writing, which by the way I now do it, you will find has been as soon as my weakness, after so violent a sickness, could permit. All the comfort I had in it was that, all the while I lay ill, had I been otherwise, nothing could be done for my Lord during that time, nor can yet, till after next Thursday, when 'tis supposed sentence will be passed against them. God almighty help us, and send us success after."

God helps those who help themselves, and when her petition to the king ("as we were forced to call him") was being considered she straightway devised a remarkable plan of escape for her husband. What is more remarkable, she carried it out with the minimum of assistance from the boneheaded Nithsdale himself.

A glance at that part of the Tower of London will show just how difficult it would have been, even with a lithe and anxious husband, really anxious to get out. Nithsdale was confined in a small room in what is still, today, the Governor's house, a room with a single window overlooking Water Lane, some sixty feet below. The only way in was through the Council Chamber and by the staircase and front door used by the Governor himself; then across Tower Green and under the Bloody Tower, to Water Lane.

At first, she had been refused permission to see her husband unless she were prepared to go in with him and stay there until the end, when they took him and chopped off his head. She naturally refused this and immediately struck up such a friendship with the guards, by her beauty, her cheerful bravery—and her money—that she seems to have had no difficulty walking in and out during the hours of daylight.

She and Cecilia Evans had taken lodgings in Drury Lane, as close as they could get to the Tower without arousing suspicion, in the house of a fat lady, Mrs. Mills. Another lady present in the establishment was Miss Hilton, who was tall and thin.

These—plus the Earl of Nithsdale himself—were the *Dramatis Personae* of a drama which would be told and retold in England and Scotland for a hundred years.

We have details of Winifred Nithsdale's journey south, in the letters she wrote her sister-in-law. Another, quite remarkable, letter written years later to her own sister, gives every detail of the escape. It is thousands of words in length, so we can only quote it here and there, and précis the plot in between, but for a really thrilling adventure story, told calmly and with restraint (the whole thing is in one immense paragraph covering eleven pages), there can be hardly anything like it.

Beginning with the observation, to her sister, that the escape is such an old story now "that I have almost forgot it, but since you desire the account, to whom I have too many obligations to refuse anything in my power, I will endeavour to call it to mind, and be as exact in the relation as possible", she describes the dreadful journey south. There is the "condemnation", then the petition for mercy to the king. But from this, Winifred goes boldly to the Tower and tells the guards that she brings good news about the prisoners, the petition has been passed in their favour. (Which is, of course, quite untrue.)

The guards, who are simple, kindly, men, are pleased for her sake—and still more pleased when she gives them money to drink the king's health.

"The morning after, I did not go (but in the afternoon) having too many things to put in readiness. When I was ready to go, I sent to Mrs. Mills, in whose house I was lodged, and told her that, finding there was now no further room for hope of my Lord's pardon, nor longer time but this night, I was resolved to endeavour his escape; that I had provided all that was requisite for it, and that I hoped she would not refuse to come along with me, to the end that he might pass for her, and begged she would come immediately, because we were full late."

So great was Winifred's charm and persuasiveness that neither fat Mrs. Mills nor tall-and-thin Miss Hilton, whom she also approached, made any objection to being involved in such a dangerous scheme. But "we went into the coach, where I never ceased talking, not to give them leisure to think, for they consented immediately to come with me, the surprise having left them no time to reflect of the consequences".

By this time, tall-and-slender Miss Hilton was wearing an extra riding cloak underneath her own, without quite understanding the reason. The three of them, with Cecilia Evans, got to the Tower; Cecilia stayed outside.

"When we arrived, the first I brought in was Miss Hilton, for I could carry in but one at once, and she brought in the clothes that was to serve Mrs. Mills when she had parted with her own; and after I had stripped her of what she had brought in for me, I conducted her out again, begging she would do me the kindness to send me my woman to dress me, for I began to be afraid I should be too late if she did not come immediately, having a petition to give, which if I were too late, having but this night, I were undone. So I dispatched her safe and partly downstairs, where I took Mrs. Mills who came in with her handkerchief before her eyes, as it was very natural for a person that came to take leave of a friend that was going to die. I made her do it, that he might go out in the same manner; and her eyebrows being a little upon the yellow, and his very thick and black, I had provided paint of that colour to dye his, and a twist of the same coloured hair; and to hide a long beard that had not time to be shaved, white paint to cover it with, and the rest of his face, and red for the cheeks, all which remained of the provision I left in the Tower when I went out."

At this point, one almost begins to sympathize with Nithsdale himself who, having cringed at his trial, had followed this up by at first refusing a rescue operation, which would be undignified. Certainly this one had many of the elements of bedroom farce, and perhaps, as Winifred painted his unshaven face a ghostly white—with red cheeks

—and he got himself up to look like fat Mrs. Mills, he might have been tempted to refuse finally. Better the block than this.

But he grudgingly agreed. Meanwhile Mrs. Mills had taken off her own ample cloak and given it to him, as planned, before going out, a different person altogether, in the cloak Miss Hilton had brought in for her. She was no longer weeping.

Once again Winifred went through the little homily about her serving maid: "I must beg you to go in all haste and look for my woman, for she certainly does not know what o'clock it is."

Throughout, there had been a number of women standing about, watching the visitors on what they believed would be the last occasion they saw Lord Nithsdale. Winifred had banked on these as part of her plan. The winter light, oozing through barred windows, had nearly gone, and the darkness and the crowd made it comparatively easy for Mills and Hilton to avoid close scrutiny. But she would have to hurry to get her husband out before candles were lit.

Mrs. Mills was allowed out by guards and women who jumped out of her way on hearing she had been charged to go out and get "my woman" for a reason which sounded highly urgent. She joined Miss Hilton for a moment in the fading light of out-of-doors, then both hastened away, their parts in the drama at an end.

Frantically, Winifred Nithsdale disguised her husband, put on some of her own petticoats, some of Mrs. Mills's; tied false ringlets into his hair, painted his face, got him into the riding-cloak.

Then, opening the door and urging her husband on in front of her, keeping close so no one would notice his odd gait, she got him down the passage. All the time she kept up a barrage of feminine chatter, not giving him time to reply (which he might well have been stupid enough to do, in a deep bass voice) until she had him in the courtyard.

Cecilia Evans stepped out of the shadows, took the fat lady by the elbow and led her off.

Winifred walked boldly back to her husband's empty cell. "When I got into my lord's chamber, I spoke to him as it were, and I answered as if he had, and imitated his voice as near as I could and walked up and down the room."

When enough of this seemed to have been done, she went to the door, and went half out of it, "holding the door in my hand, that what I said might be heard by those without, and took a solemn leave of my lord for that night, saying that I thought some strange thing must have happened to make Evans stay, she that never used to be neglectful in the smallest thing, to make her so in a matter of this consequence. But I found there was no remedy but going myself——"

Her last words to the guards were: "I pray you—do not disturb my lord. He is at his prayers."

The guards saluted.

A dash to Drury Lane to leave lodgings she knew would soon be searched. She would have liked to join her husband in the attic room to which Evans was taking him, but that was dangerous, too.

Kind Mr. Mills, husband of the fat lady who had wept on the way in and smiled on the way out, got Lord Nithsdale to the home of the Venetian Ambassador, "who knew nothing of the matter. But one of the servants kept him in his room till Wednesday, he being to go to Dover by the Ambassador's orders, with a coach and six horses, to bring his brother from thence; whom he expected by that time. He put my lord on a livery coat, and went away before day, and carried him safe to Dover without the least suspicion".

The Ambassador's servant crosses the channel with Nithsdale and is about to return to England, "without being suspected to have had a hand in it", but is persuaded to go on and join James Stuart's court, where he serves faithfully for many years.

Winifred had her husband safe—but this was not enough. Back to Scotland—on horseback again—to dig up the family papers and plate which she had buried in the garden before her ride south. She handed these over for safe-keeping to Lady Traquair and then set about selling whatever she could (and whatever her husband would not object to parting with!) in order to raise money to take to him in France. Nithsdale, throughout his long life, was permanently short of money, for he spent it the moment he got it, and usually before.

Yet Winifred gets a touching letter from Marion, the housekeeper at Terregles, her own and her husband's house, which she dare not visit again since digging up the garden. Marion offers her the sum of £18 if it will help "for your journey".

Winifred needs all the help she can get, for her husband, in France, is demanding not only money, but her physical presence, as soon as possible. He knows she is pregnant and that the trip is beset with danger as well as discomfort, but he insists; and she goes.

The faithful Cecilia (sometimes "Celia", sometimes "Cecil") will be with her mistress for the next twenty years, till her own death in Rome. From her letter home we learn Winifred had a miscarriage and nearly died, "in a cabin in the boat in which were seven other persons sleeping".

Eventually she got to Lille, in September, 1716, where her husband came to join her. There was scant sympathy for her condition, only a saga of unpaid debts. From now on the Nithsdales would be helped almost continuously by the generous and long-suffering Traquairs back home, with whom they steadily corresponded.

In 1718, both Nithsdales were at the Court-in-Exile, in Rome, and both receiving an allowance from their king— though a small one. James had at last got married to the little Polish Princess Clementina (who had to be kidnapped from Innsbruck because of her father's disapproval), and soon hopes rose that there would be a royal prince or princess in Rome. The pregnancy was confirmed and Winifred's hopes rose that she might be made governess to the child. Apart from the great honour, she desperately needed the money. She wrote in this fashion to her sister-in-law.

Nithsdale himself wrote, asking his sister, in view of the impending birth, to send him money for new clothes.

The royal birth took place on 31 December, 1720, and Nithsdale wrote his sister, under a pseudonym—"William Broun"—pointing out that he had not been able to wait for her money, but had drawn a bill for £50, "payable to Mr. Belloni's order. This is only to beg you will use your interest to get it duly answered——"

Winifred, though at first treated with suspicion by the little queen, was eventually given charge of the little Prince Charles ("Bonnie Prince Charlie" when the time came) and of his younger brother, Prince Henry, which meant a great deal to her—and not only financially. The queen had shocked Europe by deserting the two children in 1725 and retiring to a convent, and it was during the two years cloistered that Winifred had been able to help with the two princes. On the queen's return to the outside world in 1727, Winifred was confirmed in her position as governess. It was a position requiring a great deal of tact, and moral fibre; for Clementina, of whom so much had been hoped, grew into a hopeless neurotic, living a life of retirement and religion, while ignoring the children most of the time and then rallying to give absurd orders for their care and education. Winifred seems to have handled this with the calm good sense she showed in dealing with William her husband; and Prince Charlie probably owed many of his attractive qualities to the woman who looked after him so long. (Though, in fact, Winifred's official position was only that of governess to "Prince Henry, Duke of York".)

She lived long enough to follow from Rome the failure of her young protégé's attempt in '45 to regain the English throne. She also learnt with dismay of her son's, Lord Maxwell's, futility in the same enterprise. Young Maxwell had been about twelve when his father escaped from the Tower, and after a brief sojourn in France had been able to go back and take over the family estate—only Nithsdale himself being debarred (and his title is still in abeyance). Maxwell seems to have done a deal of talking about how he would help the prince, but in fact did literally nothing.

His father, the impecunious earl, would never know of this (and probably he would not have cared, for until his dying day all his correspondence, most of his conversation, and a large part of his thought, was about money), for he died early in 1744. Winifred lived on in Rome till her death in 1749.

She is famous for her remarkable exploit in getting the earl from his cell in the Tower of London (so much so that when the swashbuckling kidnapper of Clementina, Charles Wogan, was planning his feat outside the walls of Innsbruck, he wrote to a friend: "I wish I had Lady Nithsdale here, she is good at these things"), but she was also a very fine person.

The portraits extant of her, even including one painted in the convent at Bruges where she stayed after her near-fatal miscarriage in 1716, show a beautiful young woman. The whole story of Winifred Nithsdale, handed down from generation to generation, is of a brave young woman getting her older, stupider, husband out of the Tower. It has been immortalized by, among others, John Buchan, who gives her age at the time as twenty-six.

But Winifred was born in 1672 and married to Nithsdale in 1699—and of neither of these dates is there any doubt.

I would not be so ungallant as to do the sum and reveal the age of this vital, fascinating woman who released her husband from the impregnable Tower of London in 1716 and then nearly died of a miscarriage with his child, a few months later. And went on, active to the end, prolific as a letter-writer, to die, an exile, at the age of seventy-seven.

THE ADAM BROTHERS

South of the Strand in London are the dignified remains of a district made famous—indeed, *made*—by the Adam brothers. I suppose I had known the district, admired what survives of it, for years, and also been aware of the fact that it took its name from the brothers. I even pondered in my ignorance why they should have used only two letters of their honoured name in christening this child of stone.

They might, for example, have called it "Eden".

It was some time later that my lack of the Greek was made good by the vital word. For Adelphi, as no doubt the reader could tell me, is not a pale derivative of "Adam": it is the Greek word, *Adelphoi*, or "brothers".

It was by this that John, Robert, James and William wished to be remembered.

Sadly, a great deal of the Adelphi district, where men like

George Bernard Shaw, James Barrie and David Garrick lived, has been destroyed and replaced by glum, twentieth-century clusters of businessmen and typists. The streets, named after the individual brothers, are still there, though William Street has been renamed Durham House Street; some of the charm of this eighteenth-century Scottish confection still remains.

But as Garrick, who lived there, could testify, Scotsmen were not all that popular in mid-eighteenth-century England. Too many of them were coming south, taking the bread (and cake) from the mouths of Englishmen. Once, when they had been, if not popular, at least accepted, Garrick had produced a play by the Scots dramatist John Home. By 1769, when the same Home wrote his *The Fatal Discovery*, Scotsmen were so unpopular south of the border that Garrick, while purchasing the play, was forced to credit an Englishman with having written it.

The Fatal Discovery was an instant and overwhelming success. But as soon as the truth leaked out, the public stayed away in its thousands.

So although we must accept that the Adam brothers, and in particular Robert, were much admired in England for their work, we must add that the conditions under which they worked were not always ideal.

And yet this anti-Scottishness had not always been so. How many people know of the Scots architect—an Aberdonian, no less—who designed not only the lovely church of St. Mary's-le-Strand, but St. Martin-in-the-Fields, too? And a quantity of other graceful buildings which include the Radcliffe Library at Oxford. He lived a century before the Adams, James Gibbs.

Robert Adam was born on 3 July, 1728, in Kirkcaldy, the second surviving son of an eminently successful Scots architect, William Adam. Excepting those designed by his brilliant and prolific son, William Adam probably designed more of the large Scottish mansions we know than any other architect before or since.

John, the eldest of the four surviving into manhood, was born seven years before Robert, while James was born three years later. After that came William. There were also two sisters.

The four sons were encouraged to watch the father at his work, and probably the first any of them saw of this was the erection of Drum House at Gilmerton. By the time old William died, in 1748, he had designed a number of houses in Scotland, as well as the Edinburgh Orphans' Hospital and, in the same town, George Watson's Hospital and the Royal Infirmary. It was in this town that his son Robert, destined to be the most famous, got his education. He went to the High School, then the University.

The family was prosperous, and at the age of twenty-five he was sent to tour France and Italy. Already it had been decided he would be an architect like his father. He was a fine young man, tall and lean, with a strong jaw and a rugged, fighter's nose; and from what we can tell of all their portraits, of quite different appearance from his brothers.

His travels about the Continent have been little documented, though for years people believed he had published a journal—until it was proved that it related to travels, years later, of his brother James. There are fine drawings and plans he made in Italy, including the impressive "Design for a Royal Palace" done at Rome in 1757. (This was the year Thomas Telford was born; and while we are considering dates and noting that Robert Adam was an exact generation senior to Telford, we might note that in 1757 both Henry Raeburn and John Loudon McAdam were a year old. Robert Burns would not be born for another two years.)

Among the things Robert Adam studied in Italy were ruins at Spalato, and he completed the drawing of these in record time. For as he wrote later, the Venetian governor, "unaccustomed to such visits of curiosity from strangers, began to conceive unfavourable sentiments of my intentions, and to suspect that under pretence of taking views and plans of the Palace, I was really employed in surveying the state of the fortifications". He was stopped, then managed to get grudging permission to carry on. "The fear of a second interruption added to my industry, and by unwearied application during five weeks, we completed, with an accuracy that afforded me great satisfaction, those parts of our work which it was necessary to execute on the spot."

(He later published a book on the subject, with these plans and sketches in it, and England was greatly impressed. But by that time he was already a success.)

On his return from Italy in 1758 he settled in London, in the Lower Grosvenor Street house where he lived until his Adelphi was built, years later.

Almost immediately he became famed as a scholarly architect of great ability. And one can perhaps see reason for some of the anti-Scottish sentiment that arose because Scots were skimming the cream off England, when we read that Adam was invited by Lord Coventry to vet the work being done on his Croome Court by Launcelot, "Capability", Brown (who was both architect and garden designer); Lord Scarsdale asked his opinion on Kedleston which was being built; the future Lord Harewood invited his views on the embryo Harewood House near Leeds. We can only guess at what architects Brown, Brettingham, Paine and Carr thought about this.

But his first actual work in England was the designing of furniture and appointments for houses—which included all those mentioned above. He felt strongly that each piece of furniture, each carpet, each fitting, must be designed in accordance with the general scheme of the house. To prove his point, he started designing cabinets, carpets, tapestries, mirrors, fanlights, fire-grates, doors, himself.

His designs were furiously copied by others, so that today it is difficult to say who made a chair in "The Adam Style". And, in fact, many of these were made, but with permission and encouragement from his elder brother, by James Adam.

In 1773, after Robert had been practising in England for fifteen years, the first part of the *Works of Robert and James Adam* was published. In it the brothers stated, "Our ambition is to share with others, not to appropriate to ourselves, the applause of the public, and if we have had any claim to approbation, we found it on this alone: that if we flatter ourselves we have been able to seize, with some degree of success, the beautiful spirit of antiquity and to transfuse it with novelty and variety through all our works."

From interior design, the Adam brothers had gone on to plan houses. By an apparently amicable arrangement they found themselves completing Kedleston, in Derbyshire, which Paine had begun. Paine seems to have acquiesced cheerfully, owing to other work, in having the owner put "this great work in the hands of those able and ingenious artists, Messrs. Robert and James Adam——"

But while the structural work was being done, Robert Adam had much else to deal with, including the stately Shardeloes in Buckinghamshire; erecting a screen to hide the unimaginative shape of the Admiralty in London; and designing ceilings, chimney-pieces, doorways and furniture all over England.

Young James had gone on his own continental tour in 1760. Thanks to his journal, we have an interesting record of his travels and his impressions, from which we can conjecture what his older brother had done and thought.

Boodle's Club, an interesting example in London of Adam's work, was built in about 1765. While it went up, the brothers did work at Fonthill in Wiltshire and Witham House in Somerset. They also began taking on work in Ireland.

Prosaically—but prosaic in name only—Robert was appointed Clerk of the Works at the Royal Chelsea Hospital. His job was to keep all the buildings in repair and prepare estimates for the work, but he has left behind a legacy of beauty: if you were Robert Adam, your repairs involved rather more than replacing the odd slate and pointing up the brickwork.

By this time he had begun on one of his masterpieces, *replacing* the interior (not just decorating it) of Syon House, home of the Duke of Northumberland. (And with that perversity that characterizes English dukes it had been built hundreds of miles from Northumberland, near London: His Grace of Marlborough, as we all know, had elected to put his own "Blenheim" in Oxfordshire.) Syon is today one of the great show-places of England, about which Adam himself wrote:

"I endeavoured to render it a noble and elegant habitation, not unworthy of a proprietor who possessed not only wealth to execute a design but skill to judge of its merit. Some inequality of the old walls, and some want of additional heights to the enlarged apartments were the chief difficulties with which I had to struggle. These difficulties, I flatter myself, are in a great measure surmounted so as not only to procure such convenience in the arrangements of the apartments, but likewise an elegant form and graceful proportion in the principal rooms. The inequality of levels has been managed in such a manner as to increase the scenery and add to the movement, so that an apparent defect has been converted into a real beauty."

Obviously the best way to enjoy the work of an architect or a designer is to see it. Here we must content ourselves with the man alone, and fortunately a lot of him is in the written word. He was a man of many parts, destined even to be a Member of Parliament (but only, as was the pleasing custom, in his spare time). As he wrote in the Adams brothers "Works", it was important to have been to France to study the customs "of that social and conversible people". But, he went on, "in one particular our manners prevent us from imitating them. Their eating rooms seldom or never constitute a piece in their great apartments, but lie out of the suite; and in fitting them up little attention is paid to beauty of decoration. The reason of this is obvious: the French meet there only at meals, when they trust to the display of the table for show and magnificence; and as soon as the entertainment is over, they immediately retire to the rooms of the company. It is not so with us. Accustomed by habit, or induced by the nature of our climate, we indulge more largely in the enjoyment of the bottle. The eating rooms are considered as the apartments of conversation, in which we are to pass a great part of our time."

And so the eating rooms at Syon are ornate—and beautiful.

So, too, is the rest. One of the more remarkable bits is

the so-called Vestibule, the room at the south-west corner, with its ten green marble columns enclosing a central space about twenty-five feet square. The capitals and bases of the columns are gilded and carved. The shafts themselves are of a marble dredged up from the bed of the River Tiber, and they cost the duke a cool £1,000 each—way back in the eighteenth century.

And, of course, with this extensive interior re-building there had to be the designing of furniture and fitments to go with it.

The list of houses which Robert and James re-modelled and extended—and on occasion built—is enormous. One that still stands monument to their skill and taste is Ken Wood in Hampstead. Others, to name only a few, are Bowood in Wiltshire, Harewood House in Yorkshire, Luton Hoo in Bedfordshire.

And while all this was going on, the eldest brother, John, was working as an architect in Scotland. In 1767 he began Jamaica Street Bridge over the Clyde at Glasgow— and in the following year Robert himself, not forgetting his origins, was elected Member of Parliament for Kinross. In those days Kinross and Clackmannan elected a representative in turn, and Robert served until the next election when it was time for a Member to be returned from Clackmannan. After this he seems cheerfully to have given up this political sideline.

But it was at the time he took his seat that all four brothers got together to lease Durham Yard in London, off the Strand, and build their "Adelphi" on it. The yard was a hideous neighbourhood of hovels, mean streets and bad smells, sloping sharply to the river, where the stink was even worse. The brothers hit upon an ingenious but expensive plan: to avoid having to build on a slope, and to get dwellings away from the foul-smelling water, they would raise the whole of their new residential area far above the river by constructing a series of vaults in brickwork. This would be much like making a flat raft of their building land, supported on immense barrels.

They were led to believe the government would lease

these vaults from them as store houses—and this, they rashly assumed, would defray some of the cost.

In another move to keep down cost, they imported their labourers from Scotland, where wages were lower. A splendidly immoral plan, which has been adopted more than once in this century. (I know a chain of hotels spanning England and Scotland where the management finds it cheaper, more satisfactory, to load up an aeroplane in Glasgow with Scottish craftsmen and fly them to London to do repairs and alterations, than to get the same work done locally. The reason, I was told, was the "better value-for-money" of the Scotsmen.)

But the Adams had their troubles. When their Scots workmen found out what Englishmen were being paid, they immediately went on strike. At this point, so history relates, the brothers got hold of Irishmen and completed the work.

When the thing had been built, the four brothers then introduced a Bill into Parliament seeking to reclaim more land from the Thames by erecting at their own cost an embankment. Their good friend and fellow-architect, James Paine, with whom they had once competed, joined them in the petition. Against much opposition from the City of London, the Bill was passed, in 1771.

Seldom has so ambitious a scheme been embarked on by private enterprise. Had it not been so costly, the actual buildings would have been grander, more expansive, but by the time the vaults had been laid on the river bank, there was a decided shortage of money for completing the scheme. All manner of buildings had been planned, and not all were built. Among those that *were* built were the Adelphi Chapel and the School of Arts. In April, 1772, Robert Adam himself moved into one of the many private houses, one in the street that still bears his Christian name, while the names of the other three brothers were given to other streets on the site. Among the first to move in was their friend David Garrick, and as the area immediately became highly desirable, the actor was besieged by men and tradesmen who wanted to get there, too. Becket the bookseller asked him to intercede with the four Scotsmen, and Garrick wrote them:

"My dear Adelphi, I forgot to speak to you last Saturday about our friend Becket. We shall all break our hearts if he is not bookseller at the Adelphi and has not the corner house that is to be built. Pray, my dear and very good friends, think a little of this matter, and if you can make us happy by suiting all our conveniences, we shall make his shop, as old Jacob Tonson's was formerly, the rendezvous for the first people in England."

Becket got his shop. But there was trouble ahead. The government welshed on its agreement to use the vaults as storehouses, and soon the brothers were in very serious financial trouble. Yet Parliament—perhaps through the good offices of the Member for Kinross—seems to have been on their side. They were saved by a Lottery Bill, passed in 1773, which gave permission for them to dispose of their buildings by means of a lottery. The idea is not as bizarre as it seems, for in the eighteenth century Parliament often permitted lotteries to be held "for desirable purposes". One of these, twenty years earlier, had been for the establishment of the first British Museum.

The lottery for the Adelphi buildings netted a sizeable profit and the brothers were solvent again.

Their fame grew, and the Adelphi, though it had taken on some of the notoriety of a South Sea Bubble, remained a monument to the four Adam brothers for a hundred and fifty years, till much of it was pulled down in the 1930s. While they lived, the brothers went on building or decorating houses all over London and all over Britain.

Robert Adam died in 1792 at the age of sixty-three, in London. He was still unmarried, and he left his effects to his two sisters, Elizabeth and Margaret. John, the eldest, died in the same year, in Edinburgh. James followed them into the grave two years later, and William, the youngest, was left with the job of supervising all the work they had begun and left unfinished. He did this in the intervals of erecting buildings to his own design, right up to the time of his death at Edinburgh in 1822.

Quite a family. What did they achieve?

They were clannish and devoted, on the Scots pattern. Had they been English we would have heard only of Robert, for he was really the great architect of the team, and the others, though he encouraged them in their work, were basically little more than business associates. We must make up our own minds whether Robert was a genius or not. After Kedleston and Syon, we can look at Osterley; Ken Wood; Harewood; at what survives of the Adelphi, and at Fitzroy Square. And farther north, at work he did towards the end of his life, at Charlotte Square in Edinburge, and at the University.

There is a theory that all painting, architecture, of this period held the seeds of decay; that with Britain about to plunge into the horrors of an Industrial Revolution, some divine or satanic hand made architecture, in these last years of the eighteenth century, more elegant, less real. Sacheverell Sitwell, writing of eighteenth-century architecture, comes out with the theory, "Adam created so easily that difficulty must be coming. And, indeed, in a few more years, architecture was dead completely."

We may argue. But if architecture really died in that last decade of the eighteenth century, it had a lovely funeral.

JAMES WATT

"It was in the Green of Glasgow, I had gone to take a walk on a fine Sabbath afternoon. I had entered the Green by the gate at the foot of Charlotte Street—had passed to the old washing-house. I was thinking upon the engine at the time, and gone so far as the Herd's house when the idea came into my mind that, as steam is an elastic body, it would rush into a vacuum, and if communication were made between the cylinder and an exhausted vessel, it would rush into it, and might there be condensed without cooling the cylinder——"

And so great ideas are born, as men wander and ponder, taking their walks on a fine Sabbath afternoon. The idea that now occurred to the instrument-maker James Watt was to change the shape of the world. Had James Watt never lived, someone else would have invented a practical steam engine—years later. Destiny produced this quiet, simple man just at the moment when his engine and all that followed from it would put Britain at the head of the world. For the coming of Watt's engine was a mechanical revolution which in turn spawned the Industrial Revolution, in which Britain—not entirely to her credit— would lead the world. The pace would be tremendous: the huge increase in manufacturing occasioned by this noisy, gasping monster of an engine would disorganize, dislocate factory managements and all the economic systems of the western world—particularly Britain's. Men and women would flock into overcrowded towns to work in factories and bring about an overcrowding and concentration of misery with which we are still struggling.

The fault would not be James Watt's: the misery attendant on his monster would be the result of other people's greed, the greed of factory owners and of peasants, of rich men and poor.

Watt would see little of this, for he died in 1819. Five years after that, a statue of him was placed in Westminster Abbey, and perhaps the inscription on its base puts more succinctly, and at least as accurately as I can, the real achievement of

"JAMES WATT
Who, directing the forces of an original genius,
Early exercised in philosophic research
to the improvement of
THE STEAM ENGINE,
enlarged the resources of his country,
increased the power of men,
and rose to an eminent place among the most
illustrious followers of science and the real
benefactors of the world."

He was born in Greenock on the Clyde, in 1736, and there is a famous—and probably absurd—engraving of him by J. W. Steel, sitting as a small boy in that house in Greenock, watching in wonder, chin in hands, as the steam rises from a kettle on the stove. His mother is at the back of the room, chattering: she hasn't noticed the lid of the kettle being prised off by steam. Only the cat and James are watching, with clouds of the white vapour swirling about them.

The picture could really have been painted of dozens of other small boys. Robert Boyle, Edward Somerset, Christiaan Huygens, Thomas Savery, Denis Papin, Thomas Newcomen—and many others—could have been drawn in the same wondering attitude, all of them fascinated by the properties of this "steam" (though it wasn't) coming from the boiling water. All of these, and others, experimented with it: it was left to James Watt to produce a satisfactory "steam engine".

He was the fourth of five children of a skilled carpenter who went on from the building of houses and ships to be a general merchant and a town councillor of Greenock. The young James Watt was a sickly child, too weak to go to school at the right age; and when he did go he was a poor specimen who did badly at his studies and was bullied by everyone.

He was no good at studies—but his father had the insight to realize the boy could become an engineer, for he showed an interest and a natural aptitude. He was given a workshop, all his own, in the attic, and there he made working models of barrel-organs, pumps, pulleys, a crane.

His mother's death coinciding with the family's sudden financial difficulty made him realize he must give up any thought of the university: he must go out now and earn his living.

How did a boy who made toy barrel-organs set about making a living?

He would be an instrument-maker. But first he would have to find one to teach him his trade: he moved to Glasgow.

A little later, having found no one to work with, he set off for London, armed with a letter of recommendation from a kindly professor at Glasgow University.

At first, London seemed as unpromising as Glasgow. As he wrote his father, he had been to visit a number of instrument-makers with his letter of introduction, but "I have not yet got a Master, they all make some objection or other".

At last he found one, who was a businessman as well as an instrument-maker, for he demanded a fee of twenty guineas. Having handed this over, James could work with him—and without pay—for twelve months.

He agreed, and the bargain—though his father was hard put to it sending down sufficient money to keep the lad—was a success. Mr. Morgan seems to have been one of the very few men in London able to teach all the things Watt felt he must know: "Though he works chiefly in the brass way, yet he can teach me most branches of the business, such as rules, scales, quadrants, etc." And by the end of his training, in 1757, aged twenty-one, he was able to write, modestly, "I think I shall be able to get my bread anywhere as I am now able to work as well as most journeymen, though I am not so quick as many".

A brief visit with his father in Greenock, and then back to Glasgow. He went to thank the professor who had helped him with a letter of introduction and was able to help him by repairing some astronomical instruments which had been bequeathed to the university in a state of very bad repair. A little later he was invited to set up business as instrument-maker and repairer within the actual grounds of the university.

Within two years his business had so grown that he needed a partner, and he found him in John Craig, an architect with money, who undertook to handle the financial side of the venture. They needed larger premises, so moved outside the university grounds—though Watt went on living there, and doing all the work they required.

Five years later the firm was employing sixteen men and had sales of over £600 a year. There seemed nothing it was unable to do and Watt himself undertook to repair all sorts of toys, as well as violins, flutes and organs. Later he took to building all these things.

He was twenty-seven when he married—and a good catch. On the other hand, he was the least competent of businessmen and might well have got into difficulties after Craig's death the next year: difficulties from which the canny Margaret saved him.

In the year of his marriage he was handed a particularly difficult job: would he repair the university's model of a Newcomen steam engine? It had never worked properly and its recent visit to London for overhaul had made matters worse.

This was a challenge if ever there was one: a challenge not only to James Watt, but to Scotland. He set to work and stripped the little engine, re-assembled it with joints made leak-proof and the boiler enclosed in a heat-resistant wooden box. But even then the engine, with a bellows blowing like mad into the fire-box, gave a few gasping strokes and stopped dead.

At which point we had better stop and have a look at this Newcomen engine. Its designer, Thomas Newcomen, had greatly improved on the work of his predecessors. He had died in 1729, seven years before Watt was born, yet his engine, with very minor modifications made after his death, was still the best thing available in 1763. But it could only be used as a pump: there was no question of rotary motion. Its piston went slowly up and down, powered by atmospheric pressure, and not steam—though steam was needed in the process—while a lever worked by this piston pumped out mine shafts or delivered water through pipes. Newcomen's great innovation had been to provide a separate boiler, and not rely on the slow and wasteful system of heating a boiler with a piston in it, allowing the piston to move as the steam expanded, and then removing the fire so steam condensed back to water and atmospheric pressure forced the piston back again. Newcomen piped his steam into a separate small cylinder with a piston in it. When the piston had been thrust out by the steam pressure, a valve turned off the inlet of steam and at the same time a jet of cold water *inside* the cylinder condensed the steam and let the piston come back under atmospheric pressure. Previous machines (including Newcomen's own, earlier models) had experimented with a jet of water on the *outside* of the cylinder—which obviously took rather longer to have its effect.

Newcomen's engine was, in its day, of the greatest importance: the pumping of water from mines was a vital task, and without that engine, many shafts would have had to be abandoned. Many countries wanted it, and the one installed in France, at Fresnes, was pumping in forty-eight hours as much water as had been raised in a week by fifty horses and twenty men working day and night in shifts.

It did, however, need its two "engineers" from England, to operate its taps. It was still only a pump. The development of turning its up-and-down, pumping motion into a rotary one—or even of seeing a need to do so—would be Watt's.

He got the university's Newcomen model working and he now turned to his own engine. He took his "walk on a fine Sabbath afternoon", to which we referred earlier, and came back to make a separate condenser, for turning used steam back into water. The steam, having done its work, would be piped to this separate vessel, still hot. (And—which was what really mattered—it would leave the cylinder behind it still hot, so that half the next lot of steam didn't turn to water before it did any work.) In this separate condenser it quietly cooled down to water and was led back to the boiler to be used again.

This enormously improved the efficiency of the engine: a given amount of fuel produced a far greater degree of thrust, pumped far more water.

But somehow, something was still wrong. He had studied his steam (knew it was an invisible substance, that the white vapour one saw at the end of the process, the leak from the cylinder—or from the tea kettle—was steam condensed and useless) and he felt there *must* be a way to get his piston back again, without cooling, wasting, his steam.

This next idea came to him (we do not know whether he was walking on a Sabbath or any other day) and he rushed to put it into effect. Now that he had a cylinder which was kept hot, and needed to be kept hot for maximum efficiency, why not enclose it completely in an outer airtight case filled with steam straight from the boiler? Not only would this keep the cylinder hot: a simple arrangement of valves could make steam pressure exert first one side of the piston, then return it to its original position—the job which had been done by the atmosphere.

And so, at last, there was a real *steam* engine. The steam provided all the power, was not merely a means of providing a vacuum so that atmospheric pressure did the work.

Oddly enough, the innovation of using all this to provide rotative power, to turn wheels, was left to the last. Watt's next great step forward, which would halve the cost of running a steam engine and increase its efficiency, was expansive working. He found that if he let steam into his cylinder and then shut it off when the piston had travelled only a fraction of its full distance, it would still travel that full distance, with great force, simply because the steam expanded. So "one wee spoonful of steam" injected alternately on each side of the piston, did what great gusts of steam had done less effectively before.

And at last Watt developed the rotative engine we know today: converting the up-and-down motion into a rotating one. At first, not trusting the time-honoured crank of spinning-machine and foot-lathe, he devised a system whereby a planet wheel, fastened rigidly to a connecting rod on the end of his piston, rotated like a planet round a sun, around a central wheel which was keyed to the shaft that was to be driven.

Ingenious as this was, he discovered that the old spinning-wheel crank—which he had believed too weak for the engine—was better. All his later engines incorporated a crankshaft and a flywheel—terms which are familiar to us but which were apologetically introduced by James Watt.

There was one problem left. An engine with a constant speed was highly desirable, yet the steam engine varied its speed with the load imposed. He invented the centrifugal governor, in which the tendency of heavy iron or brass balls to fly outwards when whirled round like chestnuts on a string could be made to narrow the steam inlet and reduce speed.

And this was the final Watt engine: not the first steam-engine in history, but as far removed from its predecessors as the rifle from the spear. It had separate condenser, double action, expansive working and a governor. The governor alone, an afterthought by Watt, was a step into something we now call "automation"—roughly two hundred years ahead of its time. For the first time, a machine could use its own "intelligence", decide it was running too fast, slow down.

The Watt engine absolutely revolutionized industry. It came in time to operate the new cotton mills and to give power to a new range of metal- and wood-working tools. By linking the crankshaft of Watt's engine through shafting and belts, to all the machinery in a workshop or factory, it could be made to operate drills, lathes, and the rest of the equipment with a speed and an efficiency undreamed of.

But as inventors throughout history have found—the most brilliant ideas bring little reward until they are completely developed and completely commercial. Watt found himself suddenly a very poor man: he had devoted so much time—and money—to his engine that his instrument-making work had suffered.

And how did he re-coup his losses? He used the knowledge of survey work which he had acquired in repairing survey instruments, and set himself up as a surveyor. He remained an instrument-maker, but managed to find some three days a week to do the other job, and made £200 a year from it, which solved his financial problem. He surveyed the route of a number of canals, and for his work on a part of the great Caledonian, from Inverness to Fort William, he was highly commended by the architect of that scheme, Thomas Telford.

He remained solvent. A little later he was fortunate enough to form a partnership with Matthew Boulton in Birmingham, a man with wealth and influence, who was genuinely interested in the inventor and his engine. In May of 1774 Watt, still only thirty-nine, moved with wife and family to Birmingham. A few months later the firm of Boulton and Watt was making steam-engines for sale.

They soon found that while the making of one engine was a reasonably simple matter, the manufacture of many was highly complex. For a start, the accurate boring of cylinders took weeks and was often a failure. The partners were fortunate in getting hold of a man, whose name is still famous today, who was a brilliant worker in iron: John Wilkinson, and he was able to turn out the cylinders with the accuracy required. He took over the supply of all cylinders to the firm, and when another iron-worker made a bid in competition, Matthew Boulton wrote back, "Wilkinson hath bored us several cylinders almost without error: that of 50″ diameter for Bentley & Co. doth not err the thickness of an old shilling in no part, so you must improve in boring——"

Watt was fortunate in his choice of partner. He himself was highly strung, temperamental, and quite unable to deal with money or any sort of crisis—and Boulton, urbane and level-headed, was the exact opposite. There was a period of depression, which reached its worst in 1781, and Watt, puzzled and panicky, wanted to foreclose on all defaulters. Boulton managed to calm him, and by imaginative methods (as far ahead of their time as Watt's governor), like investing money in the defaulting firms to make them solvent, fight their way out of the crisis.

Both Watt and Boulton lived to a ripe old age, and retired in excellent health to hand over to their sons. Boulton died in 1809 at the age of eighty-two, and Watt, still a youngster of seventy-three with another ten years to go, was heart-broken. He wrote Matthew's son, "Few men have had his abilities and still fewer have exerted them as he has done, and if to them we add his urbanity, his generosity and his affection to his friends, we shall make up a character rarely to be equalled."

In the closing years of his life James Watt received many honours. He was a Fellow of the Royal Society of Edinburgh, and of the Royal Society in London. The University of Glasgow, where he had begun his career, made him an honorary LL.D. Other countries showered unpronounceable honours upon him. His own offered a baronetcy which he politely refused: "Sir James Watt? Never."

His closing years, away from the business—which had worried him—were peaceful and prosperous. Had he been more willing to take risks he would certainly have pioneered the steam locomotive, which would have to wait for someone else—though the hard work had already been done by Watt. Watt's interest had been to make the best possible steam-engine in the world, and go right on doing that. He succeeded—and the demand for those engines went right on mounting. They gave the spur to the Industrial Revolution, but other factors were already in operation when Watt was completing his model: a transition was taking place from the methods and economics of cottage industry and the domestic workshop on the one hand, to larger-scale factory production on the other. Watt and his machine came at the right time to hasten this.

Today steam sounds out of date, old-fashioned. It isn't "switched on" or "with it", and we speak condescendingly of "steam radio" as compared with television. But steam still plays—thanks to that temperamental Scottish genius from Greenock—a very large part in all our lives—for most electricity is generated by steam. We may talk bravely about "nuclear power stations"; we may picture in our mind's eye something like the Aswan Dam in the middle of Britain, producing hydro-electric power—but the fact remains that most electricity in Britain comes from steam-driven generators. (Only the north of Scotland has moved out of the nineteenth century into the next, with its North of Scotland Hydro-Electric Board.) Most power stations now use the fast-running steam turbine, in which high-pressure steam impels a device like a water-wheel: but this would have taken years longer to perfect without James Watt.

He was eighty-four when he died. He had been, as we saw, a sickly child. Perhaps the moral is: work with steam. Certainly inventing television sets and glass razor-blades never did John Logie Baird's health any good.

Before he died, Watt put his own achievement in words, without any false modesty:

"I have spent a long life in improving the arts and manufactures of the nation. My inventions at present, or lately, give employment to the best part of a million of people. Having added many millions to the natural riches, I therefore have a natural right to rest in my extreme old age."

SIR HENRY RAEBURN

They say—or Dr. Johnson did—that a Scotsman's fairest prospect is the road leading south. And certainly many of those in these pages stepped out along it as soon as they were able.

One who tried to but was firmly discouraged was Henry Raeburn, from Edinburgh. At the age of fifty-four, now an established painter, he came to London and called on Sir Thomas Lawrence, the President of the Royal Academy, suggesting he settle there. Sir Thomas replied firmly that in his opinion it would be a grave mistake. Raeburn acted on that advice, went back to Edinburgh.

Supporters of Raeburn maintain that Lawrence was all too obviously trying to prevent another great painter from poaching on his own preserves. Others, comparing the two men and taking note of their contemporaries south of the

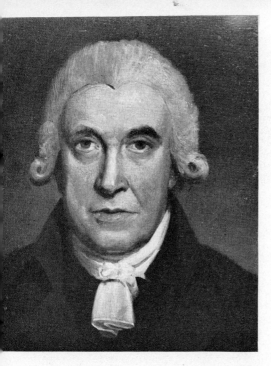

James Watt, *left,* in a portrait by Henry Howard, entitled "The Eminent Engineer, Improver of the Steam Engine". Although it is true that Watt only "improved" the steam engine, it was hopelessly inefficient before he did so, and of little practical use. Watt's improvement brought the Age of Steam and the Industrial Revolution. There are many representations of the young James Watt being fascinated by steam he saw rising from his mother's kettle, and this one, *below,* is less fanciful than many. But it seems that Watt's first real notice of steam came when he had reached manhood and become an instrument-maker. He was given a primitive engine to repair and in the process changed it completely.

Robert Adam, architect and designer, was a dandy as well, who enjoyed life in the fashionable world of London and his own "Adelphi". This painting of him, *above left,* brings the fact out. Sir Henry Raeburn, *above right,* was not: this unusual self-portrait, whose hands must have been painted in later, shows a stolid, no-nonsense, craftsman. Only the luminous eyes hint to us that he was genius as well. But this we can see from his superb portrait of Sir John Sinclair, *right,* believed by many to be one of the finest standing figures ever painted. Raeburn, unlike Adam, spent his entire working life in Scotland.

The Hon. R. M. Sinclair, on Loan to the National Gallery of Scotland border—men like Hoppner, Jackson, Archer Shee—feel Sir Thomas's advice was disinterested. A man of almost fifty-five, who is already a huge fish in quite a small pool, should stay in it.

When I was a child some friends had a number of stunningly beautiful Raeburns in their house. I watched these, open-mouthed, for as long as I was permitted, and as often as I was invited over, which wasn't often. I bought myself a paintbox.

The big Raeburns had the quality of making me feel, literally, very small. I attributed this, not unreasonably, to the fact that I was. But now I realize that this great Scots painter always rendered his subjects as if he were crouching at their feet. This has been explained by experts as his realization that portraits are meant to be hung some distance above the floor; the sitter is therefore seen from below and in commonsense he should be painted as if he were. One would not expect, for example, to see the top of a man's head if one observed him from knee level.

There seems little doubt that this was in Raeburn's mind, and it gives a majestic quality to so much of his painting. On the other hand, one so often sees his men and women from unattractive angles: we are squinting up their nostrils, watching their heads taper off to a point. This is noticeable with "Glengarry", in the National Gallery of Scotland, where the figure of the highland chieftain holding his grounded musket by the muzzle seems about to topple over backwards, seems to clutch frantically at the gun to keep his balance. Being a man of courage he does not show his alarm. But I can—sometimes—almost see it.

In "Sir John Sinclair", where the same knee-height approach has been adopted, the effect is quite different. Sir William Orpen wrote of it, that it could "hold its own with any painted man in existence. In truth, distinction, and dignity without haughtiness, Raeburn's masterpiece surpasses the elegance of Van Dyck and the supreme achievements of Velasquez."

And most of us, able or not to drop names with such assurance, would agree.

Henry Raeburn was born on 4 March, 1756, twelve years after his only brother, William. He was thus thirty-three years younger than Reynolds, twenty-nine years younger than Gainsborough, and twenty-two years younger than Romney. And thirteen years older than Lawrence. The father died when Henry was six, and William looked after him. He was sent to George Heriot's school, where it seems he made hilarious caricatures of his masters and schoolmates, till at about sixteen he was apprenticed to a goldsmith in the High Street. He was fortunate in that his new master, Mr. Gilliland, was a kind and enlightened man, and gave him much encouragement in his drawing and painting. Probably Raeburn's interest in painting was whetted by the miniatures for which he, as apprentice goldsmith, had to design frames. He copied some of the miniatures and was warmly praised for the work, but his interest all along seems to have been in the full-length portrait: as soon as he was able, he jumped straight from the one to the other. By the time he was twenty he was well known in Edinburgh for portraits and also for a few large-canvas landscapes. He had never attended any form of art school— and never would—but he had a certain amount of help from David Martin, a successful portrait painter in the town, who even allowed him to copy some of his own work.

Yet David Martin's rather insipid painting was the exact opposite of the robust, warts-and-all style which Raeburn developed for himself.

Like Gainsborough, he was passionately addicted to the open air, walking miles most days, sketch-book in hand. During one of these rambles he discovered a startlingly pretty girl in a field, and straightway sat down to build a landscape round her.

Whether he managed to attract her attention and point this out to her, whether she merely recognized herself when the picture was exhibited, we do not know, except that she presented herself at his studio to have her portrait painted. It transpired that she was the widow of a Frenchman, Count Leslie, with three small children, and also a little money. Her maiden name was Ann Edgar.

Artist fell in love with model. At the age of twenty-two Henry Raeburn was married and settled into respectable matrimony at Deanhaugh House, near the present Dean Bridge in Edinburgh.

Luck, we can see, was with him: it would stay there throughout his life. Now he was financially almost independent, would never have to paint flattering and dishonest portraits of the rich.

He also had the considerable advantage of real talent without training. He had never been "taught", he never tried to force his own ability into another's mould.

By twenty-eight he was the foremost painter in Scotland. Someone gave him an introduction to the great Sir Joshua Reynolds in London, and he hastened south to present it. Reynolds was kind to the young man, let him work in his studio, admired his work and offered advice. Among it was the suggestion that, if at all possible, the young Scot with the virile technique, the rugged style, go to Italy and study Old Masters. Sir Joshua, now almost an Old Master himself, aged sixty-one, even offered to advance money for the trip, but Raeburn gratefully, and gracefully, refused.

From the paintings he made before Italy and after, that sunny land does not seem to have altered his technique—which is probably as well—though it enlarged his ideas. He spent two years in Italy, and his success, when he got back to Scotland, was swift and enormous. The great of the land queued up to have their portraits in oil painted by him. And, on the firm understanding that they would be presented as he, Raeburn, saw them, not as they saw themselves, the painter agreed.

At this time his brother William died and left him their father's property. He was now wealthy in his own right, quite apart from that of his wife, and he could, in addition, command any price he liked for his portraits. The family moved to a larger house, and he built himself a separate studio and gallery in York Place.

From now on Henry Raeburn's life was an absolutely unbroken chain of success. As we have seen, he was soon to ask Sir Thomas Lawrence about the advisability of moving to London, and, on the strength of Lawrence's answer, to stay in Edinburgh. Honours began to tumble over him. In 1812 he was elected President of the Society of Arts in Edinburgh. Two years later he was an Associate of the Royal Academy in London, and shortly afterwards a full member. In 1822 George IV visited Edinburgh and knighted him. Not content with awarding this honour, the king raised him to the distinction of "His Majesty's Limner for Scotland".

The next year, 1823, he began a majestic picture of Sir Walter Scott. It was while he was engaged on this that he was taken suddenly ill and died. He was sixty-seven.

He had lived a good, generous life, a man with many real friends both in Scotland and in England. He was much respected. As his fellow-Scot, David Wilkie, recorded at the time of Raeburn's arrival in London on a visit, "Went with Raeburn to the Crown and Anchor to meet the gentlemen of the Royal Academy. I introduced him to Flaxman: after dinner he was asked by Beechey to sit near the President, and great attention was paid to him."

He was never involved in any sort of scandal, any dispute; and perhaps these homely virtues tend to blind us to the fact that he was not only a superb painter, but a pioneer. For in Raeburn's day and before, almost every painter of repute—Franz Hals is a notable exception, as is Raeburn's contemporary, Goya—built his work up from a careful black-and-white drawing on the canvas, a complete modelling, before any colour was used. Raeburn, quite untaught, started painting straight away, using all his colours and beginning prosaically with forehead, chin, nose and mouth which he completed before he moved to the rest. It has been said that he spent far more time looking at his sitters than in painting them, because he would stare at them for minutes on end. It unnerved not a few, but the great man was merely taking in details, trying to understand the character of his subject, before putting brush to canvas. He was one of the first great "direct" painters, and probably the life and spontaneity of his pictures could have been achieved in no other way.

They say—many critics do—that the colour of Raeburn's portraits is undistinguished, set against a Goya or a Gainsborough. But it was always in keeping with the subjects he painted: red, grey, white and black, with a certain soft green which was almost his own patent, are the colour schemes of so much he painted. There are few blue Raeburns, no rainbows of the sort Turner used when he is said to have tossed his paint-pot at the public. But "Sir John Sinclair", "Dr. Adam", "The Drummond Children"—even the toppling "Glengarry"—are perfectly presented as we know they must have been. For this reason Raeburn was less successful with his portraits of women, for he was more interested in character than charm.

As we have said, he was personally about as blameless as a man can be. He didn't keep mistresses, didn't drink to excess; he never got into debt, never quarrelled with other painters. This boring blamelessness—why couldn't he have been involved in a good lawsuit, or at least eloped with somebody else's wife?—may have helped disguise the fact that he was and remains one of the greatest British portraitists.

Every day of his life—except when travelling, which was seldom—he rose at seven, breakfasted at eight, entered his studio at nine. There he worked without break till five o'clock every afternoon. After this, on long summer afternoons, he would play a few holes of golf, or go for a walk.

How too terribly, terribly dull. He certainly wouldn't have made the grade today.

JOHN LOUDON McADAM

The girls of Sussex get their long and lovely legs through pulling them out of the mud.

This 1690 observation—in dead earnest—might have applied to numerous other English counties: and might still apply to them; for though we have roads now, which were lacking in 1690, a few strides off one of them in, say, the north of Buckinghamshire during April, will give ample scope for leg-stretching exercise.

For the fact that we have roads, and good ones, we must thank John McAdam. We have come to take them so much for granted that it requires an effort of reason to consider the bald fact that the Industrial Revolution, despite James Watt and his steam engine, despite every other invention and mechanization, would never have happened at all—without McAdam roads. Without them there could have been no transport of the goods so rapidly, efficiently and cheaply made; no sale for them. Production in England's proud new factories would have stopped almost before it began.

It seems odd that Britain should have been so starved of roads: the Romans left plenty behind, and these, with a little care and maintenance, would have survived into our present day, as indeed some do. But for the most part it is only the names that remain: Watling Street, The Icknield Way, Ermine Street and the rest of them.

The Romans built for ever—and the fact that their handiwork is still with us, two thousand years or so after they did it, seems proof enough that they succeeded. Thomas Telford built roads in the same way and they were superb and extremely expensive. Labour costs had been less in the time of the Romans.

It needed McAdam to work out a way of building roads which was really efficient and yet not prohibitively expensive. Were it not for McAdam we might still, in many ways, be back in the eighteenth century, without its charm. Our various local councils, from the Greater London down, would be arguing whether to leave Piccadilly and Princes Street, Sauchiehall Street and the Mall just muddy cart tracks till the end of time, or float a loan to pave them by Telford's method.

Which is not to denigrate Telford: he was a brilliant engineer, who made everything, and to whom we owe an enormous debt. John McAdam was only the chap who made the road. But we would have been in a bad way without him.

He was the youngest of ten children, born in Ayrshire, in 1756, and descended from landed gentry. Indeed, the family pedigree seems to have embraced the nobility as well, and to be genuinely descended not only from Robert III, King of Scotland, but also from Edward III of England. But by the time Number Ten came along, John Loudon's father's resources were thoroughly strained, and he decided, after much worry and soul-searching, to send the boy to America. There, in an up-and-coming Colony where

Mr. McAdam's younger brother was already settled, the lad would stand a chance.

He was fourteen when at last he reached New York, was embraced by Uncle William and introduced to the pleasant world of minor merchant princes, those eighteenth-century White Settlers of Manhattan. It was a good life, though it would soon be rent by civil war, the War of American Independence. It would have been unthinkable for young John Loudon McAdam to have aligned himself with the rebels, and at the outbreak of hostilities he enlisted as a volunteer in a Loyalist New York regiment. We know little about his military service during the Revolution except the established fact that the whole of Manhattan Island and Long Island remained in English hands throughout the war, and no doubt he did his bit to ensure this.

As a result of which, he and all other Loyalists were understandably in disgrace when the war ended in American victory. By an act of the Congress, all their properties were attainted and become the property of the State (exactly as had happened in Scotland with the properties of men supporting the '15 and the '45). In 1783, John sailed home to Scotland. He was a man of twenty-seven with a wife (described on their wedding day, by the *New York Gazette*, as a "Young Lady of Great Beauty and Merit with a large Fortune") and their two children. The fortune was gone and prospects in Ayrshire seemed glum, but they managed somehow to buy themselves a house and settle down.

And they fell on their feet. As John McAdam's daughter Georgina was to write, much later, "My father made many valuable friends in New York, for owing to the war it was crowded with officers of rank. . . . It was fortunate for my parents that the war sent all home together, and the American set were all very aristocratic. My father lost nothing, therefore, in point of station in the world by living so long abroad. He found his sisters in the same circle that they had always belonged to and as much visited and made of as ever."

But McAdam was a remarkable man in his own right,

and it was not entirely the work of his aristocratic friends which placed him as Deputy-Lieutenant of Ayrshire. The job was no sinecure, for it involved among other things the raising of a corps of volunteer artillery to resist the invading French armies whensoever they might come, and he did it with great enthusiasm.

Field artillery, to be effective, needs roads—and young volunteer Major McAdam discovered his country had none. None, that is, worthy of the name. They were bad enough in England: in Scotland even the good ones were "at once loose, rough and perishable, expensive, dangerous to travel on and very costly to repair".

Oddly enough, though the name McAdam now suggests to us a tarmac road, there was no question during the great road-maker's life of using tar or any other binding substance with the little stones out of which he built a road: yet one of his first business enterprises was a firm that manufactured tar from coal. Three years after his return from New York he and his distant kinsman, the Earl of Dundonald, were partners in the British Tar Co. A by-product of the tar-making was coke, and this was conveniently utilized in making iron at their Muirkirk Iron Co.

Fifteen years of satisfying work, both for himself and for Scotland, ended when he was appointed to Bristol in charge of victualling the Navy.

To his surprise, he found the roads in and around Bristol as inadequate—or absent—as they had been in Ayrshire.

He had, for many years, given thought to methods of constructing a road that would take all sorts of traffic and need the minimum of repair, and he thought now that he had a formula for it. But at first, in Bristol, his suggestions about road-making were dismissed: his job was to victual ships, not waste his time trying to improve communications on land, which had functioned adequately for hundreds of years.

But at last, in 1816, the Bristol Municipality appointed him as its General Surveyor and John Loudon McAdam began his career as a builder of roads. He was sixty years old.

Just what was a McAdam road?

It was not, as we have seen, a thing of bitumen. It differed greatly in fact and in principle from those laid down by Thomas Telford, for McAdam believed that a road should be sprung. Not for him the heavy paving which the Romans and Telford used, upon which they built up their layers of stone and binding: his road should be entirely composed of stones, none of which were more than six ounces in weight, and the total thickness should be in the neighbourhood of ten inches. Laying this directly upon the earth (which, if needed, must be first drained) made it spring when horses and vehicles used it. This, he maintained, gave a smoother journey, and a longer interval between repairs to the surface.

The road should be laid almost flat—not highly cambered as was the practice when he took over the work—with only just enough rise, say three inches in a road eighteen feet across, for the water to run off into the ditches on either side. It should not be a great stone erection, but simply "an artificial flooring forming a strong, smooth and solid surface at once capable of carrying great weight and over which carriages may pass without meeting any impediment".

To ensure that his individual pieces of stone—he preferred flint—were no more than six ounces in weight, he devised a two-inch ring measure. If the stone wouldn't go through, it was too big. The stones were broken on site by workmen (and women) sitting down to do the job with little hammers and laying them carefully. Because they were deliberately broken and were not rounded pebbles from a beach, their sharp angles made them unite into a compact mass which was entirely waterproof.

With a road built this way, about ten inches thick—and absolutely without any admixture of earth or chalk or clay or other matter—McAdam maintained any load could be carried. We can condense his own views this way, still keeping the words of a letter he wrote to the President of the Board of Agriculture on the subject:

"The erroneous opinion so long acted upon and so tenaciously adhered to, that by placing a large quantity of stone under the road a remedy will be found for the sinking into wet clay, or other soft soils and the road be made sufficiently strong artificially to carry heavy carriages though the sub-soil be in a wet state, and by such means avert the inconveniences of the natural soil receiving water from rain or other causes, has produced most of the defects of the roads of Great Britain.

"It should be well known to every skilful and observant road-maker that if strata of stone of various sizes be placed on a road the largest stones will constantly work up by the shaking and pressure of the traffic, and that the only mode of keeping the stones from motion is to use material of a uniform size from the bottom.

"It has been found that roads laid upon a hard bottom wear away more quickly than those which are placed upon a soft soil. It is a known fact that a road lasts much longer over a morass than when made over rock.

"The first operation in making a road should be the reverse of digging a trench. The road should not be sunk below but rather raised above the ordinary level of the adjacent ground, and care should be taken that there be a sufficient fall to take off the water. This must be done either by making drains into lower ground, or if that be not practicable from the nature of the country, then the soil upon which the road is proposed to be laid must be raised by addition, so as to be some inches above the level of the water.

"Having secured the soil from *under* water the road-maker should next secure it from rain water by means of a solid road made of clean, dry stone or flint, so selected, prepared and laid so as to be perfectly impervious to water. This cannot be done unless the greatest care be taken that no earth, clay, chalk or other matter that will hold or conduct water be mixed with the broken stone, which must be so prepared and laid as to unite by its own angles into a firm, compact, impenetrable body.

"The thickness of such a road is immaterial as to its strength for carrying weight. This object is already attained by providing a dry surface over which the road is to be placed as a covering or roof in order to preserve it in that state, experience having shown that if water passes through and fills the native soil the road, whatever may be its thickness, loses its support and goes to pieces.

"None of the new roads I have recently constructed on this principle are more than six inches thick, and although that on the great north road is subjected to very heavy traffic, being only 15 miles distant from London, it has not given way, nor was it affected by the late severe winter, when the roads between that point and London became impassable by breaking up to the bottom. On the roads built according to the system I have described, over 100 miles of them, there was no interruption of travelling, nor any additional expense by the Post Office in conveying mails over them."

There, more or less in a nutshell, we have the recipe for making a good road—for the "very heavy traffic" on the great north road of the early nineteenth century: and for reasonably light traffic today. McAdam did not live to see the sort of traffic, heavy lorries travelling at forty and fifty miles an hour, which would have destroyed his road.

But that last sentence in his letter is doubly interesting. He speaks of roads built *according to the system he described*—and he points out that the Post Office had no additional expense in maintaining them, for they needed no repair.

McAdam was becoming an old man and his invention of a revolutionary new method for making roads had earned him, directly, not a penny, although others, all over the land, were using the method. Even the Post Office was saving money, hand over fist. Soon he would ask—much as the inventor of radar would ask, more than a century later—whether a grateful government might not see its way to rewarding him.

Radar is not the sort of device any man can pretend to have invented; a few minutes' cross-examination before an expert committee asking questions about oscilloscopes, scanning, and optimum frequencies, would reduce most of us to a quivering wreck. But any man can build a road if he spends a little time—a very little time—finding out how. Some of us could go out, right now, having digested the recipe above, and assemble a team to make a McAdam road. We could very easily maintain that we had been using that not very complex system for years.

We could say we thought of it first.

And this is exactly what other people did, when John McAdam's case was presented, near the end of his life, to Parliament. Not only was he using other men's ideas; he had made himself a great deal of money as Surveyor in charge of all the roads he had time to supervise himself, and he had brought down his sons from Scotland to share the work and the profit.

The last part is true. McAdam was a good businessman and a good father. When he felt that his own strength was failing and that he would not be able to do all the work he wanted, he sent for his three sons. All of them were able and very soon they were in charge of long stretches of road-making all over England—and later Scotland—which rewarded them well. But John himself did a great deal of his work for no reward at all. He was frank about this when a Committee of the House of Commons examined him to see whether he was worthy of any financial grant. The chairman asked him why he had maintained in evidence that, had he charged for his advice, it would have hindered the introduction of his system, and McAdam replied:

"I form that opinion because in every case when I was written to for advice or assistance, it was preceded by a letter desiring to know what the expense would be. Upon coming to every Trust I afterwards found there was a party adverse to my being consulted—I found they had always opposed my being sent for under the pretence that it would be an enormous expense. In any case, they never consented to my being sent for until a letter came from me to say it would be no expense at all. . . . My belief is that if I had made it a money-making speculation I should have strangled the business at its birth and my system never would have been introduced in the country at all."

McAdam did succeed in getting grants in recognition of what he had done, but to the end of his life he was opposed and misrepresented. Then, and later, he was compared unfavourably with Thomas Telford, a great and uncomplicated man who was as different from John Loudon McAdam as it is possible to imagine. Telford was the genial bachelor who lived for engineering, had no home life and didn't want any; whereas McAdam was a businessman and a family man and insisted he was no engineer, just a maker of roads. There seems little evidence that the two men ever quarrelled, but their supporters did, and baseless rumours flourished about the remarks each was said to have made about the other. The poet Southey waxed lyrical about Telford, called him *Pontifex Maximus*— and dismissed the other man's work as quackadamizing. Someone else thought up the title "Colossus of Roads" for McAdam and dismissed Telford as his inferior.

But while all this was going on, Britain was getting roads. A few years back even London had been almost a beleaguered city in the winter. Lord Hervey had written from Kensington to a friend complaining that "the road between this place and London is grown so infamously bad that we live here in the same solitude as if cast on a rock in the middle of the ocean. All Londoners tell us that between them and us there is an impassable gulf of mud."

All this was becoming a thing of the past, thanks to McAdam. (The Telford road was too expensive, took too long to build, for anything other than main highways.) Slowly the streets and squares of London were being macadamized, and one great advantage of the innovation was that the roadway was not only free of mud and potholes, but almost silent when carriages and horses went over it. *The Times* wrote:

"The Vestry of St. James's parish have, with a view of lessening the noise of carriages during Divine Service, Macadamized that part of Jermyn Street which adjoins the Church."

The heavy paving stones which had been used in London, apart from their tendency to sink into the earth, made a dismal clatter when wheels or hooves went over.

Seldom has the name of a process been so swiftly absorbed into the language. A music critic was soon to complain of a virtuoso's "macadamizing a few broad, simple and impressive sounds into passages of numberless rapid notes——" A bishop was described as having "macadamized the way for his successor"; suitors tried to "macadamize" young women into conversation; the poet Thomas Hood sends out "a gondolier on smooth macadam seas".

Hood, in fact, sets out the road-builder's claims to fame quite succinctly during his lengthy *Ode to Mr. McAdam*:

> *"Dispenser of coagulated good,*
> *Distributor of granite and of food!*
> *Long may thy fame its even path march on*
> *E'en when thy sons are dead,*
> *Best benefactor! Though thou giv'st a stone*
> *To those who ask for bread!"*

In 1836, returning in his eighty-first year from his annual visit to Scotland, McAdam was taken ill and died.

If ever proof had been needed of the service he and his sons were giving in their careful supervision of the Mcadam process, it was available, in abundance, after he died. Within a year or two roads were being built all over Britain which paid lip-service to their inventor and were a travesty of the process. Stones of all sizes were being used, the roadway was being filled with earth and clay, drainage was being neglected.

The reason, one astute observer pointed out, was "ignorant vestries in league with corrupt contractors".

And here we have another clue to the real service John McAdam gave his country. From the very first days in Bristol he had noticed that contractors and sub-contractors needed constant supervision by honest surveyors. He and his sons gave that supervision, and the roads were a monument to them. They died—and the process almost died with them.

But they left behind them thousand upon thousand of miles of superb road across the face of the world. We no longer make our highways that way—but McAdam's roads fulfilled an urgent need. No motorway of the future can ever be half as important.

THOMAS TELFORD

A Scot who would have qualified for a place in this book had there been more space is Samuel Smiles. He was a remarkable man, educated for the medical profession in Edinburgh University and then tossing the idea, the training, away to become social reformer and writer.

There was no doubt in his mind; he had waded through years of medical studentship and found himself wanting; his interests lay elsewhere. Wisely, courageously, he set about doing something else.

This is a point which has often exercised me: how many of us start off in the wrong lane and have neither the courage nor the opportunity to get into the right one? How many doctors, dentists, should have been actors, bus conductors, fabric designers, head waiters? How many airline pilots should have been hairdressers or plumbers?

We will never know.

One thing that started me thinking along these cynical lines years ago was the immediate post-war period when I persuaded the RAF to teach me, a soldier, how to fly. There was a large course of us, all young, dead keen and obviously with an interest in flying.

In the first few weeks the penguins and the eagles were separated; the penguins, who had failed to go solo in the required number of flying hours, crept back to their units. The rest of us, proud and confident, settled down to a few months' hard work.

A few more dropped, winged, by the wayside. I nearly did myself, being unable to land an aeroplane in the dark, so that I went round and round, missing the flare-path, the runway, each time. Then, a panicky realization that I might run out of fuel and plunge down a factory chimney, got me down, and alive.

But I wasn't the worst. Not by a long chalk. I was a typical young man of the sort who takes up flying, with a wild urge to get airborne, and some aptitude for it—like everyone else on the course. And half of us would have been better off doing something quite different; though most of us were good enough to survive and get wings.

But if I thought today that any one of us—with the exception of, say, three—anyone from that distant Operational Training Unit, or anyone *like* them, was up in front in the Boeing Jet or the Concord—or the Piper Cub—on which I had booked a seat, I would disembark in haste.

And, of course, by the law of averages, somebody just like that *would* be there. For until someone devises a foolproof system of putting us all in the right slot we will go on having pilots who ought to have been ballet dancers or shoe salesmen; doctors who should have been airline pilots, or journalists, or bricklayers.

And engineers who should have been put on to something very, very different.

We digressed because of Samuel Smiles, a man who had the courage and the commonsense to switch his horses in mid-stream. And one of Smiles's greatest works, of which we would have been deprived had he remained a saw-bones, is *Lives of the Engineers*.

One of his *Lives*, Thomas Telford, is that rarest of birds, the man who could never have been anything other than what he was—a dedicated, brilliant, civil engineer. Perhaps Smiles, an exact opposite, understood him better than most.

He tells us Thomas Telford was born in "one of the most solitary nooks of the narrow valley of the Esk, in the eastern part of the county of Dumfries, in Scotland". The year was 1757, and "before the year was out he was an orphan". His father, a hardworking shepherd, died in November, leaving a widow and the infant Thomas.

The house they lived in was little more than a mud hut, but as all who study Scotland know, this made no difference at all to the boy's opportunities for education. There was—as there always is—an excellent village school, which he attended until he was fourteen. And by this time he had no doubts at all—he would become an engineer.

First, though, he would allow himself to be apprenticed to a mason. This was a disaster, for the man disliked Telford as much as Telford disliked the man, and the young apprentice ran home to his mother. But as the work was what he wanted, he helped his mother look round for another placing and at last was happily settled with Andrew Thomson at Langholm.

At first there was little masonry to be done, and the early months of apprenticeship were frustrating. Young Thomas Telford was put to every other sort of building task but that of mason. The reason was straightforward: in Telford's own words, the houses round about consisted of "one storey of mud walls, or rubble stones bedded in clay, and thatched with straw, rushes or heather; the floors being of earth and the fire in the middle, while instead of windows small openings in the thick mud walls admitted a scanty light".

Fortunately for Andrew Thomson and his apprentice, a new Duke of Buccleugh inherited the land for miles around. He was a young man, full of ideas, and he set about repairing and rebuilding every house on his property. Mud would be replaced by stone, straw by slate.

Soon the masons had all the work they could handle, and Telford realized that this sort of building, not for today or tomorrow, but for posterity, was the only work that interested him. There was no overtime rate in those days, but he went on working long after his employer had downed chisel for the night, lovingly shaping and facing the stones. He finished his apprenticeship but stayed on with Thomson because there was still so much work to do. Then, aged twenty-two, he headed for Edinburgh.

But before he did, he cut a headstone for his father's grave. It had been marked with only a small cairn for those twenty-two years, and now he lovingly chiselled out:

> *In Memory of*
> *John Telford*
> *Who after living 33 years*
> *an Unblameable Shepherd*
> *Died at Glendinning*
> *November 1757*

Edinburgh, for a poor boy from the country, was like one of the wonders of the world. He got work, all he could manage, rebuilding the capital of fine stone. He spent what spare time he had moving about the town, studying the buildings, the castle, Holyrood House.

But after two years, "I considered that my native country afforded few opportunities of exercising my profession to any extent. I therefore judged it advisable (like many of my countrymen) to proceed southward, where industry might find more employment, and be better remunerated."

He set out on horseback, and when he arrived, weeks later, it was to find, as he had hoped, that there was a great deal of work and very few masons to do it. An elderly spinster from his village, who had let him read books in her small library, had also armed him with a letter. This got him into the presence of no less a man than Sir William Chambers, architect of Somerset House. He got work on that building, which kept him in reasonable comfort at his lodgings, for wages were good; but each evening he busied himself drawing plans for buildings of his own.

We can say right now that Thomas Telford, though he was unquestionably one of Britain's greatest engineers, was a very lucky man. Perhaps a part of that luck stemmed from his attractive personality, for men and women liked him as soon as they met him, were anxious to help him. And though he would soon be in little need of it, a young civil engineer (qualified only as stone mason) needs all he can get. He was befriended by Sir William Pulteney, who gave him two commissions: he was to prepare plans for major alterations to Pulteney's large house, and to carry out the rebuilding of a vicarage on his property.

He did the jobs well, and prospered by them. He met the Adam brothers, much-travelled, well-off architects from his native land, and they were fascinated by this rough but charming man who told them, "There is nothing done in stone or marble that we cannot do in the completest manner".

This first person plural seems to have embraced the partner he hoped to take in with him, but that plan came to nothing. For most of a busy life Thomas Telford worked by himself. He travelled to Portsmouth where he spent another two years, part of them building a house for the Dockyard Commissioner. Already his name as one of the finest masons in Britain had spread to most of Britain's towns. But his chief interest in Portsmouth was studying the harbour, the docks.

There was a lull in the work and once again good fortune smiled upon him. His old friend Pulteney, delighted with the work on mansion and vicarage, was now able to organize a really important job for him, that of County Surveyor in Shropshire.

This was wonderful: he had been tacitly accepted as both architect and engineer, and he flung himself into the job. He found—and it pleased him—that much of it would involve bridges and bridging, for Shropshire is a land of rivers. His first bridge, though he had amused himself by planning many over the years, was at Montford, to the west of Shrewsbury. It would carry the main London-Holyhead road over the Severn, and although Telford did not know it at the time, this road and its bridges would always be associated with his name.

But in the meantime, as the Montford bridge was abuilding under his instructions, he had one of those rare "I told you so" experiences which, when they come, give such sardonic joy. As County Surveyor he was asked to inspect the old church of St. Chad in Shrewsbury town. To the anger and dismay of the churchwardens he submitted a report stating that the edifice was highly unsafe: graves had been dug so close to the foundations that it was in danger of toppling over. A patching job on the roof—which was what the wardens had had in mind—would be a waste of time and money, until the walls were made safe.

The report was rejected as too expensive and unnecessary. A local builder was put on to the patching.

And the next morning, as the builder's men stood outside the church, while someone went off to get a key, it happened. There was a thunderous crash and most of the church dissolved into ruins.

"The very parts I had pointed out were those which gave way, and down tumbled the tower, forming a very remarkable ruin, which astonished and surprised the vestry and roused them from their infatuation, although they have not yet recovered from the shock."

Telford's first bridge was of stone, but his second effort is of greater importance, for he built it of iron. It was not only efficient, but beautiful, having one long, slender span. The reason for having only one was Telford's belief that river traffic on the Severn (for this was another bridge over that river) must not be interfered with. And, though he could hardly have known it, waterways would concern him a great deal.

Canals in England were almost exactly Telford's age: he had been an infant when the first one was dug from the Worsley coal pits to Manchester. And we can skip a bridge or two to move to the next stage in Telford's career, the planning, designing, of canals.

Canals, in those days of bad roads and no railways, were the hope of the future. Nothing—not even the good roads which Telford would soon be building—would be able to carry large cargoes like coal economically. And so men began to dig them, and the navigating engineers, the "navvies", who did it, have left us a picturesque name for something quite different. Telford's first canal was the Ellesmere, joining the Mersey, the Severn and the Dee and linking Liverpool overland with Bristol. It was a daunting task, for there were high hills, deep valleys, to cross. The age-old method had been to build locks which would enable small barges to be lifted up, in the water which floated them, and be placed, water and all, on a higher level. (And, going down the hill, lowered gently in reverse.) The process was and is much like lifting a minnow from a stream in a bucket and gently pouring minnow and water into a tub. But the closing of the lock, and the slow raising or lowering of it, is a time-consuming process. To negotiate one of the valleys on the proposed canal route would have necessitated a total of sixteen locks: eight down to the floor of the valley; another eight up again, on the far side. Getting a barge or a narrowboat through this chain might easily take a day—and the horizontal distance was only half a mile.

So he planned—and built—an aqueduct.

It was a remarkable feat of engineering. There have been man-made rivers lifted up on stilts to negotiate an obstacle, but none like Telford's at Pontcysylte. It took eight years to build. The iron river-bed was lifted a hundred and twenty-seven feet, and carried on nineteen pillars. For the first seventy feet of their height these were solid: above that, hollow. The cast-iron trough they supported was seven and a half feet wide, with a four and a half feet towpath beside it.

The canal was finished in 1803 and the two aqueducts, Pontcysylte and the smaller Chirk which Telford built simultaneously, are its outstanding landmarks. To Walter Scott, the former was "the most impressive work of art" he had ever seen.

It deserved to be. From this moment on Thomas Telford's name was world-famous.

There were more canals, more aqueducts, more bridges. And in 1801, while the Ellesmere was being finished to his plans, he was asked to tour the highlands of Scotland and advise on the possibility of getting better fishing harbours on the west coast; naval bases on the east; and a canal right across the country from east coast to west.

As always, he plunged into the job, made recommendations, many of them sweeping, most of which were gratefully accepted. Telford did more for communications in Scotland than any man before him—or perhaps since. He planned no less than 1,200 bridges, all of which were built to his instructions. He charted nine hundred and twenty miles of major road, all of which was laid down.

And he built the Caledonian Canal.

It was a brilliantly executed piece of engineering, which got him commissions from all over Europe and, among other things, a Swedish knighthood. But commercially, it was a failure.

The fault was not Telford's. The Caledonian Canal was made obsolete, almost before it was finished, by the coming of steam.

The plan behind it, of course, had been avoidance of a long haul for sailing vessels, right over the top of Scotland. These, when work began, were the only ships in existence, and it was not uncommon for them to take weeks, battling with alternate storm and dead calm, to get from the east coast to the west—from North Sea to Atlantic Ocean. But by the time the canal was finished, steam ships were almost commonplace; one of these could dash over the top of Scotland in a day or so, without worrying about winds.

But it was still an astonishing feat of engineering.

It was sixty miles long—and there were others far longer than this in existence. But it was a ship canal, not a midget waterway for barges, and Telford designed it 110 feet wide on the surface, narrowing to 50 feet at its bottom, 20 feet below. The locks—for no aqueduct would be possible on this scale—were watertight chambers 180 feet by 40, and 20 feet in depth. Telford designed and built twenty-eight of these to cover the distance, including sea locks at each end which were miniature harbours.

He was sixty-five when the Caledonian Canal opened: it had taken nineteen years, from 1803 to 1822. But in the meantime he had accomplished other near-miracles. He had built splendid harbours at Aberdeen and at Wick (and made alterations to fifty others); he had built, for Sweden, the Gotha Canal linking the Baltic to the North Sea, exactly twice the length of his Caledonian; he had started work on the great bridge across the Menai Strait, linking the mainland of Wales with the Isle of Anglesey. Its purpose, of course, was, and still is, to speed up the journey from England to Ireland, via the steamer crossing at Holyhead. Telford's job was not only to throw a huge suspension bridge (one of history's first) across the Straits, but to build or re-build countless others, to make miles of road, to alter gradients, the whole way from London to Holyhead.

The Menai Bridge took seven years to build. Before it began, Telford carried out tests on the tensile strength of iron, opened up special quarries for the stone. He built his bridge with a width of 550 feet (unheard of, in those days) between two supporting pillars, and clearing high water by 100 feet. It had two carriageways 12 feet wide, with a central pathway 4 feet wide. The first London-Holyhead mail coach passed from the mainland to Anglesey on 30 January, 1826, with a beaming Telford following in a post-chaise.

One might call this superb bridge the Monument to Telford. But there are Telford roads and Telford bridges all over Britain—and in many parts of Europe, including Russia, as well as his canals. Perhaps his most beautiful bridge was the one over the Clyde at Broomielaw, a bridge without steel this one, with seven stone arches and a total length of 560 feet. It was also, at 60 feet, the widest bridge in Britain when it was completed—but Telford never lived to see that day.

What sort of a man was this *Pontifex Maximus*, as the

Poet-Laureate Southey called him, this Master Bridge-builder?

He was a confirmed bachelor, to the day he died. As we said at the beginning, he was an engineer born to the job, for he liked working, living on the site, and until he was sixty-four he never possessed a home of his own. He used as base throughout most of his life a coffee-house near Charing Cross in London, where he had rooms. Samuel Smiles tells the story in his *Lives of the Engineers* that the sight of the great engineer seated in an armchair in the coffee-house began to mean a great deal in daily takings. So much so that when the place changed hands, as it did many times during Telford's residence, he was included, as we would say today, in fixtures and fittings. When Telford at last decided to take a house of his own, and gave notice, "The landlord, who had but recently entered into possession, stood almost aghast. 'What, leave the house!' said he, 'why, sir, I have just paid £750 for you!'"

And so he had: the man before had paid a mere £450, but Telford had grown in importance. But he left and settled at a house, No. 24 Abingdon Street. He still travelled extensively, going annually to the highlands to inspect his work, but Abingdon Street remained home until his death on 2 September, 1834.

He was, perhaps, a lonely man. He never had any interest in marriage and he seems to have had few relatives. He left all his money to charity. But he had many friends, and he was always eager to meet and help young civil engineers. He had no enemies, despite the tales that he disagreed violently with John Loudon McAdam. His disagreement was one of principle, and a major engineering principle, too, but there was no personal animosity. Perhaps the two men were so totally different in background and outlook that they could never have quarrelled. They were never near enough.

What was this difference of principle?

Telford built for ever: McAdam for the immediate future. Telford's roads were expensive, works of crafts-manship which had borrowed much from the Romans. His road might be anything up to five feet deep, with big stones at the bottom, carefully fitted together, the whole rising through smaller, but still tailored, stones to the surface. McAdam's road were simpler, and, in fact, he sincerely believed that a soft bottom and nothing but six-ounce stones above it, the whole way through, would last longer. Perhaps it did—but the McAdam road, though its name has lingered, is of little use in today's heavy vehicular traffic.

Telford's roads, had they been wide enough, could have lasted for ever, wherever he laid them—as, in the highlands, many of them will. His canals today take little traffic, but times may change and bring them back to popularity. But his hundreds of bridges, from mighty stone castles to his "little spider's webs in the sky", remain his monument.

ROBERT BURNS

Probably more nonsense is said and written about Robert Burns than of any other national hero. I shall try not to add to it.

But, as pointed out elsewhere—in the article on Byron —the only things worth knowing about a writer—about Burns—are what he wrote. Our image of Burns as a man, however accurate or inaccurate it may be, has nothing to do with Burns as a writer. And it is as a writer, a superb writer, that he has survived in men's hearts. Had he been only the amorous ploughboy, the conscientious, puzzled farmer, or the Edinburgh intellectual (take your choice), he would have vanished from the pages of history many years ago. If indeed he ever got there.

And though one may be used to hearing sentimental Burns declaimed, through a mouthful of haggis, he didn't only write this way. He was a man of education, sensibility, common sense. And, above all, imagination. So was Byron. So was Scott. And though we tend to read each of them with the physical picture of the man in mind, it is not beyond reason that much of Burns could have been written by Byron or Scott. And vice versa, etc.

If it had been, it wouldn't matter.

But before we get too involved in this line of argument let us just look at the man himself. For however irrelevant his behaviour to his memory and his work—he was a remarkable fellow.

He was born, as everyone knows, in the Alloway cottage which his father built with his own two hands. The year was 1759. That father, who originally spelt his name Burness, had come to Ayrshire from the east of Scotland, from Kincardineshire, to improve his fortunes.

He was to fail. He worked desperately hard on his two leased farms, first Lochlie, then Mount Oliphant, but died bankrupt and beaten in 1784. But Burns by this time was twenty-five and thanks to his poor father's industry, and determination that the boy be educated, he knew a great deal more than most people of twenty-five today. The farmers of the neighbourhood had hired a good teacher, as was the custom, and that teacher, John Murdoch, had transmitted, to all farmers' boys who would listen, a knowledge of Latin and French and Dryden and Milton and Shakespeare. Robert Burns had absorbed all this like a sponge, and with it geography, history and grammar. To say nothing of subjects he read up by himself, like physics, astronomy, botany.

When his father died, Robert found himself tenant of the farm of Mossgiel, to which his father was transferring, in yet another disastrous move, just before he died. Robert was the eldest of seven children and therefore head of the family of Burness—a spelling which he retained for many years.

He might well have remained tenant of Mossgiel and perhaps a man of substance if Elizabeth Paton had not joined the Mossgiel establishment as servant girl. Love, and the rest of it, happened, and he was soon the father of his first illegitimate child, a daughter, whom he dearly loved, and greeted with a pretty poem. Later he was to write, "There is certainly some connection between love and music and poetry, for I never had the least thought or inclination of turning poet till I once got heartily in love. And then, rhyme and song were, in a manner, the spontaneous language of my heart."

We know much of Burns through his *Commonplace Book*, styled bravely "Observations, Hints, Songs, Scraps of Poetry, &c, by Robert Burness——" Into it in 1785, a year after his father's death, he inscribed "The Death and Dying Words of Poor Maillie". It was a mock testament, purporting to come from a dying sheep, and full of biting humour; a very Scottish piece. It was only one of a series of entries, some good, some bad, all interesting, which he made during 1785 and 1786, while still trying to run a farm.

Then in 1786 he met Jean Armour, fell madly in love. As was always the case with Burns, a child was soon on the way, but there seemed no great problem. Jean said she loved him, he knew he loved her, and by Scots law mutual consent followed by consummation was a legal marriage. Then old Armour, a master mason, persuaded his daughter to go back on her promise.

Burns, miserable, angry, almost unbelieving, turned to another girl, Mary Campbell, his *Highland Mary*. To add to his troubles, the farm was doing badly and he now planned to emigrate, with Mary, to Jamaica. The plan was thwarted by Mary's death, at about which time Jean Armour was delivered of his child—which turned out to be twins.

Upsetting. Confusing. And now old man Armour, who had prevented the legitimate birth of his own twin grandsons, made matters worse by threatening to sue Burns to provide for their upkeep. In the nick of time there emerged a thin volume of verses which he had sent to a printer in Kilmarnock. It came out on 31 July, 1786, and was entitled "Poems Chiefly in the Scottish Dialect".

A huge, and startling, success. Everyone loved it. Edinburgh critics lauded it to the skies, simple country folk bought it. So great was the demand to meet this young poet that Robert Burns, not quite twenty-eight years old, set out for Edinburgh. It was the first time he had left his native county of Ayr.

There was good stuff in that Kilmarnock volume—some of it taken from the *Commonplace Book,* like the "Death and Dying Words of Poor Maillie". There were also the now-famous "To a Mouse" and "To a Louse", with several other first-rate Scots poems, "The Holy Fair", "Scotch Drink", "The Twa Dogs". Burns wrote many "English" poems during his life and one or two of the less successful ones, like "Man was Made to Mourn" and "Despondency, an Ode", were also included.

There was also "The Cotter's Saturday Night" which brought tears to every eye, in 1786, but to us today seems contrived and bogus, a self-conscious presentation of the "peasant life" Burns thought he understood, for the edification of the sort of man he really was; in other words, a sophisticated literateur.

"To a Mouse" and "To a Louse" were gems—with honours going to the latter. The poet watches an over-dressed and self-assured lady in church, where he suddenly notices a louse upon her bonnet. He plays off the horrible insect ("How dare ye set your foot upon her, Sae fine a lady!") against the fine lady, for verse after verse—until suddenly the fine lady is just "Jenny—dinna toss your head——"

And the poem ends with the words we all know:

> *"Oh, would some Pow'r the giftie gie us*
> *To see oursels as others see us!*
> *It would from many a blunder free us*
>   *And foolish notion:*
> *What airs in dress and gait would leave us,*
>   *And e'en devotion!"*

In Edinburgh, Burns was received eagerly as an equal and more, by men like the Earl of Glencairn, the poet Hugh Blair, the historian Robertson, the philosopher Dugald Steward. Being an educated man, if largely self-taught, he moved easily into the circle, and his natural charm did the rest. As for what he looked like, let us consult Walter Scott, who was then a boy of fifteen, but remembered him vividly in later life: "He was of manners rustic, not clownish. The eye alone indicated the poetical character and temperament; it was large and of a dark cast, and literally glowed when he spoke with feeling or interest."

Two years of Edinburgh was enough; by 1788, Burns was on his way back. It had been good fun, with a number of amorous adventures thrown in but Ayrshire was his real home, and to Ayrshire he returned. He had at last persuaded his Jean, Jean Armour, to marry him, and with the money from both Kilmarnock and Edinburgh editions of his work, he was able to rent a new farm, Ellisland, on the banks of the River Nith, near Dumfries. It was a larger farm than what he had been used to before Edinburgh, and the experiment failed, despite the devoted help he got from Jean. Life was socially complicated, because the gentry and aristocracy fell all over themselves to be on terms of equality with the great Scots poet; and yet poetry is never a rich man's game, and he was struggling hard all the time to keep himself, as tenant farmer, out of bankruptcy.

In despair, after only a year out of Edinburgh, he left the farm and moved into Dumfries as an exciseman— surely the least edifying of jobs for a poet. But, with Jean's help, he remained solvent and, to the very end, much in demand both socially and as a writer.

The end was not far off. But the last years of Burns' life were happy ones, collaborating in the sort of work he loved. He refused to take payment for it, insisted it was "work for Scotland". It consisted of finding, editing, improving and re-writing old Scots songs for the collector James Johnson, an Edinburgh man. To this, unpaid, period of Robert Burns' life we owe, among others, "Auld Lang Syne".

Throughout this—indeed throughout his life—Burns corresponded with, visited, the greatest in the land. They may have been, and of course they frequently must have been, of a higher social order than the Burness family of Alloway, but they were eager to be on terms of intimacy with him, and he responded easily and happily. He wrote marvellous letters; he was a brilliant conversationalist.

He died—but not of drink or women, though he enjoyed both to the full. Compared with Byron, who also died of something quite different, he was probably abstemious in both; he just wouldn't have had the time. With women, his problem was that he made them pregnant, a hazard His Lordship—usually—avoided. And he was a good man, who was kinder to his own flock of little illegitimates than Byron to his singleton, Allegra.

Burns died, quite straightforwardly, of rheumatic heart disease. He had suffered from it since childhood, and probably the hard work on his father's struggling farm, coupled with a meagre diet, were responsible. Not women, not drink. Very dull.

He left behind an absolute treasury of work—yet a surprising amount of it had been written by the time of the great "Kilmarnock Burns" of 1786. Although he did not include it, for fear of his audience's suceptibilities—no fool, this Burns—he had already written down his greatest satiric poem, "Holy Willie's Prayer". Picture, if you can, the sanctimonious Scot whom so many other Scots from Burns to Buchan have loved to mock. He is, of course, a strict Calvinist. He says his prayer, convinced that he is predestined to salvation; he has his human failings, but to Willie they are not failings at all. He is lustful, but, of course, that is God protectively reminding him that he is a man. He has personal enemies, but he asks God's help in dealing with them, for to Holy Willie his own enemies and the Lord's are one. As for the prosperity he demands in this world, coupled with the same in the next, this is his right, for God must obviously prove to the heathen that He supports his own.

> "O thou that in the heavens dost dwell!
> Who, as it pleases best Thysel',
> Sends one to heaven and ten to hell,
>   A' for thy glory!
> And not for any good or ill
>   They've done before Thee.

Robert Burns, *left,* with his barefoot "Highland Mary". The painting could be of any of the many girls Burns loved both passionately and honestly. Byron, *below right,* was a different, more complex, character, who could scarce remember the names of his women. The painting shows him in one of the many flamboyant outfits he affected during his travels. The picture, *below left,* of Sir Walter Scott, was painted by Sir Henry Raeburn. It shows the writer near the end of a fantastically productive life—a life which he tragically shortened by overwork in order to settle a debt which his conscience told him he must discharge in full.

Sir James Young Simpson, the cheery, chubby fa*left,* is owed a debt by t world as great as that ow the inventor of penicillin, Alexander Fleming. He in ated the use of chloroform an anaesthetic in surgery a in his own branch of me cine, gynaecology. His urge advocacy of it, his success work with it, eventually p suaded a reluctant medi profession to follow s Although his first experim with the unknown chlorofo was in the civilized surrou of an after-dinner gather in his own home, there w occasions when he did m testing, and one of these shown dramatically belo

> *"I bless and praise Thy matchless might,*
> *When thousands Thou has left in night,*
> *That I am here before Thy sight*
> *For gifts and grace,*
> *A burning and a shining light*
> *To a' this place."*

Can there be any Scot who doesn't recognize this—perhaps in himself? It is, regrettably, almost a national characterestic, and Burns tore it gleefully to shreds, not only in "Holy Willie", but in "The Ordination", "The Holy Fair", "The Twa Herds", "Address to the Unco Guid", "Death and Doctor Hornbook", and others.

A favourite pub of mine, in Glasgow, down Byers Road, has a splendid mural of one of Burns' greatest narrative poems, "Tam o'Shanter". It was a technical *tour-de-force*, based on a folk legend of his childhood, and it seems a pity he should only have written one of its sort. Even to those who never read it, Burns gave the legacy of a Tam-o'-Shanter bonnet, and a Cutty Sark, or short shirt. The latter, of course, lent its name to one of the greatest of the clipper ships: the *Cutty Sark* is still to be seen in her permanent, concrete dry-dock near the Thames at Woolwich.

As the critic Gregory Smith put it, everyone sniggers over the private life of Burns, and "the comment on intrigue and whisky rolls on, involving us all in irrelevance". And irrelevance it is, though tempting. The simple fact is that Burns was not only the finest poet Scotland has ever produced, but the greatest British song-writer ever—which is quite an achievement.

The songs, of course, were written to be sung, and it would be pointless to reproduce them here, for they go with a melody upon which they depend, without which they are nothing. "A Red, Red Rose" is as lifeless as his "Auld Lang Syne" without the music—but Burns collected and arranged the music, too.

We may perhaps take leave of him with four lines of the last song—the last words—he ever wrote. He was dying, and a girl, Jessie Leward, was helping to nurse him. She had a favourite tune she hummed, and to it Burns set these words. They tell of his gratitude, tell Jessie that, if *she* were the one in distress, caught in the cold blast of life, he would shelter her:

> *"Oh were thou in the cauld blast,*
> *On yonder lea, on yonder lea;*
> *My plaidie to the angry airt,*
> *I'd shelter thee, I'd shelter thee."*

No, this was not a Byron, having them and leaving them, kissing and telling: this was Burns.

And, to Robert Burns, Byron and the whole of the English Romantic Movement owe an enormous debt.

Burns was the man who cared.

SIR WALTER SCOTT

For years—more than thirty of them—I have cherished a tiny book. It is four inches by three and admits to no publisher, though on the last page, just below the "End of the Notes", it seemed to have been printed by "Ballantyne, Hanson & Co., Edinburgh and London".

It is *The Lady of the Lake* given to me "with best wishes for your stay in Scotland, from Doctor Tolmie".

I have lost touch with Dr. Tolmie in America. And, in fact, our relationship when I was fifteen and about to return and stay in a Scotland I hardly knew, had not been awfully close. He had been too old to be an intimate and I too well to be a patient. I suppose he was fifteen years my senior. He is of interest here, apart from Scott's *Lady of the Lake,* because he was part of that brain drain which is believed to be such a recent phenomenon. He was, of course, a Scot; and no doubt now, at the age of sixty-odd, he will be a towering figure in American medicine. American papers, please copy. For though we Scots talk with absolute sincerity of our nostalgia for the old country, few who make the grade in other lands come back to stay—not while there is strength in their bodies.

So I read *The Lady of the Lake*. I began it without marked enthusiasm, for I failed to see how a story, even about Scotland, could sustain interest if told in six cantos and 204 pages of *verse*.

I was wrong of course. *The Lady of the Lake* holds our attention from the start. Well, not perhaps from the very start, for the lady, like many of Scott's brain-children, is a bit slow off her mark. But once into the tale one finds it hard to put down. Fascinated by the tale, the imagery and imagination, one even glosses over McGonagalesquerie like:

> *"And now to issue from the glen,*
> *No pathway meets the wanderer's ken,*
> *Unless he climb, with footing nice,*
> *A far projecting precipice."*

But, *pace* Dr. Tolmie, who after all introduced me to the great man, it is in the novels that Scott comes into his own. Novels of which he was ashamed to claim authorship, for like Buchan and Byron and others he felt himself very much the amateur writer. He was, like Buchan, a successful barrister, and though Buchan had no shame about being a writer of adventure stories on the side, Scott did. Shame, not for himself, but for the dignity of Scotland's courts of law; shame that a learned man who was, among other things, Clerk of Session in the High Court of Edinburgh, should dabble in such things.

The resemblance to Buchan was, as we shall see, quite considerable. No one could conceivably have been less like the feckless George Gordon Byron than Walter Scott —and yet much of their work, and attitude to it, was conditioned by the fact that both were lame from childhood.

But back to the beginning. He was born towards the end of the eighteenth century—in 1771—at Edinburgh, where his father was a solicitor, a Writer to the Signet, and the family claimed connection with a number of noble houses. The fact was drummed into young Walter's head from an early age. In fact, as he remarked in later life, "every Scotsman has a pedigree"—and the fact obsessed him. He liked to believe his ancestors were "merry men all, of the persuasion and calling of Robin Hood and Little John". Nothing less like this jolly pair can be imagined than his mother and father, and this conflict, helped by a paralysis which struck him in infancy, had a profound effect on what he wrote, and how he wrote it. He took, early on, a great interest in listening to tales of feuding in the border country, many of which he committed to memory. In fact, though he seems to have had little interest in the broad spectrum of literature, he gorged himself on history and the romantic poets of England. He also read extensively in their native tongues—for he was an educated man— the work of French and Italian authors, particularly historical works dealing with war, knightly tournaments, chivalry.

He was called to the Bar at the age of twenty-one, and five years later married a girl whom he'd met on a visit to the English Lake District. They settled happily into matrimony in a house in Edinburgh, and Walter worked hard at the Law, yet found time to scribble what he called "metrical tales".

In 1799, when he was twenty-eight and newly-appointed Sheriff-Depute of Selkirkshire, the first metrical tale was published. It was a translation from the German poet Bürger. This attracted some attention, which pleased him, for he had no objection to being known as a part-time translator and editor, even a versifier. The attention was heightened later with the publication of *Minstrelsy of the Scottish Border,* based on "the forays and predatory excursions made upon the Border". He had laboriously collected these from country folk, scribbling them down in a large exercise book.

Neither of these works, of course, was original: both were works of translation and compilation. But in the meantime he was working on original stuff, and in 1805 he published his first narrative poem, *The Lay of the Last Minstrel.*

This was a huge success. It was followed soon after by *Marmion,* after that by *The Lady of the Lake.* Tastes have changed, and a paper-back *Marmion* today would hardly cause a run on the bookstalls, but in the early nineteenth century, with its verse tailored to the taste of the age, it was a thundering success.

Though we quoted, unkindly, a piece of near-doggerel from Scott at the beginning, to show it was the story, the atmosphere, that mattered with his verse, there are plenty of examples of beautiful, moving writing. Much of it has a strange, underlying, sadness:

> *"Now is the stately column broke,*
> *The beacon light is quenched in smoke;*
> *The trumpet's silver sound is still,*
> *The warder silent on his hill."*

The poems brought their young author not only fame but wealth. He was soon able, aged just forty, to retire to the stately home he had dreamed of and now bought: Abbotsford, near Melrose. He was a family man, as we have seen, in the sense that he thought deeply about his family's past and its future: it had been his dream for years to found a new branch of the Scott family, with a firm base on the land. Now, with Abbotsford destined to be centre of a great estate, he would be founder of the Abbotsford branch.

To an Englishman this, though perfectly natural, may smack of buying up Lordships of the Manor, and setting oneself up as local squire. Though there must have been an element of this in Scott's behaviour, the underlying purpose was different. Scott was trying to pay a debt to his forebears and to re-establish the family name—not his *own*—for the posterity from which he felt accidents of time and fate had displaced them.

And for the Laird of Abbotsford, respected lawyer, part-time versifier, a new-fangled role of novelist was less than attractive. He had turned his attention to prose, and his first Romance, *Waverley*, came out in 1814. Anonymously.

Like the narrative verse, it was an instant success, and read as avidly on the Continent as in Britain. It dealt, as so much of his work did, with Scotland's history, the romantic adventures of an earlier day, before the need of lairds to be circumspect and canny, before the need, in fact, for Writers to the Signet.

Six books followed hard on the heels of *Waverley*, all of them still anonymous, and all describing to an ecstatic public the romance of Scotland in the seventeenth and eighteenth centuries. And most certainly, though literary styles have altered and we find these *Scotch Novels*, as he first called them, a bit difficult to get into, they suddenly seize one, like the Ancient Mariner, and refuse to let go.

So the money tinkled, then poured, in; with the author sagaciously exploiting the rich vein he had tapped, and at the same time buying more land for his Abbotsford. He was still unknown except as a popular, romantic, part-time poet (and, of course, a Writer to the Signet), and he intended to remain this way. All writers must dream of standing in a corner of a bookshop watching the public clamour for their latest best-seller: Scott had the added delight of being able to attend gatherings where he was well known and be asked his own opinion of his own "exciting new literary talent".

Perhaps, for Scott, this was no delight. For in his heart he despised literary people, unless they were, like himself, a great deal more besides. Certainly literary fame meant nothing. He was the respected Laird of Abbotsford, doing the various kinds of work he enjoyed.

But he knew his Scottish tales could not sell indefinitely and he hunted round for some other subject to exploit. He had discovered that his new commitments made it vital he remain a best-seller, and he was lucky in that he found other subjects and other periods which attracted him

—and attracted the public. There seems little doubt that the Scots romances, particularly when he dealt with ordinary folk and put their own words into their mouths, were his best work. Of that long series of anonymous novels starting with *Waverley*, and thus ultimately called *The Waverley Novels, The Heart of Midlothian*, published in 1818, is probably the finest. Here Scott eschews upper-class hero and heroine to put his finest writing into the broad Scots tongue of Jennie Deans.

By now, though, he had taken the disastrous step of investing money in the publishing firm of Ballantyne. To a lesser man the outcome might have been less disastrous, but to a man with the moral sense, keen sense of duty, which belonged to the Laird of Abbotsford, this was tantamount to sentence of death. Death, not from shame, but from overwork, trying to pay off his debts. He can hardly have anticipated this when he handed over the first few thousand pounds to James and John Ballantyne to become a keen but unskilled partner.

Before the debacle, however, there were happy, delightful years, with book following book, and affluence at Abbotsford. By this time there were a number of people aware of the identity of the *Waverley* author, and when he publicly revealed the fact at an Edinburgh dinner there was polite applause; but hardly anyone in the room was surprised.

He was created a baronet and in the same year elected President of the Royal Society of Scotland. Men and women started making pilgrimage from all over Britain —indeed, the world—to see Abbotsford, home of their favourite author. He in the meantime had his public in the palm of his hand, knew exactly what they, and his publisher, wanted. He also knew just how much he needed to write to keep abreast of expenses. If the publisher wanted an extra two hundred pages, Scott took the manuscript home again and dashed the pages off, as exciting as the rest. To devoted students of literature he was an embarrassment, for he laughed at its techniques and the bogus mystique behind so much of it. As he wrote in the introduction to *The Fortunes of Nigel*, "I have repeatedly laid down my future work to scale, divided it into volumes and chapters, and endeavoured to construct a story. But I think there is a demon who sits himself on the feather of my pen when I begin to write, and leads it astray from my purpose. Characters expand under my hand; incidents are multiplied; the story lingers, while the materials increase. My regular mansion turns out a Gothic anomaly——"

Many present-day critics would agree with this unashamed self-analysis by Sir Walter: but the public of his day went on clamouring for more.

And now, in 1826, the beginning of the end. Messrs. Ballantyne, the publishers of which he was a partner, went bankrupt. They owed rather more than a quarter of a million pounds.

We do not know to what extent Scott was responsible for this. Certainly he was no businessman. At any rate he set himself the fantastic task of paying off at least his share —perhaps £100,000—of this sum. There was only one way he could do it: write more. "This right hand," he declared, "shall work it off."

And so for the next—the last—six years of his sadly shortened life he literally worked himself to death, paying off the firm's creditors. Books poured from his pen, and two of these, *The Fair Maid of Perth* and *Anne of Geierstein*, written at enormous speed to earn enormous money, are among his finest work.

Some though were not: his powers of invention were not keeping up with his output. More serious still, his health was failing. In 1832 he took himself to the Continent, absolutely exhausted, in the hope that a change of scenery might restore both health and imagination.

But he could not stop, for so much as one day, the business of writing. He rushed through *Castle Dangerous* and *Count Robert of Paris*: I have read neither, but it seems they were much inferior to anything else he wrote.

The continental trip did him little good and probably much harm, for it tired him. He returned, and died, in

1832. He had begun working himself to death at the age of fifty-five: the process had taken six years.

Sir Henry Raeburn had painted him nine years previously: it had been the last painting Raeburn did before his own death, and this is still at Abbotsford, with Scott's antiquarian collection, and his library. Both that portrait and the one done a year later by Landseer, and now in the National Portrait Gallery, show a strong, determined man in the prime of life and strength. I know of no subsequent portraits—and perhaps this is just as well.

As we have seen, Scott contracted a paralysis in childhood. It was probably poliomyelitis, and although his parents sent him down to Bath for treatment with the waters he was never cured. But, unlike Byron, who was obsessed by his disability, Scott seems to have suffered no psychological effect from it.

His private life, unlike that of every other writer in this collection, from Burns to Buchan, was uneventful until the last six dreadful years. He spent the early years of his marriage living in a house in Edinburgh, though he and his wife Charlotte stayed as often as they could at a cottage in the nearby village of Lasswade.

Scottish authors have always been partial to children; with, I suppose, James Barrie the most striking example. My father has a delightful letter sent to him as a very small boy by Andrew Lang: they had met briefly and somehow my father had extolled a children's book called *The Lost Squire*. The next day he got the letter, in which the great man, having pondered the idea and come to a conclusion that the book "seems to be a masterpiece", asks to borrow it.

And Scott seems no exception. For years I have had a child's album of piano pieces, the setting to music of poems written by "Majorie Fleming, the Little Friend of Sir Walter Scott". Marjorie died on 19 January, 1811, just four days after her *eighth* birthday, and her little poems would be amazing from one twice her age. This was Scott's last year in Edinburgh, for he moved to Abbotsford in 1812, and he was quite overcome by the talented, pretty child, his "bonnie, wee, croodlin' doo". To him she was "the most extraordinary creature I ever met with, and her repeating of Shakespeare overpowers me as nothing else does". She wrote "literary" verses, with lines like:

> *"Death the righteous love to see,*
> *But from it do the wicked flee,"*

but perhaps was happiest with the exuberant, little-girl, stuff she wrote so enchantingly, like:

> *"I love in Isa's bed to lie,*
> *Oh such a joy and luxury!*
> *The bottom of the bed I sleep,*
> *And with great care within I creep;*
> *Oft I embrace her feet of lillys,*
> *But she has goton all the pillys——"*

She had a little vocabulary all her own, as in the "Ephibol" she wrote to this same sister Isabella, and quite probably some of Scott's expression and thought may have been coloured by Marjorie's verses.

His work, of course, had a tremendous effect on all British writing, in particular Scottish writing. Not only did he awake interest in the past of Scotland—hardly anyone had considered it might be interesting enough to write about—so that learned societies popped up everywhere to study it; but his whole approach to writing gave rise to imitators. Or at least, men inspired by his example. Particularly was this true in France, where writers like Victor Hugo and even painters like Millet openly acknowledged their debt to Sir Walter. Nearer home there are many successful writers who owe him a debt of gratitude, for the historical novel, still one of the most popular forms of expression, was entirely Scott's creation.

He died at his beloved Abbotsford, and over the last few weeks of life the brutally overworked mind and body ran slowly down, like a clock. His friends would wheel him about among his roses, which gave him the greatest pleasure, but it was not only the roses, but the very earth itself, of the family home he had built up.

Day by day he grew feebler, yet as appreciative as ever of the little journeys on which he was taken to see a rose-bed here, a young plantation there. He had increasing difficulty with his speech: he was too exhausted, too weak, to make himself understood.

On the last day of life, as he was wheeled through the grounds, he whispered—so feebly that his friend could scarce hear the words,

"I have seen much, but—but nothing like my ain house."

GEORGE GORDON BYRON,
LORD BYRON

"Byron lay, Lazily Lay
Hid from Lesson and Game Away,
Dreaming Poetry, all Alone——"

So we sang, and they sing, at Harrow. Like most school songs, the words of this one were capable of infinite, *sotto voce*, variation; and Byron, during the course of four longish stanzas, could be put in the strangest of situations, without being able to protest. Which was as well, for, as we knew, he was a hot-tempered chap, who throughout his life carried two small loaded pistols.

And now I must stop involving others: I have no idea at all whether my school friends had read all or any of Byron. I myself had read scarcely a word, but his story fascinated me. He seemed so colourful, there was no need for him to have written anything.

We have our mini-Byrons today.

But Byron did write, and though his physical beauty, his title, his wealth, his sexual excess and his spirit of rebellion would have earned him a small place in history somewhere between George the Fourth and James Dean, only the written word could improve on that placing. And Byron wrote like an angel.

He knew, too, the power of words:

> *"Words are things, and a small drop of ink,*
> *Falling like dew upon a thought, produces*
> *That which makes thousands, perhaps millions, think;*
> *'Tis strange, the shortest letter which man uses,*
> *Instead of speech, may form a lasting link*
> *Of ages; to what straits old Time reduces*
> *Frail man, when paper—even a rag like this—*
> *Survives himself, the tomb, and all that's his."*

The words are from Byron's *Don Juan*, Canto III. Seldom has poet written a better epitaph for himself.

Perhaps he was the greatest of all the English Romantic poets, greater than Shelley, Wordsworth, Keats. Which, for one who spent so many of his formative years in the north of Scotland, is quite an achievement.

The English, as all good Scotsmen know, are perfidious. Eight years before his death he had been almost literally thrown out of their country, for Breaking the Eleventh Commandment, for Being Found Out. English society, in one of those moods of straight-laced virtue which alternate with periods of astonishing licence, had drummed him out, and at Dover a huge gawking crowd of Englishmen and women, some shaking their fists, others grinning with a frank admiration which none dared put into words, watched him embark with his retinue.

And eight years later when he died—romantically, if a little pointlessly—in Greece, all England wept. Howls of anguish rent the air, the papers, choking back their tears, pointed out for their readers, who already knew, that

Byron's death "came upon London like an earthquake". A bright light, a beacon, the rest of it, had gone out——

Little Alfred Tennyson, aged fifteen, galloped weeping into a wood to scratch three words on a rock: "Byron is dead."

And so he was. But what on earth was there about the man to occasion these violent shifts of public opinion?

He had spent his earliest, most formative, years in Aberdeen. The foundations of his education, his love of words, of mountain beauty, even of Scripture, were laid there, at school and from his nurse. And from that nurse, May Gray, he learnt more than that: the odd devotion they shared was to alter Byron's emotional orientation for ever.

He was grandson of another remarkable man, Admiral John Byron, who had been shipwrecked on the west coast of Patagonia and held prisoner for three years before returning to England in 1745. He too was a writer of sorts, for his *Voyage Round the World* has been extensively read, studied, translated. His son, the poet's father, was a captain in the Guards, and a splendidly potent womanizer.

And we must mention one other antecedent: the fifth Lord Byron was the poet's great-uncle. From him, in the fullness of time, would descend the title which would so endear him to English society; and indeed to the inhabitants of France, Italy, Greece. Even Scotland. As we can see on another page, William McGonagall thought highly of him.

He was born of this stock, and with a Scottish heiress for mother. The year was 1788. Catherine Gordon was related—all Scotsmen have pedigrees, as Walter Scott points out—to the Stuart kings. Already his father had squandered her fortune and left her in a small furnished room off Cavendish Square in London, to bear her child.

He was born with a club foot.

Almost immediately Catherine took him home to Aberdeenshire. There, as he grew older, the boy absorbed a stern Scots education, and grew to love wild Highland scenery. (He spent much time around Ballater.) He also learned to love—in a decidedly precocious way—his young nanny.

After ten years of this he learnt his great-uncle's title was now his. "The Wicked Lord", men had called him, and with reason; for his morals, his profligacy, were as renowned in their way as George's one day would be. The Wicked Lord was dead. George had inherited not only the title, but the family seat in Nottinghamshire, Newstead Abbey.

This, though it was in an alarming state of disrepair, still had an income to go with it. Byron and his mother made haste to move there.

From Newstead he was sent to a preparatory school at Dulwich, thence in 1801 to Harrow. He was thirteen.

He hated it at first. Discipline was strict and most of the classroom subjects were a crashing bore. And there were no women. Somehow he managed to endure it, and Harrow too endured four years of mutual acquaintanceship. But towards the end of these years he was not only enjoying the opportunities for reading which the school gave him, he was astonishing his friends by deeds of schoolboy bravery—a gallant attempt to overcome the handicap of a crippled foot. He made friends here, and later, at Trinity College, Cambridge. He seemed obsessed with a desire for love. Not mere sensuality, which he displayed later, but emotional love, and he directed it at school friends, university friends, his cousin Mary Chaworth during the holidays. He shocked some, amused others.

At Cambridge he struck up an emotional relationship with John Edleston, while at the same time excelling at boxing, riding, swimming. By now he knew he was handsome, even beautiful, that this outweighed the physical disability of his foot; the consideration, the balancing, of these two attributes occupied a great deal of his life.

He did little work, but made strenuous efforts to keep his weight down, keep his perfect profile unmarred by lines, his hair thick and black. The effort was needed, for Byron at Cambridge drank, gambled and womanized to a degree at which we mere twentieth-century men can only marvel. On more than one occasion, so much did youth and beauty obsess him, he signed the Age column in an hotel register as 100. He made sick little jokes when he walked across a room and showed his hated limp. He practised daily with the two pistols he carried everywhere. But, apart from good friends, he derived little benefit from the ancient establishment: his record at Cambridge is merely one of dissolute living and a mounting tide of debt.

So far in this tale there is little for us to study. But now, in 1807, comes the first sign of a genius which has been there all along. In that year he publishes—he is nineteen —a volume of poems, *Hours of Idleness*. Many like it, some do not. Some do not even like *Poems Original and Translated* of the following year. The *Edinburgh Review* dismisses all of it loftily, and this provokes his *English Bards and Scottish Reviewers* in 1809, where he satirizes the Editor—and yet manages to say a great deal, favourable and otherwise, about *English Bards*.

In this year he came of age. He had already received his inheritance, had taken his seat in the House of Lords. Now he would go with his latest, closest friend, John Hobhouse, on The Grand Tour.

They went, and visited Portugal and Spain, thence via Malta and Greece to Albania. From Albania Byron went back to Greece, which exercised a fascination for him, and there he began the long autobiographical poem, *Childe Harold's Pilgrimage*, which would soon bring him the most astonishing fame. (In fact, he began it under the title *Childe Burun's Pilgrimage*, then decided against such blatant autobiography.) In the second year of his tour he visited the Middle East and in particular Constantinople. We have seen that he was a good, strong swimmer, and now, to prove it, prove himself equal to the heroes of antiquity, he swam the two miles across the Dardanelles— swam from Asia to Europe. He also found time to finish Cantos I and II of *Childe Harold*. He wrote *Hints from Horace* and *The Curse of Minerva*. All these were published after his return to Europe, and *Childe Harold's Pilgrimage*, appearing in February, 1812, took London by storm. Its author was just twenty-four, and "awoke one morning and found myself famous". This was an age when poetry really struck to the heart, whether it be frankly romantic, like "Music arose with its voluptuous spell, Soft eyes looked love to eyes which spake again" (from Byron's *Waterloo*), or adventurous like Scott's. Nothing in our day has struck anything like the same chord, with the tiny, tinkling exception of Dylan Thomas's *Under Milk Wood*.

Byron's gratification at being suddenly famous was marred by the death of his mother. She had died at Newstead before he was able to get back to her, and he never forgave himself. They had quarrelled often—in a frightening way, for they both had terrible tempers and the good lady drank to excess—but he was heartbroken when she died.

For a short time he began to be seen as a rising young statesman. He made a few remarkable speeches in the House of Lords, delivered them in his beautiful voice (his strongest subject at Harrow had been "Declamation") and brought tears to many a noble eye with his support of Nottingham weavers. Outside the House, indeed everywhere he went, for the beauty and the crippled foot were alike unmistakable, he was fawned on like royalty.

But in 1813 he chanced to re-meet his half-sister. His profligate father, before ruining Catherine Gordon, had been briefly married to the Marchioness of Carmarthen and the daughter of that union had always held a strange attraction for Byron. She was now Mrs. Augusta Leigh; she returned his affection and there seems little doubt that he began an incestuous affair with her.

But not content with this, he began a simultaneous affair with Lady Caroline Lamb. He was at the height of his fame—his *Corsair* of Oriental Tales had sold ten thousand copies on day of publication—and what might have been ignored in a lesser man became society's chief topic of conversation. Never reticent, the poet discussed his amours with all who cared to listen, and Augusta, already trying to break a relationship which would soon be a major scandal, was horrified to learn its details, no doubt magnified, from some good friend who, like all this sort of good friend, felt she ought to know what was being said.

So the horrified Augusta was one of several women who decided to marry Byron off, but fast, before other reputations as well as his own had been compromised. The girl chosen was Miss Annabella Milbanke. A blue-stocking perhaps, but with charm. And—which perhaps clinched the deal—a sizeable fortune of her own. A marriage was arranged. Byron, while perfectly aware of the reasons for matrimony, procrastinated and changed his mind for many, many months. Then, in a flash, the deed had been done.

The marriage lasted a year and there are probably more conflicting tales about that one year of matrimony than of any other union in history. It is quite possible that the marriage, though dull, was successful for most of those twelve months: on the other hand, Byron is supposed to have told his Annabella, on their wedding day, that now he had married her he hated her.

Whatever he told her, she was soon taking medical advice about him, believing and hoping that he was temporarily insane. The doctors refuted this, and as by now the scandal about Augusta Leigh was at its height she planned to leave him.

Right after the birth of their only child, a daughter, she did so and fled to her parents.

It was, for London, the biggest scandal on record. Within a week *Childe Harold* and the rest of Byron's work, all of which women had swooned over, was forgotten. There were few to defend Byron—these only materialized like Robert Edgecombe and his *Byron, the Last Phase,* many years after the man was dead—and many to blame him. There was a separation which was legally satisfactory, and it seems that Byron was genuinely shocked and sorry that his wife had left him. But London society howled for blood. He was ostracized—and yet dragged into functions where he could be publicly disgraced, like Lady Jersey's party. There he was cut by almost everyone, including all his old "friends".

And on 25 April, 1816—fifteen months after contracting marriage—he sailed from Dover, never to return again. As we have seen, there were those at the dock, several rows of them, waiting to sneer. Many great ladies, unwilling to be recognized in the crush, borrowed their maids' clothes to do so.

Probably Byron had an intention at the back of his mind that some day he would return. But he never did.

More problems—most of his own manufacture—now assailed him. He fled in the grand manner, no midnight flit for Lord Byron, and among his entourage was a young and faintly ridiculous Italian doctor, Polidori. No mysterious affection here—merely that Byron, as was often the custom, felt he would require a reliable doctor with him on his travels. Polidori appeared to Byron's publisher, John Murray, to be sufficiently intelligent and trustworthy to be entrusted with a commission: if he kept an exact record of their travels, he, Polidori, would earn five hundred guineas.

The doctor managed to produce a record and collect his five hundred guineas, though his service with Byron ended temporarily when the poet found him too boring. Our only interest in Polidori is in the words which were cut from the first chapter of his journal. These were ultimately replaced by an editor less prudish. The party, according to Polidori, had arrived at Ostend and gone to the hotel, whereupon,

"As soon as he reached his room, Lord Byron fell like a thunderbolt upon the chambermaid."

And so it was to go on, right across the continent of Europe, with chambermaids, merchants' wives, countesses, all collapsing under him, and one unfortunate—but very foolish—English girl joining their number. She was the poet Shelley's sister-in-law, Claire, who joined Shelley's quite different continental entourage for the sole purpose of pursuing Byron into Italy. She had an illegitimate child by him and was then utterly and cruelly rejected. The child, Allegra, was born in 1817 and kept in a convent by her father. He felt some affection for the little thing, but none for the mother, and was shocked and distressed when Allegra died at the convent, aged five.

Much of the remainder of Byron's life was spent in Venice, where the pattern of chambermaids, grooms' wives and the nobility was maintained. The longest period of fidelity in that life was the four years from 1819 after he had met and wooed the Countess Teresa Guiccioli. She remained his mistress throughout that period. He went on writing—as he always did, faithful or no—and his master-piece, *Don Juan*, took shape slowly, in Italy. He worked at other poems, *Mazeppa, Sardanapalus, The Prophecy of Dante*. The work was by no means all introspective and he seized on all sorts of different subjects: *The Island, or Christian and his Comrades*, was based on the mutiny aboard H.M.S. *Bounty*, which was then only about thirty years in the past.

He led an active life by day, whether it be philandering, or taking violent exercise out of doors, and much of his writing was done in the evenings. Night after night—or at any rate, on some nights—he wrote stanza after stanza of delightful verses, lubricating his imagination with gin and water. Often the gin and water was the only thing he con-sumed during the day, for he was vain till the end, and fighting a steady battle with age and obesity.

He had always, since strange distant days in the English House of Lords, taken a lively interest in world affairs, and in particular the question of Greek independence. There had always been the urge to do something about it, not just write on the subject. At last, feeling time slip by, with so many friends fallen by the wayside—Shelley had just been tragically drowned and he had helped cremate the fish-gnawed body on the beach—he set off for Greece. Already he had given help to that country's cause, with money, advice, propaganda.

What he thought his actual presence could do is not clear, but he arrived at Missolonghi in January of 1824. The Greeks were naturally overjoyed that so famous a man should so publicly have come to their aid. But by now a lifetime of dissipation—and also overwork, for he never spared himself, in love or labour—was fast catching up. It is almost as if he knew his days were numbered, that he must go out in a blaze of glory, a rebel as ever, supporting the fine cause of independence for a nation from whom the whole of western civilization had sprung.

Perhaps the behaviour of those he befriended speeded the process: the Greeks were fighting absurdly among themselves, and there was no concerted plan, however much he might try to impose one. Greed and jealousy ruled supreme. Byron fell ill—and in his weakened, dissipated state his body could do nothing about it. On 19 April, 1824, he died, in his thirty-sixth year.

The news took a month to reach England. And then, as we have seen, the land which had banished him wailed piteously, beat its breast.

It is pointless to take up a moral stance about Byron. Almost everything he did was morally deplorable. He used women and discarded them cruelly; did the same with men when their use, their attraction, whatever it might be, was over. And still he was almost universally loved—and not only for his poetry. His self-imposed exile had been occasioned by a wave of English self-righteousness, and when that wave had vanished out to sea, in the wake of his own departure (probably even as he fell upon the Ostend chambermaid) a new love welled up for him.

It would have been impossible to write about Byron—as impossible as it is of Burns—without discussing him as a flesh and blood man. Which, paradoxically, has been quite the wrong way to approach either of them. For neither of these men—a randy peer, a randy ploughman—would have survived a generation in men's memory, were it not for what they wrote. And *pace* Ernest Hemingway, who at least pretended to believe no man can write of what he hasn't physically experienced, there is seldom much connection between a writer as the world sees him and a writer as he writes.

There are plenty to drink to Burns and Byron, who have never read a dozen lines of either: but the men they cheer are nothing. It has been a joy writing about His Lordship.

But to understand the first thing about him you must close this book, forget everything you have read in it, and start reading what Byron wrote.

But to understand the greatness about him you must also know this book, before reading on you feel as if you were reading what Lister wrote.

SIR JAMES YOUNG SIMPSON

The eyes are almost startling with their compassion. Most medical men, inured perhaps by the sufferings of others, seem to have brisk, no-nonsense, businessmen's eyes. But James Simpson was a man of quite a different stamp; he felt, suffered, understood.

He did not invent anaesthesia. But he developed it, forced its use where others would not have bothered; made it sure and safe.

The medical profession throughout history has been conservative, reluctant to change. (Two of the greatest exceptions, Fleming and Simpson, are in this book.) It has been said that though it is not history's oldest profession (and, sadly, we have no sparkling representative of that one in this volume) it behaves as if it were. For fourteen hundred years it believed—or made no effort not to—an hypothesis about the behaviour of the blood which is so ludicrous, and so demonstrably so, that William Harvey, when he came up with the right answer in the sixteenth century, found it hard to believe the rest had subscribed to it so long. From Galen's time, in the second century A.D., doctors had believed that blood was sucked up out of the liver (which made it) by the heart, and then despatched to the extremities where it was used up entirely and vanished. The lungs were explained away as an ingenious cooling device, like the radiator of a car, to lower the temperature of this sizzling hot blood from the liver before it got out to the muscles and skin. And disappeared.

Harvey, with a few strokes of a pen, showed that if this really happened a man would be eating three times his weight of food every day, just in order to keep alive.

The medical profession, while quite unable to refute this, muttered that Harvey's theory of the Circulation of the Blood was "wicked and heretical".

And so it was that, two and a half centuries later, James Simpson found himself one of the pitifully few pioneers of surgical anaesthesia—a problem to which every surgeon should have been devoting at least half of his waking hours since the dawn of time.

Before we continue, read this:

"The morning of the operation arrived. There were no anaesthetics in those days, and I took no preparative stimulant or anodyne of any kind, unless two cups of tea, which with a fragment of toast formed my breakfast, be considered such.

"The operation was a more tedious one than some which involve much greater mutilation. It necessitated cutting through inflamed and morbidly sensitive parts, and could not be despatched by a few swift strokes of the knife. I do not suppose that it was more painful than the majority of severe surgical operations, but I am not, I believe, mistaken in thinking that it was not less painful, and this is all that I wish to contend for.

"Of the agony it occasioned, I will say nothing. Suffering so great as I underwent cannot be expressed in words, and thus, fortunately, cannot be recalled. The particular pangs are now forgotten, but the black whirlwind of emotion, the horror of great darkness, and the sense of desertion by God and man, bordering close upon despair, which swept through my mind and overwhelmed my heart, I can never forget, however gladly I would do so. Only the wish to save others some of my sufferings makes me deliberately recall and confess the anguish and humiliation of such a personal experience; nor can I find language more sober and familiar than that I have used, to express feelings which, happily for us all, are too rare as matters of general experience to have been shaped into household words.

"From all this anguish I should, of course, have been saved had I been rendered insensible by ether or chloroform, or otherwise, before submitting to the operation. On that point, however, I do not dwell, because it needs no proof, and the testimony of the thousands who have been spared such experiences by the employment of chloroform is at hand to satisfy all who are not determined not to be satisfied.

"During the operation, in spite of the pain it occasioned, my senses were preternaturally acute, as I have been told they generally are in patients in such circumstances. I watched all that the surgeon did, with a fascinated intensity. I still recall with unwelcome vividness the spreading out of the instruments; the twisting of the tourniquet; the first incision; the fingering of the sawed bone; the sponge pressed on the flap, the tying of the blood vessels; the stitching of the skin; and the bloody, dismembered, limb lying on the floor."

The letter, of which this is but a small part, was addressed to James Simpson. Apart from the poignant detail, every bit of which Simpson knew to be true, and its plea for a more widespread use of chloroform—recently invented by Simpson—it held a number of deliberately misleading clues to the writer's identity and was signed merely, "An Old Patient". But Simpson knew only too well who it was. The writer was a man who could either have become a great physician or a great chemist—until an accident called for the amputation of his leg. He survived the ghastly experience set out in his letter, but his health was ruined. Shortly after writing the letter he died.

The search, among a few devoted men, to discover some form of anaesthetic to kill the pain of surgery, had been going on for many years. Some of the discoveries were moderately effective. Homer wrote of nepenthe, which must have been hemp; the Romans took mandragora in their wine to dull the pain of wounds; and later on people took opium from the poppy. But none of these was found really efficient. However drowsy these drugs might make the patient, it needed only the cold touch of a knife to have him awake, alert, and screaming.

The first substance to make patients really insensible to pain—whether or not it sent them to sleep—was nitrous oxide, or laughing gas, discovered by Sir Humphry Davy in 1799. It was reputed to be a deadly poison, but having discovered accidentally that a sniff of it made him laugh, the brave Sir Humphry went on to inhale quantities of the stuff. And apart from inducing uncontrollable mirth (and not killing him) it seemed to deprive him of sensation in his limbs.

And now we are back where we began, having a go at the medical profession. For Sir Humphry Davy wrote, in 1799, that his new gas, which any fool could make, was "capable of destroying physical pain". Cautiously, he added —because the medical profession was not only conservative, but took itself seriously, "It could *probably* be used with advantage during surgical operations". Sir Humphry was only a physicist.

A million corpses later, give or take a few, the profession sat up and thought about this. Half a century had gone by.

And in 1844, a young American dentist, Horace Wells, strolled into a demonstration of popular science in Hartford, Connecticut. The demonstrator was a failed medical student who was making a few dollars by such stunts as The Effects Produced by Inhaling Exhilarating or Laughing Gas. This always brought down the house, as Gentlemen of the First Respectability from the audience sniffed the drug and then made fools of themselves, laughing, scampering about the room, falling down.

And, as Wells now noted, never hurting themselves.

He got the demonstrator and his gas round the next morning and had one of his own teeth drawn by a colleague. No pain at all. His remark, on opening eyes after this first effective administration in the world's history, was a gem of understatement.

"Oh——" he gasped. "A new era in tooth pulling!"

Sadly, Wells failed to convince anyone else. He gave a public demonstration which ended in confusion and shouting because someone removed the bladder of gas too soon and the patient woke up. Wells died a few years later, in abject poverty, and people still had legs sawn off, organs removed in full, screaming consciousness. Others, wiser, just refused and died in peace.

But eventually Wells's partner, Morton, bullied Medicine into giving him a chance. It is typical of the profession's attitude to an innovation which if successful would revolutionize surgery (and if not, nothing had been lost by trying) that when Morton arrived a few minutes late it was to find surgeon and students bitterly hostile. He had been delayed with adjustments to his new dispenser and now, while he frantically set it up by the operating table, the surgeon hummed, rolled his eyes, tapped his foot.

At last Morton put his mask over the patient's face.

The surgeon, hot with anger and resentment, made a sudden, deep incision. This was the moment—he had experienced it a hundred times or more—when the patient screamed. He would go on screaming till exhaustion stopped him.

Had there been screaming he hardly would have noticed it, for this was a part of life; a patient who submitted himself for surgery expected to scream. But there was no screaming. Not a sound.

There was a gasp from the audience. The surgeon, mouth agape, stopped for a moment, and his beads of sweat continued to splash down on the sleeping patient. Then he went on, completed the removal of the tumour.

The operation was successful; the patient, quite unaware of what had happened, woke up when Morton wanted him to, and made a full recovery. The date was 16 October, 1846.

The substance Morton used, which had similar properties to nitrous oxide, was sulphuric ether. It had worked, no
man could gainsay that, and in front of a large and qualified
audience. Surgical anaesthesia existed, had been proved.

James Young Simpson, over in Edinburgh, was just thirty-
five. He was a brilliant doctor who had attained the Chair
of Midwifery in that city at the early age of twenty-eight,
having begun life as the youngest of seven sons born to a
baker in Bathgate. In contrast with surgeons who questioned
the advisability of anaesthesia even for the removal of a
leg, James Simpson wanted some sort of anaesthetic for
the considerably less harrowing pains of childbirth. When
he heard of Morton's success with ether, he shouted "It is
a glorious thing—I can think of naught else!"

He was to find, as did others, that ether had disadvantages. It had a foul smell and an irritant effect on the lungs:
a sufficient dose for really deep anaesthesia made the patient
ill for days; there were problems in dispensing it. But now
that something so effective had been discovered, it
behoved doctors and chemists to make improvements to it.

A Liverpool chemist, knowing his interest, sent off a
small sample of a drug called chloroform. It was believed to
have some anaesthetic property, but few men were anxious
to experiment with it, for so many of these gases were
poisonous. Simpson, like Humphry Davy, had no fear, and
he managed to imbue his assistants with the same courage,
in the cause of science. And so, quite late one evening in
November, 1847, we find him and his two assistants about
to embark on a hazardous experiment with drugs, including the chloroform from Liverpool. Being civilized men,
they are doing it in Simpson's Edinburgh dining room,
after a pleasant meal, and in order that an impartial view
may be taken—and if necessary a rescue operation undertaken—they have allowed others into the room to watch. In
fact, no one apart from the three is aware of danger.

Here is an eye-witness report: "Having inhaled several
substances but without much effect, it remained to
Dr. Simpson to search for and try the small bottle of
'chloroform'. Search was made and it was recovered from

beneath a heap of waste paper. And with each tumbler newly charged, the inhalers resumed their vocation.

"Immediately, an unwonted hilarity seized the party; they became bright-eyed, very happy, and very loquacious —expatiating on the delicious aroma of the new fluid. The conversation was of unusual intelligence, and quite charmed the listeners, some ladies of the family and a naval officer, brother-in-law of Dr. Simpson.

"But suddenly there was talk of sounds being heard like that of a cotton-mill, louder and louder. A moment more, then all was quiet—and then, a crash.

"On awaking, Dr. Simpson's first perception was mental. 'This is far stronger and better than ether', he said to himself. His second was to note that he was prostrate on the floor and that among the friends about him there was both confusion and alarm. Hearing a noise, he turned round and saw Dr. Duncan beneath a chair. His jaw had dropped, his eyes were staring, his head bent half under him; he was quite unconscious and snoring in a most determined and alarming manner. More noise still, and much motion. And then his eyes overtook Dr. Keith's feet and legs making valorous efforts to over-turn the supper table, or more probably, to annihilate everything that was on it."

Even on Burns night, few parties can have ended more dramatically.

Chloroform worked—and James Young Simpson was not the sort of man to put it on the shelf and forget. Within weeks he was using it regularly in midwifery, and a little later surgeons were using it for major operations. Like ether (but unlike nitrous oxide, the old laughing gas) it was a liquid, highly volatile, and powerful in its effect. Only a few drops on a cloth were needed to produce deep anaesthesia, sufficient even for abdominal operations, where the patient, although unconscious, might contract his power- ful abdominal muscles at the first incision and make further surgery impossible. With the new chloroform this was no longer a problem. So great were its advantages that it almost completely superseded the earlier two anaesthetics.

Later, chloroform, too, was found to have disadvantages,

and it was supplanted by ethyl chloride, cyclopropane and, as recently as the Second World War, trichlorethylene, all three of which are in use for different types of surgery. And there are, of course, the local anaesthetics since developed, which deaden only one area of the body.

So, with Simpson's chloroform discredited now for anything but international spies in the cinema, what have we to remember him for? After all, he didn't develop the *first* effective anaesthetic; William Morton had done that the year before.

Simpson's contribution—and it was an enormous one—was to push and popularize the use of anaesthesia in all sorts of surgery and in his own midwifery. Such was the conservatism of his profession that years would have gone by before anaesthesia became general. But Simpson, who was a man of towering personality and of towering stature in his work, dragged Medicine, screaming, into the nineteenth century. What Simpson—soon to be Sir James, for his contributions to gynaecology—did, others copied.

In his own words, after paying tribute to the men who worked on the first two anaesthetic drugs, he went on to say that "chloroform swiftly superseded in Scotland and elsewhere the use of sulphuric ether. *It extended rapidly and greatly the practice of anaesthesia in surgery, midwifery, etc.*"

The italics are mine.

He was a remarkable man in more ways than one. For though we remember him as the great developer of anaesthesia, he is best remembered in his own profession as a brilliant gynaecologist and obstetrician. He invented all manner of tools for the job, from a new type of obstetric forceps to a lubricating oil more frictionless than science said was possible. On a scale which gave full friction as 100, olive oil 38, sperm oil 18, Simpson's derivative of paraffin registered a mere 6.

Perhaps, had he lived a century later, he would have been a spare-time mechanical engineer, as well as everything else. For James Simpson tried his hand at many things, and, his writings on archaeology are classics in their field.

But there was one obsession with him, right until the time of his early death, aged fifty-nine, in 1870—and for this above all else the world owes him gratitude. He would not allow needless suffering.

And his life was devoted to ensuring that it was just that —needless.

DAVID LIVINGSTONE

Everyone in this book is, by definition, "famous". Some are goodies, a few perhaps are baddies, and we are concerned only with their achievement. Mary Garden is in these pages because she was a superb artist and gave the greatest joy to thousands of people; Sir James Simpson is present because he developed the use of anaesthetic and millions were then able to endure the unendurable; Baird invented television so that millions of people——

Never mind. The fact is, they did the things, they were interesting as people. Beyond that, it is probably none of my business or yours to pry.

But almost alone of the assembled men in these pages there is one who was above all else a good man, whose claim to attention lies as much with the fact that he was good as that he happened to discover a lot of Africa.

He was in many ways as near a saint as makes no difference. But he, too, as we shall see, had his faults.

He was born on 19 March, 1813, in Blantyre on the
Clyde, in the street Shuttle Row where his entire family
lived in a single room fourteen feet by ten. The accommodation had been built for cotton-factory workers by a
paternal industrialist, and though the conditions would be
unthinkable today, they were regarded as decent in 1813:
Blantyre was a model village.

At ten, young David started work in the cotton factory,
marching about and tying up the broken threads on the
jenny. His hours were from six in the morning to eight at
night, after which he attended classes. But no opportunity
passed him by for improving his mind, even while actually
working in the factory he put a newly purchased book of
Latin Grammar on the frame of the spinning jenny, and
"thus kept up a pretty constant study undisturbed by the
roar of the machinery. To this part of my education I owe
my present power of completely abstracting the mind from
surrounding noises, so as to read and write with perfect
comfort amidst the play of children or near the dancing
and songs of savages."

Always to the adult David Livingstone the Africans—
for whom he sacrificed his life—were savages. And yet he
loved them as much as man ever has.

But not all his youth was spent in the cotton factory.
There were summer evenings and holidays, and then he
loved to play about the burns and braes, collecting wild
flowers, fossils—and fish. For the young Livingstone, soon
to become a pillar of the Church, was an expert poacher,
not averse to getting a salmon home by dangling it inside
his brother Charlie's trousers as they walked, very close
together, back to Shuttle Row.

But as a contemporary remarked, he had other interests:
"I didna think muckle o' that David Livingstone when he
worked wi' me. He was aye lyin' on his belly readin' a
book——"

A really Scottish devotion to knowledge, almost for its
own sake, had seized him. By eighteen, promoted to spinner

in the factory, he was using the wages to attend lectures in medicine and divinity. And, needless to say, he bought or borrowed every possible book on both subjects.

At the age of twenty, the call came. He applied to be a communicant member of the Independent Church at Hamilton. His father had held the office of deacon in that church for some years, having been gripped by religion while serving as a tea vendor. He also—for some reason known best to himself—altered the spelling of his age-old Scots name Livingston and added the final "e". The father cautiously left it to the kirk elders to decide his son's fitness or not for the honour, and these insisted on a study period of five months before the lad was considered a worthy entrant to that church.

Life is a chain of accidents—and it was the brand-new idea of medical missionaries that made the young man decide to go abroad. How very fortunate it was that he had elected to study both Medicine and Divinity, such normally disparate subjects!

But being a medical missionary required a wider knowledge than contained in those two subjects. He would need to know Greek (of all things) and Chemistry, and he would also need a far deeper knowledge of the other two than he already possessed.

Undaunted, he got his father's permission to study these subjects in Glasgow and moved into the only lodgings he could afford, for two shillings a week. The plan was that he would earn the money to keep himself in Glasgow by doing work at the Blantyre cotton factory during his vacations.

Somehow he did, and in the summer of 1838, when he was twenty-five, he was accepted by the London Missionary Society. He had chosen that body because it was the only completely non-sectarian one. He was sent for final studies to England, to London first, and then a parsonage in Essex —and here he very nearly failed to make the grade. His appearance, he learnt, was most unprepossessing, his manner uncouth. He had, furthermore, absolutely no ability to orate, to sermonize, from the pulpit.

This last charge was absolutely true. During the Essex

training he was asked to deputize for a parson who had been taken ill. He was given adequate warning and he carefully prepared his sermon. But when the time came during the service for him to read out his text and then deliver some thoughts on the subject, he only just managed the text. After embarrassing seconds of total silence, he gulped and said, "Friends, I have forgotten all I had to say". A moment later he was out of the pulpit and heading for the door.

But somehow his real charm, his huge intelligence and his capacity for work won the day. He managed to keep well during these studies on a regular three hours sleep each night and at last they passed him as fit in every way for overseas service as a missionary.

What was he like at the start of his career? Two colleagues can tell us a bit about him: "He was middle-sized, firm upon his feet, light in the under-trunk, round and full in the chest. I have to admit he was not bonny. His face wore at all times the strongly marked lines of potent will——"

The other found that: "There was a truly indescribable charm about him which with all his ungainly ways and by no means winning face, attracted almost everyone."

They say we have no control over the faces the good Lord gives us until we are forty. Then what is writ on them is entirely what we have written ourselves. And David Livingstone is a comically perfect example. Pictures taken of him in his thirties show a puzzled bigot's face half hidden behind its walrus moustache. Without doubt it is a "by no means winning face". But the pictures later in life show a face of compassion, understanding, quiet strength.

Missionaries were needed for Africa. His ambition had been to go to China, but as Britain was at war with that country this was impossible, and he agreed to be sent to the Dark Continent: "I will go at once to Africa". The London Missionary Society felt—with commendable insight—that he would be best suited to the task of opening up new ground, and that therefore he should not remain at a mission station.

While much of this was going on, Livingstone managed

to take his medical degree in Glasgow, so that when he sailed in December, 1840, for Africa, he was as fully qualified as a man could want to be: a medical practitioner and ordained minister.

Halfway out, the sailing vessel *George* steered into a vicious storm, lost her foremast and had to limp across the South Atlantic to Rio de Janeiro for refit. Here he busied himself studying the Brazilian people, rather recklessly trying to convert a few of them to his own True Christianity. Yet he wrote home that the Roman Catholic Church in Brazil was beautiful and they really did things in style. "If ever I join an Establishment it won't be either of the poor degenerate 'sisters' at home, but the good mother herself in Brazil." Yet, a few lines farther down we realize he was pulling our legs, for he adds earnestly, "When will the beams of Divine Light dispel the darkness of the beautiful empire?"

Eventually—in March, 1841—he arrived at Capetown. A few weeks later, after staying with a wise older man, Dr. Philip, he and William Ross went on by ship to Port Elizabeth. Ross was a married man and in fact he and his wife had travelled out with Livingstone on the *George*. At Port Elizabeth the three of them waited another month for the ox-carts which would take them north to their destination, and during the month Livingstone pursued his study of both the Dutch and Sechuana languages.

The journey, when they eventually got their ox-carts, need not have taken ten weeks. But it did, largely because of the new medical missionary's determination to heal all *en route* who felt they needed it. But at the end of July, 1841, he reached the mission of Kuruman, in Bechuanaland, which had been established by Robert Moffat. It was a snug place—too snug, perhaps: smug, almost—and he admired its comfortable houses, its fine church, the forge, the carpenter's shop and so on. It had an air of prosperity and contentment. But David Livingstone knew his role would be to press on, do his work much farther afield. Perhaps he irritated the inhabitants of the Kuruman mission by suggesting there were too many contented missionaries in residence and that they should be scattered miles apart. They should go out, one by one, and with what he called "native agency" convert and succour the savages. Native agency, he felt, "is the only thing that can evangelize the world". He would stay only just long enough to master the Sechuana language and then go north to live "excluded from all European society".

And so began a lifetime serving Africa. He found that not only did the remote northern Africans need instruction more than those at hand, for they were totally ignorant, but that in fact there were far more of them. Kuruman mission seemed to have been dumped down in a remarkably under-populated spot. He began making expeditions into the bush, spending a few days here, a week there, and sometimes recruiting an interested man to spread the Word among his own people.

But it was not until 1843 that he got permission to open a new station. By now the ceaseless double quest for know-ledge and for willing recipients of what he himself had to offer, had made him into an explorer as well as a missionary. He began having his share of adventure, and quite early on was hideously savaged by a lion. The experience, coupled with his disappointment at the attitude of so many Africans towards his teaching, might have severely discouraged a lesser man, but not Livingstone. They asked him what he felt at the moment the lion leapt on him, and he said, in his dry way, "I was wondering what part of me he'd eat first".

Livingstone had always been a good shot, and would remain one: but from now on he would be unable to fire his gun from the right shoulder, would be forced to use the left, and sight with the left eye.

Perhaps it was the long convalescence following his near-fatal experience which warmed his heart towards the oppo-site sex. And perhaps the fact that he was an invalid had a similar effect upon the girl he was soon to marry. She was Robert Moffat's twenty-three-year-old daughter Mary, and now in 1844, when he himself was thirty-one, he married her.

Up to a point it was a successful marriage—though it

has always seemed to me that David Livingstone should never have married at all. Certainly he approached the partnership with eyes unromantically open. His betrothed, he wrote to a friend, was "not romantic, but a matter-of-fact lady, a little, thick, black-haired girl, sturdy and all I want".

For this matter-of-fact little lady he built a house in his new, up-country mission of Mabotsa. His salary, as married man, was raised to £100 a year.

The work he and his wife did lives after them. Over his many years in Africa, Livingstone was to heal and, from time to time, convert Africans. Those he healed and helped in many, many ways must have run into hundreds of thousands. One of his greatest achievements—in the missionary sphere—was his exposure of the slave trade, which resulted in its abolition. But though it is as a selfless Christian that he left his mark on Africa, it is as the world's greatest explorer of modern times that he is remembered outside it.

The big journeys began in 1849. Some time previous he had made the acquaintance of the English explorer William Oswell (Mr. Moffat had urged the explorer to press on another two hundred miles beyond Kuruman to Livingstone's mission and pick his son-in-law's brain), and in 1849 he joined him, and Mungo Murray, in a search for a great lake. No white man had ever seen it, but natives knew where it was. It was believed to be simply enormous, to stretch from horizon to horizon in all directions. Livingstone agreed to join the Englishmen: his knowledge of Africa would help them, and he would have the opportunity, with this well-equipped caravan, of opening up still more territory.

The journey was hazardous and unpleasant, but at last, on 1 August, 1849, they reached the enormous lake, Lake Ngami. He was excited by the discovery, but his chief interest remained in spreading the Word of God and healing the sick bodies of the Africans who now came up to him and asked his help. Already the great Livingstone's fame had preceded him, to a land no white man had ever seen. He busied himself getting his "native agency" going in this unfamiliar part, getting others to learn a little religion, a little medicine, from him and go out to help their own people. To do this Livingstone had to learn yet another language, but he did so at speed.

The expedition made its way home and months later he was delighted to receive the Royal Geographical Society's award for discovering the lake. It was £25, and though he and Mary were very poor he blued the lot on a handsome watch for himself. As for the award, he wrote, tongue in cheek to his parents: "It is from the Queen. You must be very loyal, all of you. Next time she comes your way, shout till you are hoarse."

And where is Lake Ngami now? It has evaporated, vanished: it is a vast green plain. But Livingstone's mapping of the area and his route to it threw light on an absolutely unknown, unvisited part of Africa.

The next year Livingstone took Mary and the three small children north from their mission at Kolobeng, to show them his lake. (He noted that the level had already fallen three feet in the twelve months.) And now we come to see the one great fault in his character: he was quite unable and unwilling to see that his wife should not be subjected to this sort of hardship. His desire to have her with him, have her help him in his work as she did at the mission, completely over-ruled common humanity which would surely have insisted she stay at home.

Mary was pregnant with her fourth child, and she suffered greatly from the journey. She got back to Kolobeng in August, more dead than alive, and lost the child.

Livingstone in his journal wrote cheerfully: "It was just as likely to have happened had we remained at home, and we have now one of our number in heaven."

Mary's recovery was slow and only partial, and after— incredibly—an arduous trip with her husband to the Upper Zambezi during which she had another child, it became obvious even to her husband that she and the children must leave Africa, at least for a while. This personal matter, however, was overshadowed by Livingstone's great discovery that the Upper Zambezi River had been wrongly placed on the map—and by the fact that there were natives galore in this area who badly needed his help, and got it.

For Mary, who was a very brave girl, it was a terrible wrench to leave her husband and Africa; she loved them both very deeply. But she and the four children sailed from Capetown on 23 April, 1852.

Without his wife and children, the tale of Livingstone becomes more of a geography lesson. He went on, opening up the country, leaving his native assistants everywhere he could, to carry on his missionary work, and it was in 1855 that he made perhaps his greatest discovery.

He was following the great Zambezi to its mouth in Delagoa Bay, travelling in a light canoe, when suddenly he reached a small island. It was almost hidden in clouds of spray. He disembarked on it and then discovered that the island was projecting right out over a precipice. Over this a gigantic waterfall was tumbling, and he crawled to the very edge, lay down and watched in wonder. "It had never been seen before by European eyes, but scenes so lovely must have been gazed on by angels in their flight." He was always, throughout life, horrified by exaggeration and now he estimated the length of these falls as "not less than six hundred yards". They are, in fact, 1,900 yards in length, with a drop of up to 350 feet at the deeper end.

He named them after his queen, perhaps remembering his quip about "shouting till you are hoarse" in her honour.

At the end of the next year he returned to England, to be acclaimed as the greatest explorer of the age, the man who had accomplished the most marvellous journeys on record and necessitated the complete re-drawing of the map of Africa. All this was true.

Perhaps this was the finest hour of his life. For soon, owing to a difference of opinion with the London Missionary Society, he resigned from that body. When he set sail a second time for Africa it was with the appointment of Consul to Quelimane in Mozambique, near the mouth of the Zambezi. He was also in charge of an expedition with orders to explore east and central Africa.

This second visit to that continent was in many ways a failure, and the expedition, mismanaged by himself and beset by every sort of bad luck, was recalled. His wife, who had bravely and eagerly rejoined him in Africa, died in 1862 on a ship at the mouth of the Zambezi. The interminable delay in that fever-ridden spot—which caused her death—was largely the result of Livingstone's own total inability as an organizer. One of the ship's officers wrote, "I have rarely seen a man so easily led as Dr. Livingstone. I never saw such constant vacillations, blunders, delays and want of common thought and foresight."

He was heartbroken at Mary's death, but still able to do valuable work. He now pointed out the horrors of slavery as practised by the Portuguese and was instrumental in stopping it. He found time to discover Lake Nyasa and lay the foundations of what would some day become Nyasaland. His name is still reverenced there, though Nyasaland's name has changed to Malawi: its capital is still Blantyre, after the explorer's birthplace in Lanarkshire.

He returned to Britain in July, 1864, and spent a whole year at home. His third and last visit to Africa began with the declared intention—sponsored by the Geographical Society—of discovering the sources of the Nile. He was completely lost to the world for five years, from 1866, and it was during these years that at last advancing years and the rigours of his life began to take their toll. Disasters followed each other: his goods were stolen, his medicines lost, he nearly died half a dozen times from disease or starvation. And it was at his lowest ebb that he was found by Henry Stanley, sent by the go-ahead editor of the *New York Herald*.

Stanley was in almost every way the antithesis of Livingstone. He was brash and boastful. But the two men conceived a great respect for each other. Their friendship began, as everyone knows, when Stanley got to Ujiji and saw this walking skeleton, "pale and wearied, with a grey beard, wearing a blueish cap with a faded gold band round it, a red-sleeved waistcoat and a pair of grey tweed trousers". Stanley's first words were: "Doctor Livingstone, I presume?"

The two men stayed together till March, 1872, exploring still more of Africa, until Stanley reluctantly had to go home. He urged the explorer to come with him, but Livingstone refused: now, with Mary dead, the continent was more than ever his life, his work. Ill with malaria and dysentery, he set off again for the sources of the Nile which he fancied were near yet another lake he had discovered, Bangweulu.

He never got there. In April, 1873, he scribbled in his journal, "Tried to ride, but was forced to lie down, and they carried me back to the village exhausted".

It was the end. When he reached the village—Chitambo —his grief-stricken attendants built him a hut, and there he died.

And now these devoted Africans, who could easily have left the body where it lay, endured the most dreadful hardships, including battle and bloodshed, to get it to the coast. There it was taken by ship to England and a hero's burial in Westminster Abbey.

Perhaps we can sum up David Livingstone and his life, with its selflessness and yet complete lack of consideration for people—like Mary—whom he did not understand; its fantastic courage and complete lack of organizing ability; with his words:

"I am a missionary, heart and soul. God had an only Son, and He was a missionary and a physician. A poor, poor imitation I am or wish to be. In this service I hope to live, in it, I wish to die."

But no—we cannot leave him as just a saint. He was not a saint: he was a good, yet sometimes selfish man. He even had a sense of humour—at the expense of the ladies:

"I notice that the mongoose gets lean on a diet of cockroaches. That would be invaluable to fat young ladies at home——"

WILLIAM McGONAGALL

"Oh mighty City of New York! You are wonderful to behold,
Your buildings are magnificent, the truth be it told,
They were the only thing that seemed to arrest my eye,
Because many of them are thirteen storeys high."

Lines from the *Poetic Gems* of
William McGonagall, published in 1890.

Who was this man, almost universally acclaimed as history's
worst poet? And was all his poetry all *that* bad?

To answer the second question first: no, not *quite*. Some
of his verse has lyric quality: all of it has something to say.

Which is more than can be claimed for a lot of poetry.

Some of the verses, re-punctuated and set out so that the
jingling rhythm goes, would pass as poetry of the nineteen-
sixties: might even win a prize. The Hawthornden has
gone for less.

It has become fashionable in Britain to yelp with mirth when the name McGonagall is mentioned. Comedians like Spike Milligan give recitals of his work (and do it superbly). We glance at him here, not because he was just a bad poet, but because there is something basically noble and appealing about him. He was a man of courage; and he had a soul which he tried hard to put into words. The thought was there: the words were missing. William McGonagall is a cautionary tale to a schoolboy, for he was crippled by lack of vocabulary. Just as within every fat man there is a thin one trying to get out, so within McGonagall there was a poet, and a real poet, without the words to let his thoughts escape. Learn your words, Johnnie, or you'll be like poor Mr. McGonagall.

He was born in Edinburgh in 1830 and, like so many others within these pages, had a father who was a handloom weaver. There was depression in the cotton trade in Edinburgh and the little family moved west to Glasgow. Here they kept themselves just alive, but there could be no question of young William staying at school: his education ended at the age of seven.

After this, the family moved east again, to Dundee, and William went to work in a jute mill. Here, like David Livingstone, Mary Slessor and others, he started reading books on the job. One wonders how cloth was produced at all, during the nineteenth century. He read avidly, and practised his handwriting.

"The books that I liked best to read were Shakespeare's penny plays, more especially *Macbeth, Richard III, Hamlet* and *Othello*; and I gave myself no rest until I obtained complete mastery over the above four characters. Many a time in my dear father's absence I enacted entire scenes from *Macbeth* and *Richard III,* along with some of my shopmates, until they were quite delighted; and many a time they regaled me and the other actors that had entertained them to strong ale, biscuits and cheese——"

And now one begins to see, even before William McGonagall had committed words to paper, had written a first line of verse, that he was a figure of fun. So unconsciously comic was he that people were prepared to pay good money to come and laugh at him. Mr. Giles ran an Edinburgh theatre and was happy to let McGonagall perform in it, on payment of one pound. McGonagall, for his part, was happy mounting a stage to recite some of his Shakespeare, was quite prepared to pay for the privilege. His workmates eagerly chipped in to make up the needed pound.

On the night, the theatre was packed, standing room only. "When I appeared on the stage, I was received with a perfect storm of applause, but when I exclaimed, 'Command, they make a halt upon the heath', the applause was deafening, and was continued during the entire evening, especially so in the combat scene."

This was the funniest thing that had ever happened to Dundee, and word got around. The tragedian gave three performances, and by the third audiences were fighting to get in and witness something which might never again happen. "What a sight it was to see such a mass of people struggling to gain admission! Hundreds failed to do so, and in the struggle numbers were trampled underfoot, one man having lost one of his shoes in the scrimmage——"

It was a most satisfactory arrangement: Mr. Giles was delighted at having his theatre full—and getting a pound from the artist; the audience had never laughed so much or applauded so loudly, in its life; and Mr. McGonagall was overcome at the realization that overnight he had become a box-office draw. The show was repeated, and this time there were queues stretching down the street.

But the biggest event in McGonagall's life was still ahead. His forty-seventh birthday had come and gone, when suddenly, as he sat in his room in Dundee, "A flame, as Lord Byron has said, seemed to kindle up my entire frame, along with a strong desire to write poetry: and I felt so happy, so happy that I was inclined to dance. Then I began to pace backwards and forwards in the room, trying to shake off all thought of writing poetry; but the more I tried, the more strong the sensation became. It was so strong, I imagined that a pen was in my right hand, and a voice crying, 'Write! Write!'"

So he did. He wrote straightway a few lines on a man he admired, the late Reverend George Gilfillan. Then he folded the paper, took it along to the offices of the Dundee *Weekly News*, and dropped it in the letter-box.

To his delight, the poem was printed. The editor's note about it showed the great man had taken a personal interest, and this was particularly pleasing. McGonagall carefully cut out note and poem and kept them as a memory of the first verses he ever wrote. The column in the paper began:

"*W. McG.*, Dundee, who modestly seeks to hide his light under a bushel, has surreptitiously dropped into our letter-box an address to the Rev. George Gilfillan. Here is a sample of this worthy's powers of versification:

> '*Rev. George Gilfillan of Dundee,*
> *There is none can you excel;*
> *You have boldly rejected the Confession of Faith,*
> *And defended your case right well.*' "

The *Weekly News* went on to print the whole poem, for which we have no space, but which ended with the moving words, "May all good angels guard him while living, and hereafter, when he's dead".

Fame at last—or more accurately, still greater fame, for McGonagall was already notorious for his readings from the drama. Now he was not only tragedian, but poet as well. Within a few months he had written enough to fill a slim volume, and others followed hard on its heels. By 1890, aged sixty, he was able to choose a selection of *Poetic Gems Selected From the Works of William McGonagall, Poet & Tragedian.*

The fan mail flooded in, including a "Tribute from Three Students at Glasgow University", which McGonagall gratefully published in the second volume of his *Gems*. To most people but McGonagall it would have been offensive, but the sarcasm passed him by and he was most grateful for the "Ode" they had composed in his honour. One cannot help noting a faint similarity between the idea behind this "Tribute" from three students at

Glasgow University and that behind the "Testimonial" offered by another three at the same place, to someone else within these pages. Be that as it may, the "Ode" began:

"Among the poets of the present day,
There is no one on earth who can possibly be able for to gainsay,
But that William McGonagall, poet and tragedian,
Is truly the greatest poet that was ever found above or below the meridian."

After twelve stanzas in this vein, the three students ask him a number of questions, to all of which McGonagall conscientiously replied: Would the most intellectual benefit be derived from a study of the McGonagallian or Shakespearian school of poetry? Would he recommend them to write direct to the Queen as a patron of poetry, or should they go to Balmoral to see her? If they went to Balmoral, what route would he recommend?

Poor man, he had been to Balmoral, and this seems the only time in his life that his work brought physical and mental discomfort to him. Some wag had sent him a parchment scroll purporting to come from Her Majesty and virtually appointing him Poet Laureate. Thrilled, bursting with gratitude, he prepared to set off and thank her.

It was a very hot day in July, and after walking throughout it, he got to the village of Alyth. For fourpence he was given lodging for the night and hot water to wash his badly blistered feet. The next morning he limped off again and got as far as the Spittal of Glenshee when a thunderstorm of tropic intensity burst upon him, drenched him to the skin. He got to a shepherd's cottage and was refused entry: no room for lodgers. He dragged out his soggy parchment from the Queen, with its royal seal. The shepherd was so impressed that he invited the poet in out of the downpour and made him welcome. McGonagall went to bed in the barn and dreamt of Her Majesty.

The next morning, thrusting a volume of his verses into the shepherd's hand, he set off towards Braemar and Balmoral. Nothing untoward happened until at three in the afternoon he reached the porter's lodge of the castle.

He knocked boldly on the door and two constables popped out. "One of them asked me in a very authoritative tone what I wanted, and of course I told him I wanted to see Her Majesty, and he repeated, 'Who do you want to see?', and I said I was surprised to think that he should ask me again after telling him distinctly that I wanted to see Her Majesty. Then I showed him Her Majesty's royal letter of patronage for my poetic abilities, and he read it and said it was not Her Majesty's letter."

Undaunted, McGonagall assures the constables that it is, and to humour him one of them pretends to go to the Queen with it. He returns, says she thanks him, but that she is too busy to grant him an audience. "Well," says the poet, "it cannot be helped." He then embarks on a short rendering of his verses and is hastily quietened: what is his charge for that volume of verse, and if they buy it will he go? "I said '2d.', and he gave it me, telling me to go straight home and not think of coming back again to Balmoral."

Quite content, the poet trudges three days back to Dundee, arriving there "footsore and weary, but not the least discouraged. So ends my ever-memorable journey to Balmoral."

I find it hard not to like William McGonagall.

In 1887 he made another ever-memorable journey, to New York, a visit which spawned many lines of verse, four of which are quoted earlier. Why he went there is unclear, as there were no professional engagements during his stay. This, as he solemnly records, was because "the New York theatre managers didn't encourage rivalry". The poet and tragedian returned to his native land. A few years later, rich in years if not in wisdom, William McGonagall died.

It is tempting to end with his ludicrous Ode to Robert Burns, of whom he considered himself a rival. But I prefer to use the last lines of another McGonagall epic, not because I think they are funny, but because they catch the essential goodness of a pious, homely, man, with a lot to say, but without the means to say it.

"Whatsoever God wills must come to pass,
The fall of a sparrow or a tiny blade of grass;
Also, man must fall at home, by his command,
Just equally the same as in a foreign land."

A good man, and a happy one. He gave more pleasure to more people during his lifetime than most of us do. What greater praise can one offer?

ANDREW CARNEGIE

He embodied much that is fine in the Scots character—and quite a bit which is not. He was an economic wizard, persuasive, charming and fantastically hard-working. When it suited him, he was fantastically generous. He had the common touch, so that even when he was many times a millionaire and exploiting his workmen, they would do whatever he told them—so long as he told it personally. They would rise in revolt against an unpleasant order, if it were handed down by an underling.

He was embittered, childishly embittered, against all those born with the proverbial silver spoon in the mouth, and this included all royalty, all aristocracy. He was boastful; the science of Public Relations, Image Building, which was unknown in his day, might have been thought up by Andrew Carnegie. Other rich men might have retrospective qualms about the way they made their money. Never Carnegie. We may compare him with John D. Rockefeller, who made more money and gave more away.

To do so, let us creep aboard an ocean liner which is just about to sail from New York. Gangways are being removed, gongs are sounding, there is an atmosphere of noise and excitement. Yet down below in his cabin sits Mr. Rockefeller, with the door locked. He is deeply ashamed of the money he possesses, conscious that there has been a deal of unpleasantness recently about the way he is alleged to have made it. He has crept aboard under an assumed name and slunk down to his cabin. He may well not leave it throughout the seven-day journey to Europe.

Above his head—some four decks above it—stands Andrew Carnegie, four years his senior and another multi-millionaire about whom unpleasant questions have been asked. But the round-faced, jolly Scot is the man everyone loves, and the press is clustered round him like bees at a honey-pot, busily scribbling down his views, his opinions, on philosophy, the world situation, and himself. By tomorrow morning half the newspapers in the world will have columns about the great philanthropist.

There will be nothing about the grasping Rockefeller.

And we must admit that Andrew Carnegie, ruthless maker of money, inexhaustible giver-away, is a more interesting character than John Rockefeller, who was both these things, only more so. For that he can thank the fact that he was born in Scotland.

The event took place in a cottage at Dunfermline. The year was 1835. Like the cottages in which so many of our famous men and women were born, it contained a hand-loom, and on it Thomas Carnegie made table-cloths.

His hard-working wife, Margaret, who will figure throughout much of the Carnegie story, made shoes and sold them in her own little shop to supplement Thomas's earnings. She also ruled the family with an iron hand.

A predilection for revolt has long been a Scots characteristic, and the Carnegies were no exception. They quarrelled with their church, their neighbours, the local laird. In this they were surpassed only by Margaret Carnegie's family, the Morrisons, who got so acrimoniously involved with the laird of Pittencrieff that he swore no one of Morrison blood should ever enter his grounds. Young Andrew took this to heart and immediately became a rabid hater of all lairds. The hate, as life wore on, would extend to royalty.

His mother, staunch, determined woman with a mind of her own, kept his thoughts in this direction. Her control over her son till he was an elderly man is one of the oddest facets of an odd career.

Years before, a member of the family had emigrated to America and settled in Pennsylvania. Now, with their fortunes low, the Carnegies decided to follow. It was 1848; Andrew was thirteen, his brother Tom just five. They packed their few belongings, said goodbye to their neighbours and set off across Scotland to Glasgow. Here they embarked and sailed west.

Once across the Atlantic they moved inland to settle near Uncle Willie in the township of Allegheny, in Pennsylvania. It was a primitive place, unconnected by rail to anywhere and supplied only by river steamer up the Monongahela River. Thomas and Margaret Carnegie were discouraged, for the place seemed even less promising than Dunfermline. Young Andrew found his first weeks, working in a cotton mill, thoroughly depressing; but he kept eyes and ears open and within a month of arrival had transferred to the Telegraph Company as messenger boy.

The job only involved carrying telegrams from the receiving station to the addressee, but he set himself to work learning the Morse code. Soon, like other young and ambitious telegraphists of the period, he was able to listen to the clickerty-clack of the sounder and read off whole sentences out loud, without putting pencil to paper. This was Thomas Edison's proudest achievement as a young man and, at the time, it was wee Andrew Carnegie's.

For he *was* wee. A wee blond mannie with a round face and large eyes. Not Rockefeller eyes that stared through one, but round, innocent, visionary orbs that seemed to be looking at something far off, in the future.

Or in the past. Andrew Carnegie built his life, as soon as he was rich enough, round the memory of Scotland. As luck would have it—for luck, as with all of us, good luck and bad, makes a difference—he was rich enough remarkably soon.

His father died and he was now alone with his canny, doting mother, and young Tom; the responsibility determined him to be more than just the best telegraphist in Pennsylvania. He remembered the land from which he had sprung, made up his mind to be a worthy descendant. As he wrote later, "Every Scotchman is two Scotchmen, as his land has the wild barren stern crags and mountain peaks, and also the smiling valleys where the mildest foxglove and bluebell blossom, so the Scotchman with his rugged force and hard intellect has a heart capable of being touched to the finest issue."

The luck? Ah, yes. The railway, when it reached Pittsburgh, was one of the wonders of the world, and its arrival coincided with the maturity of a boy who had become not only a superb telegraphist, but the most promising young man in the neighbourhood. The new Superintendent of the Pennsylvania Railroad in Pittsburgh signed the boy up as his personal assistant and sent him off, for a start, in charge of gangs of men repairing the track, track which in those early days needed constant attention.

Then, one day, there was a nasty train crash. It coincided (luck again here) with the absence on business of Mr. Scott and brought about total confusion. The line had been blocked and no one knew how to disentangle the mess. One after another, goods trains were coming to a halt all over Pennsylvania.

The young assistant took charge instantly. He sent telegrams to each train, giving the driver an exact time to move off, and signing each message "Thomas A. Scott". Such a method of telegraph control had been tried, but no one yet understood it. Under Andrew Carnegie it worked beautifully; the railroad paralysis ended and the Pennsylvania got back on the move.

Thomas A Scott, when he got back to Pittsburgh, could only gasp at the success obtained by his "white-haired Scotch devil".

The Scotch devil had become, overnight, a man to be reckoned with. And now, another stroke of luck. A mysterious stranger walked in, carrying an ingenious wooden model which turned out to be a folding bed, suitable for putting inside a rail carriage. By day the carriage would be comfortable, seated; at night it converted easily into a honeycomb of little private alcoves for sleeping. Carnegie persuaded his firm that this would be the design of railway carriages in the future, and they not only agreed to manufacture them, but formed a separate company to build them *en masse*. Young Andrew, having discovered the design, was allowed to be majority shareholder. By this time a gifted carpenter had been found to supervise the manufacture of these cars, and he added his own improvements. His name was George Pullman.

And now, somehow, Andrew Carnegie found himself the new Superintendent of the Pittsburgh Division, Pennsylvania Railroad. Thomas A. Scott faded from the picture.

With inside information about where the Railroad would go and when, Carnegie got into the lucrative habit of buying the right stocks and shares cheaply in the knowledge that they would soon be worth a great deal more. His wealth grew every month, and well before he was thirty he found himself a millionaire. Under the eagle eye of his mother, every penny was carefully reinvested.

Came the American Civil War and he was able to give valuable assistance to the northern side by his handling of the railways. Tracks and bridges were kept in first-class repair and troop-trains were slotted in, one after the other, with a skill that puzzled and delighted the military authorities.

And then, at the end of the war, this rich young man took a trip back home to Scotland—and he realized that his heart belonged there. His aunt in Dunfermline, delighted to see that the lad had made a bit of money, suggested kindly that he open up a wee shoppie in the town of his ancestors. He smilingly declined.

Back in Pittsburgh, he took stock and pondered the question of culture. He had always read copiously; now he set himself to doing it like a military exercise. The whole of Shakespeare was consumed within weeks, much of it committed to memory. He joined a debating society, met men more sophisticated than himself and studied them, their behaviour, what made them tick.

He was invited to one of their houses, far grander than his own, and there in the library he saw words carved over the fireplace which he committed to memory on the spot. He would remember them for the rest of his life:

> *"He that cannot reason is a fool,*
> *He that will not reason is a bigot;*
> *He that dare not reason is a slave."*

He swapped heavy boots for a gentleman's shoes, mastered the art of small talk, became much in demand in Pittsburg society. Girls who had once fought shy of the ponderous little man now found him attractive, wondered why their interest was not returned. They had forgotten Margaret Carnegie.

As a millionaire, Andrew had no need to remain an employee of the Pennsylvania Railroad, and he resigned. He invested in iron and in a new device called a trip-hammer which shaped pig-iron more simply and effectively than any other method. The inventor, a man called Kloman, had no business acumen and soon Carnegie and his mother were partners in his enterprise.

The Kloman firm, now with all these limitless funds behind it, was set for a prosperous future. And then one day, Kloman, never quite sure what hit him, was out in the street.

From iron, by easy and obvious stages, to bridges. The Carnegie-financed Keystone Bridge Company crossed the Ohio at Cincinnati, the Missouri at Plattsmouth, the Mississippi at St. Louis. And with new bridges, new lines were opened; the rails for them were made by another Carnegie enterprise, the Union Iron Works. The middle west had begun shouting for everything the east could send it, and demanding railways to transport it; Carnegie made it his job to see they got them.

Young Tom now got married and Andrew moved with his mother to New York, to a hotel off Broadway. He had discovered that his talent lay in persuading others to do what he wanted; this he could do more comfortably, more effectively, from New York, while leaving the humdrum work of building bridges, making rails, to subordinates.

He realized suddenly that if he never worked again he would still have a tax-free income of fifty thousand dollars a year. At the same time he realized the difficulty of spending such an amount on himself and his mother.

He would leave America immediately, go to Britain and study at Oxford. There he would get a degree—and he would have been educated. The feeling of inferiority which crept up on him in the company of people with culture would vanish.

On second thought, it could wait. He would go to Oxford in two years' time.

The lure of profit intervened. And to be fair to Carnegie, we must add that it was not simply the glitter of gold; it was the shimmer of steel. On a visit to England he had been to a factory where the new Bessemer converter, for making pig-iron cheaply and efficiently into steel, was being used. It was a revelation; the molten pig-iron was brought to white heat simply by bubbling air through it, without any further addition of heat. And then, with air cut off at a predetermined point—a white and bubbling liquid which was steel. Childishly, magically simple; it would revolutionize the nineteenth century, change the world of iron into a world of steel.

Henry Bessemer, the cheerful English wizard who invented more things than Baird, and far more profitably, was allowing this particular brainchild to be operated anywhere under licence, for a very reasonable figure. Carnegie was genuinely fascinated by the process and he now plunged into the steel business as if it were the only thing in life that mattered. His young brother Tom had an option on a site called Braddock by the Monongahela River which would be ideal for a Carnegie steelworks. Andrew made haste to take the option up.

In his autobiography he wrote that an inspiration came to him in bed, telling him this great new enterprise would be sited at a place to be called Braddock.

You may take your choice.

He built his steelworks where Tom and the Lord told him. And now we get a glimpse of the sort of insight which really made Carnegie rich and great. He learnt that another steelworks, not far off, was on strike, that the leader of the strikers was a man called Bill Jones, whom the men would follow whatever he asked them to do. Carnegie signed him up immediately and put him in charge of his own labour relations. Bill Jones might have his troubles today, but in nineteenth-century Pennsylvania he worked wonders. The men, at his suggestion, were paid very high wages and divided into teams which competed against each other in productivity. (The very thought makes a mid-twentieth-century mind reel.) At the end of the day the furnace which had produced the most was allowed to hoist a flag and keep it aloft for twenty-four hours, egging on others to get it pulled down. It was made clear, too, that any man good enough could become a boss. As for Bill Jones—Captain Bill, as he was universally known—he refused Carnegie's offer of a partnership and settled simply for the role of "the highest-paid working man in the United States of America". At 25,000 dollars a year he was.

Carnegie came to a friendly agreement with the railways about transporting his steel, much the same arrangement that Rockefeller had reached about oil: cheap transport meant cheap steel for the railway, and it also in effect meant no transport for anyone else's steel. Such action today would be illegal, but in the forceful nineteenth century it was accepted business practice; no sort of bribe or blackmail was considered out of order.

By 1880 the Carnegie steel interests were producing more steel than any firm had ever done, and their steel was being rushed about the U.S.A., at cut rates, to build bridges, and to lay down rails on which to carry more steel. And, of course, to carry the wonderful Pullman car, which Carnegie owned.

He certainly didn't need any more money. But now it was exciting, and there could be no question of swapping the world of steel for Oxford. What he would do, and did do, from 1880 onwards, was spend half of each year in Europe. For the first of these European visits he took a party of friends in a stage-coach. He wrote the exploit up in a little book called *An American Four-in-Hand in Britain*, and the writing of this, his first book, seems to have meant as much to him as any of the take-overs, the successes, of the past. "To do things," he now proclaimed, "is not half the battle. Carlyle is all wrong about this. To be able to tell the world what you have done, that is the greater accomplishment."

Hence, we might almost say, Public Relations.

He bought up a prettily named rival steelworks, Homestead, a few miles away. Homestead had suffered a lot of labour troubles and Carnegie watched till these were at their very worst and made a very low bid—which was thankfully accepted. He put in a manager, Henry Frick, and retired for six months to Scotland.

And in his absence a strike far worse than those which had afflicted Homestead in the old days descended over the whole of Carnegie Steel. A union had been formed, The Amalgamated Association, and it demanded better conditions. Earnings on piecework could be very high, but men worked a twelve-hour shift and sometimes a non-stop twenty-four. This, Amalgamated said, just wasn't good enough.

The first threat of a strike met strong-arm tactics from Frick; to prevent victimization of men who stayed at work, he took the fantastic step of ordering three hundred men from the Pinkerton Detective Agency in New York— virtually a private army.

News of this got out, and when a tug came up the Monongahela drawing behind it two barges full of Pinkertons and crates of rifles, a barrage of small-arms fire greeted it from the shore.

Panic on board, for the rifles were still in their crates. And a knotty legal problem to solve—with bullets whistling past: the local Sheriff was on board, and he had been expected to give a straightforward blessing to the Pinkerton invasion, but he did not. Each man would have to be individually sworn in as Sheriff's Assistant. Furthermore, this could not be done until they were on dry land. The cursing Pinkertons lay flat on the deck while bullets screamed overhead.

The tug cast them adrift, beat a hasty retreat. The strikers poured burning oil on the river. The Pinkertons slowly unpicked the crates—from their horizontal position —and prepared to do battle.

But they were forced to surrender; and although the strike leader gave them safe conduct to get ashore and escape, the unfortunate Pinkertons were attacked with stones and broken bottles.

This was civil war: and unlike the one of a generation previous, it was devoid of profit for Carnegie. The massacre became a national scandal. Carnegie, who had been sending contradictory orders from Scotland, where he was fishing salmon, rushed back and settled the affair. It is an indication of the man's charm, his common touch, that whereas his manager Frick, who had done most of what he did because Carnegie either suggested it or acquiesced, was nearly murdered by the men, one of them said to Carnegie, "The men would have let you trick them— but they wouldn't let that other man stroke their hair."

Whether this influenced the next, astonishing stage in Carnegie's career—the chief one we remember—one cannot say. He became a philanthropist. He had acquired an education from his own reading; he would now offer that same opportunity to all the world. He gave a magnificent library to Allegheny, another to Pittsburgh. He announced that *any community in the English-speaking world* might have a library, but it would have to prove to Andrew Carnegie that it intended to stock it with books and set aside a reasonable sum each year for upkeep.

Libraries sprang up in Britain and America—and with them art galleries, technical colleges.

He took time off to write another book. This was a very odd book, setting out to prove that because Andrew Carnegie was an ordinary man, only ordinary men were capable of achieving greatness. Only ordinary men could discover minerals, build railways, plan cities. The book was called *Triumphant Democracy* and it asserted that republicanism was the answer to the world's ills; that no nation could prosper under a monarchy or an aristocracy.

It is a strange twenty-four chapters worth of egotism: an ode to materialism. America, he points out, is O.K. because she has avoided the Frenchy corruption of Europe. A union between America and Britain would be a good thing, but impossible of achievement while Britain hangs on to its outmoded monarchy: the monarchy must go. The aristocracy must go.

And up in Carnegie's great Scottish home, his castle of Skibo in Sutherland, where some of this has been written, the most honoured guests are from the British peerage.

Margaret Carnegie died when her son was in his fifties. Tom had died some years before that. Only now did Andrew Carnegie feel himself free to marry. He was over sixty when his daughter was born.

And now, at last, the great man, with a little girl playing about his feet at Skibo, had become a human being. The philanthropy, of course, had started years before, but it went on now, redoubled. He went on with his giving of libraries (and the total spent on this alone soon reached £10,000,000) and now he gave £2,000,000 for Scottish education. This was followed up by vast sums to American and English universities. For his old home of Dunfermline he set up a trust with an annual income of £25,000.

In 1904 he hit upon the imaginative idea of a Carnegie Hero Fund. At first it was for the U.S.A. and Canada, but it was extended to cover Britain as well, by 1908. Its laudable purpose was "to place those following peaceful vocations who have been injured in an heroic effort to save human life in somewhat better positions pecuniarily than before, until again able to work".

Carnegie Trusts, Carnegie Foundations, Carnegie Endowments, poured out money, all of it for excellent causes—more money than most small nations earn over the same period. There was the Carnegie Foundation for the Advancement of Teaching, the Carnegie Endowment for International Peace, the Carnegie Trust for Universities of Scotland, the Carnegie United Kingdom Trust——

Till the end of life he would spend spring and summer in Europe—most of it at Skibo, where that representative of effete monarchy, Edward VII, was an honoured guest— and the autumn and winter in America. As time ran out and age crept up, Carnegie's attempts to do something really worthwhile with his money grew ever greater. He disbelieved in churches, but he liked hymns—and the number of church organs he gave in the last years of his life rose into the hundreds.

He died, universally mourned, at the age of eighty-four, having given away some 300 million dollars. Here, men knew, was a man, a real man like themselves, who had been doing just the sort of thing they would have done themselves, had they been in similar circumstance.

Here, in fact, was a man no better and no worse than any other: a man like one or two others who had made a fortune and gave a lot of it back again. But the larger-than-life image of that man, putting paid to heresies about Scotsmen being tight-fisted with their bawbees—this has ensured that the name of Andrew Carnegie will be remembered, with gratitude, till the end of time.

MARY SLESSOR

It is the face of a humorous, intelligent girl of the nineteen-sixties. The hair is cut short like a man's, and the smiling eyes set well apart in that oval, handsome face, with the high cheek-bones, have an almost oriental look about them.

Only the leg-of-mutton sleeves which one notices after one has stared into the face itself, only these set Mary Slessor firmly in the nineteenth century.

When she was forty-three—which is some time after this particular photo was taken—a young man of twenty-five died of a broken heart because she refused to marry him. Perhaps men don't die of broken hearts, but Charles Morrison pined away, was invalided out of Africa, grew steadily worse and died while trying to recover his health in North Carolina.

She converted blood-streaked savages twice her size, by

rushing at them with her umbrella, beating them over the head. She dealt with the sex life of cannibals. She went everywhere barefoot.

A man at one of her lectures, when she was on furlough in Scotland, would upset her so much that she would ask that he hide himself behind a lady: in Africa, she was surrounded, unmoved, by naked men; watched sex orgies of a sort to make even our own permissive age gasp in horror. Calmly, she went on to explain to ageing savages, after her umbrella had stopped them beating their young wives, just why it was natural that those wives should feel an urge to fly into the jungle with younger men. She explained, too, after hundreds of years in which twins were killed at birth as being the result of union with the devil, that only a man of the utmost virility could produce two at a time; she brought pride, lasting joy, to parents—and life to twins.

She died in 1915, and her name in West Africa means more even that David Livingstone's, more than those of others who gave lives to the Dark Continent. Livingstone was almost a saint (though in some ways he was less than human, as the death of his wife bears out): little Mary Slessor was as human as they come, and within the narrow geographical limits in which she worked (no explorer, this girl) she was as fine a missionary as ever lived.

She came from Aberdeen—and if readers may be noting that we seem to include a fair number of Aberdonians, may I assert that I had no idea, till I began to study the little missionary I admired, that she came from that Granite City. And perhaps Aberdeen has little cause to be proud of its connection with Mary Slessor, for she lived in a slum and was reared by a drunk. Slessor was a cobbler and the sad little sums he earned in the shoe factory were squandered each Saturday, so that when he awoke on Sunday to the sound of church bells and an inner clanging of the skull, it was to discover that a handful of coppers stood between his family and starvation by the end of the week. Mrs. Slessor went out to work to keep that starvation at bay; one by one the children started dying.

Mary was the only one to survive into old age, and few

David Livingstone, the boy from the Blantyre cotton factory on the Clyde, who gave Blantyre's name to a great African town, was a man of stern and stubborn principle. He also had a sly sense of humour coupled with a determination to spread the Christian gospel, which not only Christianized a sizeable part of Africa, but opened up vast, unknown tracts of it. Livingstone in effect completely re-drew the map of the Dark Continent, putting in lakes and mountain ranges, shifting rivers from one valley to another, hundreds of miles away.

ivingstone was lost to e world for five years, ntil a resourceful and naginative Editor of e *New York Herald* nt the journalist enry Stanley to frica to find him. istory relates that the st words of their counter were (as very schoolboy nows), "Doctor Livgstone, I presume?" hat moment is represented here in a conmporary drawing. At e time, Stanley's disvering of Livingstone as front-page news in ery newspaper in the orld — not least the *New York Herald*.

Robert Louis Stevenson is s[o] often shown as a long-haire[d] effete that it is pleasing to fin[d] this picture of him as he reall[y] was, a vital man of action – though suffering cruelly fro[m] ill-health—who could pursue th[e] woman he loved half-way acro[ss] the world and win her for him[-] self. He could also dash o[ff] masterpieces like *Treasure Islan[d]* to amuse her small son. Later h[e] collaborated with the son i[n] writing, as a family game, son[e] of his best work. He had worri[ed] about his health and finance[s] but life was a good game f[or] much of the time. In the end h[e] confounded himself and th[e] physicians by living longer tha[n] they expected and dying a ri[ch] man.

Andrew Carnegie, the fair-haired, blue-eyed youth who by a combination of luck, genius and ruthlessness took over control of the great Pennsylvania Railroad, is shown here, *right*, many years later. He is still "that white-haired Scotch devil": but by now, as his astonishing career nears its end, he has begun to devote time and fortune to a life of giving—philanthropy on a vaster, yet more discerning scale, perhaps, than ever before in history.

of the six even reached adulthood. She was born in 1848. Her mother was a God-fearing woman who pinned hopes on her eldest, Robert: Robert would be a missionary. But he died at the age of sixteen, at the same time that his father was sacked from the shoe factory. They decided to start a new life, move to Dundee.

The mixture in Dundee was much as before. Mary, now ten, was a half-timer in a factory (as were others, at other times, in these pages), doing one day's work among the jute, and another at school. A little later she was doing twelve hours a day, every day, in the jute mill—and, exactly like the man she most admired, was propping a book against the loom to study. Just like David Livingstone.

The second son, John, the one who would be missionary after Robert, died two years after him.

Suddenly, Mary realized she was the one; she, Mary Slessor, must become the family's missionary. And in an instant she had chosen not only her vocation, but the scene of her endeavour. It would be Calabar, on the west coast of Africa.

There is, in the way they decided exactly where they would work, and insisted on it, and in what they did when they got there, a striking resemblance between Mary Slessor and Gladys Aylward, the "small woman" missionary in China.

Why had Mary chosen this unhealthy coastal region?

Because of the odd, fascinating way the Calabar mission had sprung up. It was an area rich in slaves; the land on both sides of the Calabar estuary in Nigeria teemed with potential slaves and many men had made fortunes in the trade. (In fairness to the white man, it must be pointed out that the slave trade throve long before he got there, with African tribes busily selling themselves and their neighbours into slavery with other African tribes and with the Moslems of the north.) It was an occupational risk to a white man that if his slaver were wrecked on the coast he would be butchered by the natives.

And so, when the slave ship on which Dr. Ferguson was ship's surgeon perished in a tornado, and the wreck was flung against the shore, a terrified crew hid themselves in the jungle.

Africans came in their hundreds to loot what was left. After a few days, with the hulk picked dry, they vanished, but by this time the white men were dying like flies of disease, starvation, crocodiles.

Then, round a bend in the river, came a war canoe. The wrath of Africa was better than starvation and the survivors waved and shouted.

The war canoe picked them up, took them to a native king. And he made them welcome. The white men were nursed back to health, taken to the nearest port. When the next English ship came in, they were taken back to England.

Dr. Ferguson was profoundly moved by all this—as well he might be. He determined to set up a mission, in token of his gratitude. And eventually, after many difficulties (the ungrateful blacks didn't *want* a mission), Calabar was set up, in 1843.

The natives, though reasonably friendly with these white interlopers, persisted in two deplorable practices. They massacred wives and slaves when a great man died; and, as we have seen, they slaughtered new-born twins. These were just two of the wrongs Mary Slessor was determined to put right.

But for several more years there was no opportunity. Her father died, her mother was ailing, the survivors of the family, apart from herself, were too young to work: she had to keep the lot.

She was twenty-six when David Livingstone died—and now, with two other sisters just old enough to work, she could go out, take his place. She would send home money from Africa, she would need none herself. Her mother agreed and Mary went to the Foreign Missions Board.

The Board wrinkled its brows over her insistence on going to Calabar and nowhere else, but they gave their permission.

She sailed on the *Ethiopia* of the African Steamship Line. A humdrum voyage was livened by a squall as they rounded the western bulge of Africa, but all of it, squall included, was fascinating to a young girl just out of Scotland. They came to the estuary of the Calabar river, entered it. There were canoes everywhere, so it seemed the *Ethiopia* must run them down, feed shouting black men to the crocodiles, but they dodged the ship and went on shouting.

The villages of Old Town and Duke Town came in sight. They dropped anchor and the Mission Boat from Duke Town came out to them, a white thing with an awning, propelled by four native rowers in neat shirts and trousers, with a prim pair of missionaries, one of each sex, in the stern.

They came aboard, introduced themselves as Daddy Anderson and his wife, Mammy.

Ten minutes later, Mary Slessor was on the soil of Africa, in the Duke Town Mission grounds. There were twelve white people and a larger number of doubtful African converts helping in the work. She was shown her tiny white-washed room. There were prayers straight away, in the Efik language, and an unrehearsed—and therefore terrifying—lecture by Mary ("Right, my dear, you tell them all about yourself, *now*——") which was translated, sentence by sentence, from broad Scots into Efik.

And almost immediately young Miss Slessor shocked everyone. She laughed, she sang, she ran races with the natives—and, horror of horrors, she climbed trees! She was a scarlet woman: it was made clear that unless she buckled down and made herself an example—of the proper sort—to the heathen, she would be bundled off home.

There was less tree-climbing after this, but Mary continued to go for long walks, often alone, finding out what she could about the savages—and, much as she learnt to love and understand them, they were this and worse—and their customs. Every rich man had slaves, she saw, but the slaves for the most part were happy and well-treated.

She noted with disapproval the absurd European clothes of the Mission ladies, their hats, their veils, their long, wide skirts. She resolved, just as soon as she dared, to go hatless, shoeless, petticoatless.

One day early on, when she was out walking, miles from the Mission compound, there was an outbreak of *Egbo*, the hateful cult which came to the surface from time to time. When it did, people were murdered, tortured, mutilated.

A gong sounded—and the village through which she was passing seemed to empty itself in an instant.

Into the emptiness burst a naked woman. She was screaming, a high-pitched, terrifying sound; and seconds later a huge man, painted from head to foot, rushed at her with a ten-foot whip. She screamed, ran faster, stumbled, fell.

Other men, in various stages of undress, ran in from the jungle, all with whips. One seized the woman by a leg, started dragging her towards a hut.

This was too much for Mary Slessor. Clutching her umbrella, she tore into the centre of the village. A painted, naked man stared at her in amazement, then slashed with his whip. He missed, she got in under his guard, dealt him a murderous blow with the point of the umbrella. He groaned and she brought it down with all her strength on the top of his woolly, mud-streaked head. He staggered off, and the others, after watching open-mouthed, went too. The whipped woman crept away.

The Mission, when it learnt, was horrified.

By 1880, after one home leave, she was back and in charge of Old Town, at her own request. Here she would be away from other missionaries, able to get on with the job as she saw it. She lived alone in Old Town, which, despite its name, was a small and stinking village on the river bank, a few miles away from Duke Town and the Mission.

On the surface, Old Town's inhabitants were law-abiding, but everyone knew atrocities still took place in the blackness of the jungle. These Mary would deal with, but in the meantime, away from the primness of Mission life, she cropped her hair like a boy's, discarded shoes and underwear. And, of course, stays. The first Mission visitor to come her way was aghast at finding her in the shapeless mother hubbard prescribed for the modesty of African ladies.

She set about building her community. There would be a church here, a school there—and until she had trained her helpers she would officiate in both. And, of course, in the hospital.

Shortly after her arrival in Old Town, she attended a birth. She came barefoot, carrying towels and antiseptics, to find everyone in the hut dead drunk, except for the pregnant girl who lay spread-eagled on the filthy mud floor, held tight by four women, while a witch doctor postured above her.

As Mary took in the situation, another woman appeared from nowhere, straddled the girl and jumped with all her weight on the distended belly.

Amid screams, a child was born.

Then to more screams and a deadly silence, another.

Half the people in the hut tore out into the night. Mary, shaking her head with annoyance, knelt down to look after the girl and her twins. After she had cut the cords and made the mother as comfortable as possible, she quickly wrapped the tiny black babies in a cloth and ran back with them to her own compound.

Her family of adopted children had begun. The real mother was never seen again.

From now on, every sort of horror descended on her. She watched a man, tied to a stake in shallow water, being eaten by a crocodile. He was only a slave, sacrificed to improve the fishing, and she had been too late to save him. She was too late to save a number of other men, women and children from similar hideous fates. But she did succeed in rescuing the two young wives of a chief. They had been caught in adultery with slave boys and would have been indescribably mutilated, savaged with knives and boiling palm oil, before being put to death. Mary Slessor, eyes flashing with rage, stopped the ceremony before it began.

"*Stop that!*" she screamed. It stopped as if a thunderbolt had struck the village.

Then, recovering her composure and her breath, she explained that this sort of behaviour was absolutely forbidden and that *she* would not permit it. As for the erring girls, she would deal with them herself.

As for the pot-bellied old lecher who kept wives locked up because his own attractions were insufficient to keep them at home, he was beneath contempt. Was he not ashamed of himself? Was he a man, able to hold his women like a man? Or was he not?

There was shocked silence, then laughter. The meeting broke up in confusion.

She had found that here, in her own community, she was able to live on the proverbial smell of an oil rag; with tidy Europeans in Duke Town, it had been expensive, paying one's share of unnecessarily lavish catering, keeping oneself respectable. Now, in Old Town, she was able to send her salary home.

But in 1886 her mother and the last surviving sister, Janie, died.

Mary Slessor was thirty-eight and alone. And now there was no reason for not going up-country, to the dangerous, forbidden areas, where no white person had been. She was a missionary, and although exploring held few attractions for her, she knew her job was to look after the bodies and the souls (in that order) of the African people. Those who most needed her help were a hundred miles inland, murdering each other.

After much argument, the Mission said she might move to the Okoyong district. Mark you, they pointed out, it was entirely at Miss Slessor's request. On no account was she to involve the Mission in expense.

And so she moved north, by canoe. An interesting sidelight on the character of Mary Slessor is that she was throughout her life terrified of canoes, snakes, wild beasts. But it never hindered her in anything which she knew was her duty. She got to the land of the Okoyongs and they were unable to believe this lone white woman would dare to move in among them. She did, and they accepted her with reluctance.

Then, when they saw she would teach their women to cook properly, to care for their children and to sew, they made her welcome.

There were dreadful occasions when, despite the promises she had wrung from them, they slaughtered their slaves and their wives, broke the arms and legs of children and threw them screaming into their mother's graves. She saved many, many lives—but there were many for whom she was too late.

But in the end she was successful—and succeful where probably no other missionary would have been. Living with them, completely as a native—yet keeping herself scrupulously clean as an example to them—she was able to understand their thinking, get inside it. Before she left Africa the practices she abhorred had been done away with.

There had been undeclared war between these inland, bush people and the coastal Calabars, for hundreds of years, since the advent of slavery, when the Calabars had started raiding the bush for slaves. Now Mary Slessor began what had always been thought impossible, began to open up the inland region to peaceful trade.

She travelled a great deal, visiting hidden villages, helping and teaching their inhabitants, and the years crept by. For the most part, other missionaries left her alone to get on with her work, but there was one young man who began to pay regular visits from the Duke Town Mission.

She was forty-three—and Charles Morrison was twenty-five. He asked her to marry him.

She considered it. Of course, he would have to come and settle among the Okoyongs, there was no question of her going back to the Duke Town Mission—or anywhere else. He agreed: he was eager to come. And it would be convenient, too, for the continuity of the work; they could take their furloughs separately, thus ensuring that one or other was always there, ready to deal with the sudden, life-and-death emergencies which arose so regularly.

The Mission authorities, who regarded Okoyong as a dubious hinterland, came to the decision that Charles Morrison could not be spared from his work at Duke Town.

Perhaps they made a mistake. For Morrison, from that moment, went steadily downhill. His health, his work, grew worse: he was sent home. He got better: the doctors advised against his returning to Africa. He resigned, went to North Carolina, died.

But, husband or no husband, Mary Slessor had need of an assistant. The work, the bouts of fever and dysentery, had aged her. She asked for one or more female helpers, and her appeal gives an idea of the sort of woman she herself was. She wanted women, "not afraid of work or of filth of any kind, moral or material. Women who can nurse a baby or teach a child to wash and comb as well as to read and write; women who can tactfully smooth over a roughness and, for Christ's sake, bear a snub. If they can play Beethoven and paint and draw and speak French and German, so much the better, but we can want all these latter accomplishments if they have only a loving heart, willing hands and common sense. They will not need fine English, for there is none to admire it——"

She dealt, almost single-handed, with a smallpox epidemic which wiped out nearly half her community—and her problem was a thousandfold worse than that of a doctor in less superstitious lands, for she had to avert the orgy of human sacrifice which was waiting to be unleashed to appease the sickness devils.

She was shipped home, sick and weary. A year later she was back, and now, having civilized Okoyong, she went on into still less tractable lands, to cannibal country. She went, amazed the cannibals, won them over.

But this indomitable little creature could not go on for ever. She became crippled by arthritis, suffered constant fever. At last, in 1915, she died.

What had she done? What had she achieved, apart from the saving of lives in a land where life is cheap?

Many things. Above all, she completely altered the status of women in her part of Africa—and the movement is still spreading. She civilized a part of the world unique for its barbaric cruelty, a savagery with which Livingstone hardly came in contact. She left behind a nucleus of hospitals and schools which are a credit to all Africa.

She died, as she would have wished, among the people to whom she had given her life. She was buried, while hundreds wailed and tore their clothes, at the Duke Town cemetery.

In Nigeria—and elsewhere—the little, short-haired, barefoot woman with the flashing eyes, the eyes that sometimes smouldered, often laughed, will never be forgotten.

What would Stanley have made of her, this faintly comic little figure in a shapeless Mother Hubbard, brandishing her rapier of an umbrella? "Mary Slessor, I presume?"

But even without Stanley to make a journalistic legend of her, Mary Slessor stands as monument to generations of selfless missionaries who lived and died for Africa.

ROBERT LOUIS STEVENSON

They say he should never have married; that the fine,
tender, blossom of Stevenson's thought was crushed by the
cares of matrimony and a materialistic woman. Fanny
Stevenson—what a name for a start! —was both a divorcee
and an American, never a popular combination in the
British press. In order, they said, to keep herself in the
comfort to which she had been accustomed, she forced him
to write at ever-increasing speed, even getting her son, his
stepson, to collaborate with him from time to time, just
to speed up the process and get things to the publisher. She
killed him, and he died of overwork at the age of forty-four.

This sort of tale, simply because it *is* malicious, dies hard.
But, of course, it is utter nonsense and about as far from the
truth as it is possible to imagine. The legend of R.L.S.
abounds with nonsense: let us deal with this bit first; and

let the others, as we look at the man himself, speak for themselves.

After he met Mrs. Fanny Osbourne in France, and after
he subsequently married her, he wrote almost everything
for which we remember him. *Jekyll and Hyde, Catriona,
Kidnapped, Treasure Island, The Master of Ballantrae*, for
a start.

Before that he had written a handful of essays, *The New
Arabian Nights*, and *Travels with a Donkey*.

With his stepson, Lloyd Osbourne, he wrote, among other
things, *The Wrong Box*, ultimately made into a hilarious
film; also *The Wrecker* and *The Ebb Tide*. With Fanny,
he wrote *Dynamiters*, a sequel to his early *New Arabian
Nights*. For to Stevenson, so different to Scott, though both
excelled in historical romances, the business of writing was
an exciting, technical challenge. He was a stylist: the
game, like a superior crossword puzzle, was one he eagerly
shared with others.

The pictures extant show him for the most part with
hair which would do justice to a nineteen-sixties' pop group.
Though the face amongst all that hair is too sensitive, too
intelligent for us to envisage behind microphone or guitar,
the effect is misleading. Why these photos are almost the
only ones no man can tell: we know there were others
taken during the last four years in Samoa, photos of a wiry,
short-haired man chopping down trees, galloping on horseback, doing a thumping great job of gardening in the early
morning before settling down to a full day's writing, and
apparently thriving on it.

As for his youth—and we have few pictures of that either
—it must have been quite unlike the long-haired invalid
of the pictures, with the wan, and pallid smile. (Though
that youth may well have contributed to the serious illness
of middle-age; for the young R.L.S. was a rip and a rake,
and worse. His father, dour lighthouse designer, who had
so wanted this literary-minded son to take after him and
dot the coast of Britain with beacons, was appalled.)

R.L.S. was born on 13 November, 1850, in Edinburgh.
Both father and grandfather were designers of lighthouses.

From birth the boy was sickly, prey to every wandering germ, so that he spent much of his childhood in bed. It was this that reluctantly decided his father not to try and make him a lighthouse designer: the open-air work would kill him.

And yet, when the family moved from Edinburgh to the Pentland Hills, the boy spent most of his time on long walks with his father, and loving it.

He went on to Edinburgh University to study Law and, at least for the time being, forgot about the writing which, since childhood sickbed, had been such a hobby. His health had improved: there seemed no reason why he should not make a success of his studies.

But he behaved disgracefully. It would have been disgraceful anywhere, to say nothing of within that stern, Calvinist environment. Edinburgh is not a town one thinks of in terms of the brothel industry, but there were sufficient in Stevenson's time, and he found them all.

Somehow he managed to get his Law degree, though with much less speed than either Scott or Buchan, also in these pages. Fortunately for the legal profession, and certainly for that of letters, he never practised it. Almost immediately he fell seriously ill, which is hardly to be wondered at. And it was while he convalesced with cousins in England that he met two people who were to have a considerable effect on his life: Mrs. Sitwell and Sidney Colvin. They urged him most strongly to become a professional writer, go where his talents and interests led him. Colvin was instrumental in getting his first work, *Roads,* published in a magazine.

For this first professional contribution, Stevenson signed himself as others did by initials. R.L.S. was to become a signature for the rest of his life. In some quarters this was seized upon as affectation: who did this man think he was? Was the world expected to bow down before three little letters, know whose they were?

Stevenson survived this sort of thing and more. But in the meantime, his health still in need of repair, he was packed off to the south of France. He went on writing, and at his return was able to offer essays to the *Cornhill*

Magazine, essays which were eagerly accepted and which laid the foundations of his career.

In 1877, aged twenty-seven, he went with his cousin Bob Stevenson on a long ramble over northern France. Much of this was by canoe along inland waterways and formed the basis of his first book. It was published the following year under the title, *An Inland Voyage.*

And it was during this summer that he met an attractive woman, considerably his senior. She was from Indiana and she was staying at an inn in the Forest of Fontainebleau with her two children. He fell instantly in love with Fanny Osbourne and with the children, Isobel and Lloyd.

He also fell on his feet. For his love was returned, and he was able, while the spirits of Calvin and of Knox spun furiously in their graves, to move in with her. He spent the next two summers with her, his winters in Edinburgh. He was happy and he wrote a great deal. His reputation grew.

He was distraught when Fanny decided to go back to her husband in California, but tried to make up for the loneliness of the next summer by going on a long, lonely trip in France with a donkey—an expedition which produced the attractive *Travels With a Donkey* in 1879.

And in that year he made his wild dash to California. He had learnt that Fanny Osbourne was seeking a divorce from her husband: if this were so, he was determined to marry her himself. His friends and his parents were appalled: everything about the proposed expedition, from its length and his health, to the moral turpitude of both California and Fanny, made it outrageous.

Not only that. The career in Law, which his parents and R.L.S. almost believed he might take up, would be finished if he cut adrift now.

He cut adrift. As he had little money, he travelled to New York by steerage on the ship, which made him as ill as he had ever been. He followed this up by immediately crossing the entire continent in an emigrant train of unexampled squalor, and arriving in the West nearly dead. In fact, he was given up as lost by physicians in Monterey and in San Francisco, but managed to thwart both.

By the time he got to Fanny, having kept himself alive by writing what anyone would buy, he was a doomed man. Not, however, as doomed as the California doctor assured him. All medical opinion pointed to the certainty that this gaunt Scottish scribbler would be dead within the year, aged thirty. He married Fanny and survived another fourteen, to the age of forty-four. By this time he had done more great work than most writers do in longer lives.

From now on, though he never made complete recovery, he had the loving care, the inspiration—and the money—of a devoted woman to keep him alive and writing. He had feared that after the furious separation from his father and mother the year before, the mad dash to America, they would never speak to him again, but a reconciliation came about and he returned to Scotland with his wife and young Lloyd. His parents fell in love with them both.

Although the intention was not to return to America, they soon found that Stevenson's lungs were unable to stand the damp and cold of Scotland for more than a few months at a time. He and Fanny began to spend summers in Scotland with his parents and winters in Switzerland. It was in order to amuse a rather bored young stepson during a miserably wet summer afternoon in the Highlands that he began work on an adventure story. He finished it after many interruptions, many months later, in Switzerland.

He decided then to call it *Treasure Island*.

Young Lloyd enjoyed the book which had been written for him, but not everyone else felt the same way. Its publication by Cassells in 1885 brought fame and fortune to the author—yet it is not so generally known that its first publication, as a serial in the magazine, *Young Folks,* was a flop. None of that publication's young readers enjoyed it.

Like many other writers, Robert Louis Stevenson was able to keep two or more irons in the fire at once, and while he amused himself in finishing this tale of adventure he embarked on a labour of love, *The Memoir of Fleeming Jenkin.* Jenkin had been the Professor at Edinburgh University who had stood by him—as Stevenson put it, "in the coiled perplexities of youth"—and known that somehow, inside the debauched body, was a beating heart and a genius.

In that year, 1882, he and Fanny moved to the south of France, and though his health became critical again he wrote most of *A Child's Garden of Verses*. As a sick child he had had a nurse, and it was to her that he now dedicated the work: "From the sick child now well and old"—in a mood of brave exaggeration.

Then, still unwell (and he would never be old), he rushed home with Fanny to settle in a house at Bournemouth. They had learnt that his father's health was failing; were resolved to stay near the old man for however long his illness lasted: the south coast at Bournemouth was as close to Scotland as R.L.S. dared live, if he himself were to survive.

Three years went by, in which he was an invalid, almost always in bed, and his father died. Nevertheless he managed to write *Kidnapped* and *The Strange Case of Dr. Jekyll and Mr. Hyde*, two huge and instantaneous successes, which arrived in the nick of time, when his fortunes were at their lowest ebb. The latter book appeared in America and gave such joy (as well it might; it had been pirated) that he was persuaded to go over again, with his mother, Fanny and Lloyd, to face his admirers. The strain was too great, however, and he found himself seriously ill again, trying to stage a recovery in the Adirondacks.

To this pleasant resort we owe *The Master of Ballantrae*. As we have seen, he loved sharing the game of writing with others, and it was here that he and Lloyd plotted the hilarious *Wrong Box*.

A sudden stroke of good luck—which probably earned him a few more years of life. His American publishers asked him to do a travel book on the South Seas, gave him a handsome advance. With this he was able to charter a yacht and sail—still with mother, Fanny and Lloyd—from San Francisco into the wide, uncharted spaces of the South Pacific.

Scotland's climate has driven many good Scotsmen from her bosom. To that fact we owe the invention—in America —of the telephone by Alexander Graham Bell, and the development in England by another fervid Scot, John Logie Baird, of television. And Robert Louis Stevenson is one of the best examples of this trend. From the moment he embarked on the chartered *Casco,* his health changed dramatically for the better. Within a week his bewildered, delighted family found it hard to realize that this energetic, wiry man of thirty-seven, bounding about the decks, rushing inland at each port of call to strike up improbable and lasting friendships with dusky rulers, was the invalid who had embarked at San Francisco.

From this week on, though in fact mortal illness was still with him, the long-haired invalid was a thing of the past. It was too hot for long hair, and it came off: the pallid dreamer's face grew brown, and jollier with each new friendship.

So enthusiastic was he that, having paid off the yacht and sent it home, having sent his mother back to Scotland, he stayed in Honolulu with Fanny and Lloyd for a further six months. They began taking passage here and there in other vessels, eagerly investigating the unknown lands to the south-west.

And it was on the island of Opolu, one of the Samoan group, north-east of Fiji, that they fell in love with the place and bought an estate. It was beautiful and balanced halfway up the side of a blue and shimmering mountain. To this admirer of Sir Walter Scott, it would be another Abbotsford; an Abbotsford in the only climate where its owner could survive.

Though, of course, it was unthinkable that he and Fanny should leave Europe for ever. They would divide each summer between England and the Continent.

Fate stamped on this plan within a month. They were on their way home for the summer of 1890 when another serious bout of illness flung him into a hospital bed in Sydney. This time there was a major haemorrhage of the lungs and the doctors were adamant: not only could Mr. Stevenson not continue his journey to northern lands; he could never go there again, if he wished to survive a few more years.

Life for Stevenson had always been a series of jerks, blows and surprises, good and bad. This was just one more. He accepted the verdict calmly, sent Lloyd on to collect the family furniture. Then he went back to his island and started to re-build the house on his new estate, the estate which henceforth would be his home. He named it *Vailima*.

The next four and a half years—his last years—would be as fruitful as any in his life. His mother followed Lloyd and the furniture to the South Seas, and a little later Stevenson and Fanny were joined by Fanny's daughter Isobel, who was now grown-up and married. She brought husband and small son. Surrounded by a devoted family, his health began to recover and he started another series of writings, which included *Catriona* and *The Ebb Tide*.

For these last years he was a Samoan laird. He was happy, healthier than he had ever been, and with nothing but a few money worries to disturb him. Many of these worries were unjustified, but Samoa is a long way from the nearest publisher, and he worried often about his sales, his royalties, and all the things that authors do concern themselves with. (Though most authors are able to put themselves out of their misery in rather less than three or four months.) In this respect he resembled Scott, whose last years at Abbotsford were plagued by money troubles.

The Samoans worshipped their laird and he became deeply involved in their troubles, to the exclusion of his own. His Samoan involvement embraced everything from local politics to full-scale war. He managed in the intervals of this life to begin and continue a long correspondence with J. M. Barrie, a correspondence that ended only on his own death, and to Barrie's deep grief. He had discovered an article the younger man had done about him in *An Edinburgh Eleven*, and wrote, tongue-in-cheek, chiding him about it. Barrie was thrilled; wrote back by return.

Pilgrims came, literary pilgrims from all over the world, much as they had gone to Abbotsford. The trip was far longer for most of them, but still they came, devoted ones and twos, to *Vailima*.

He had cheated death for years—but it caught up at last.

On 3 December, 1894, he was shaving when he suddenly turned round from the mirror and said, "Do I look strange?"

Before an answer could be given he fell down. Cerebral haemorrhage.

He died immediately after, was buried on the mountain he loved, Mount Vaea.

As we said at the beginning, there is a remarkable absence of Stevenson portraits near the end of his life. Perhaps nobody in Samoa had a camera. But when the familiar photo, with the long hair and the pallid face, was shown to a small Samoan boy who had known the original, he squealed with rage:

"I will not have that—it is the face of a pig, a pig! That is not the shadow of our chief!"

A statue was erected in his memory at Edinburgh. Not at first, for there were many good burghers still deeply shocked by the poet's behaviour at University, by his action in running away with—or was it *after*?—a divorced woman. Barrie and others fought for the statue, and at long last it went up.

But the real Stevenson was thousands of miles away. We Scots may claim him as our own, but he was happiest in Samoa. Perhaps he had never been happy anywhere before, happy and well. Above his grave on Mount Vaea are the words he wrote as his own epitaph:

> *"Under the wide and starry sky*
> *Dig the grave and let me die:*
> *Glad did I live and gladly die,*
> *And I laid me down with a will.*

> *"This be the verse you grave for me:*
> Here he lies where he long'd to be;
> Home is the sailor, home from the sea,
> And the hunter home from the hill."

KEIR HARDIE

Saints are pretty thin on the ground in politics. Indeed, sanctity and politics are about as incompatible bedfellows as we could invent.

Perhaps bearded, horny-handed, trouble-making, old Keir Hardie is about as close as we have come, in this century, to having one in the House of Commons.

I would probably have voted against him, were I voting in any of the several constituencies he represented during his career: but I would probably have respected him more than the man who got my vote.

He was born on 15 August, 1856, in a one-roomed house —not the two-roomed luxury of Ramsay MacDonald, on another page—near Holytown in Lanarkshire. He was the eldest of nine children, with a father who was a ship's carpenter and a mother who worked on a farm. It was from this mother, Mary Keir, that he derived not only his name but all the education he acquired before reaching manhood. Apart from a few, isolated, months he never went to school. His mother taught him to read, taught him the Christian virtues: his father was a fervent, dedicated agnostic, yet he imparted a habit of intellectual honesty which stayed with the boy all his life, and would enrage others throughout it.

He worked at a variety of jobs, earning pennies, until he went down the mine, aged ten. Here he was happy, for the miners were kind, good friends, and the fact that for months on end he seldom saw the sun did not distress him. He was underground by six every morning, up again at five; and working a part of every Sunday as well. His first work below ground was driving a pit-pony, Donald, for whom he developed a real attachment, with whom he shared his bottle of cold tea.

Later, as muscles and frame expanded, he was made coal-hewer, hacking the stuff from the seam. But by now there were other thoughts in his mind: he was twenty, he had seen so many drunken men abuse their wives, squander their wages in a night's debauch, that he began a campaign for temperance, a drive against drunkenness.

He also gave much thought to Christianity. He had experienced the hypocrisy of those who went to church on Sunday and had family prayers at home, yet didn't care whether their servants or employees starved. He'd had his own vivid personal experience of this, working for a bible-thumping baker. But he was still a devout Christian and he began to preach on street corners, urging, not just temperance, but the word of God.

The word of God—yes: its advocates on earth—no. "They have never," he wrote of the clergy, "have never originated any great movement. Whether it be the abolition of slavery, the abolition of the drink traffic, the abolition of child labour; no matter what the question, the pulpit has always kept aloof until some mere worldling has educated the public and made the new cause safe, profitable and respectable."

A stinging indictment—and written in anger. "There have been splendid exceptions, but these only serve to bring the fact as here stated into more general prominence. That the masses will in time be quickened into a healthy state of activity, I have no doubt; but when that time comes, it will be the work of Socialists, not of the clergy, which will have brought it about."

No wonder many hated him. But let us go underground again. Ironically, it was here that the underground mine-worker came nearest to being at peace with his world. There was good-humoured comradeship, even laughter, and the miseries of poverty in an overcrowded one-room cottage could be temporarily forgotten in the all-embracing dark. But Keir Hardie knew that something must be done, some day, about the miners' life, and it came to him, down the mine, that he might be the man to do it. By his own exertions he was now, at the age of twenty, far better educated than any man in any mine in Lanarkshire—and his workmates knew this, began to listen to him when he spoke, to adopt him, almost unconsciously, as their leader. If a meeting were held to discuss some real or fancied grievance, Hardie was pushed forward to take the chair.

Soon his name, to the mine-owner, meant Labour Agitator. He was sacked. But in fact the most that Keir Hardie wanted—though it may have seemed like heaven then—was a living wage for miners, better conditions of safety under the ground, and some sort of better accommodation above it. Miners in Lanarkshire almost all lived in one-room houses, with their entire families, and Hardie was right in seeing this as an affront to civilization. On the other hand, the mine-owners were not too far from the truth when they protested that most miners were "quite content with their lot". Ruefully, Hardie would bear this out in an anecdote he constantly re-told. It was a true story of the cheerful miner's wife who was asked by a visitor where she did her washing, her cooking, and the rest of it, in that one room. Where, for that matter, did she and the family sleep?

The miner's wife patiently pointed out the various corners of the room where these functions took place. And, in any case, it wasn't bad; there were only two wee bairns so far.

"But what will you do when there are more?"

"Och, that?" She smiled. "We'll just tak' in a lodger tae help pay the rent." And she meant it.

The mine-owners maintained that without agitation from "professional trouble-makers" like Keir Hardie, life in a mining community would be peaceful, prosperous and happy. And before we scoff at this, for it is obviously quite wide of the mark, let us look at the words of another miner of the period, from the same mines. Harry Lauder—whose story is on another page—wrote, years later: "I was a member of the Lanarkshire Union of Miners, a strong supporter of men like Keir Hardie. But politics were not mixed up in industrial affairs as they are today. Besides, there seemed to be a far greater measure of freedom for a man to work as hard as he liked and as long as he liked for the benefit of his own payroll and the increased comfort of himself and his family which the fat payroll represented. With few exceptions, every man in the pit in those days was a hard, conscientious worker. He worked hard, and he played hard. I would not go the length of saying that we were all contented with our lowly lot, but we seemed to believe in the old Scriptural injunction that only by the sweat of our brows could we eat bread. And by God, we sweated right enough!"

A point of view, and perhaps conditioned by time and prosperity; a fatter "payroll" than any miner could dream of. But worth noting.

Keir Hardie was glad to leave the mine: there was more time now to plan on the miners' behalf. He started a small shop and at the same time became local correspondent of a Glasgow newspaper. He still talked at street corners, but now, rather than press the virtues of temperance, he harangued the miners, pointed out their disabilities, told them what to fight for, how to fight. He advocated no violence—but he called for unity, and with it strength. The response was slow. There were too many Harry Lauders down the mine.

He married, moved into Ayrshire, to the town of Cumnock, and there became editor of the local paper, the *Cumnock News*. At the age of thirty he realized one of his dreams: an Ayrshire Miners' Union came into being, with himself as secretary. By this time he had become disenchanted with the Liberal Party, of which he had believed himself a supporter, for the Liberals, even those who styled themselves Radical and were more Liberal than the rest, were remarkably like Tories. Perhaps this was not surprising in the days before a Labour Party, even before a Labour movement, because no M.P., whichever label he affixed to himself, was paid a parliamentary salary, and therefore, with a few, specially subsidized, exceptions, only a rich man could be a Member of Parliament.

Hardie stopped writing for Liberal newspapers. He could see his goal: he would get the representatives of real working men into Parliament. He might be their representative himself.

At this time Scottish miners were taking home twelve shillings a week. Depression had set in over all of industry, and there was hardship everywhere, not only among miners.

He left the *Cumnock News*, founded his own paper, *The Miner*, in 1887. It became the mouthpiece for his views, Keir Hardie's forceful point of view, with an ever-growing readership—and a name that changed, within twelve months, to *The Labour Leader*. He was convinced, now, that he must get into Parliament. There were a few other men of similar background to himself, within those august walls, but they were supported by Party or other funds which virtually deprived them of freedom of action. As he now wrote in *The Miner*, this type of M.P. was not a success, "because he is afraid to offend the proprieties by being considered extreme. He thinks more of his own reputation in the eyes of the House than of the interests of his suffering brethren in mill and mine. He desires to be reckoned a gentleman fit to take his place as a member of the first club in the world."

He stood at a Lanarkshire by-election in 1888 and

received a tenth of the total votes. He would have to wait for another opportunity.

That opportunity came in 1892—and to many social historians it marked, eight years early, the start of a twentieth century. He was adopted for Independent Labour by the London borough of West Ham, and got in. It was not a Labour Party that he represented: merely the idea, the novel idea, of working men, men who Laboured, being in Parliament and quite Independent of any other party.

So his was a party of one. His arrival at Westminster to take up its duties has gone into history. The other Members of Parliament arrived, most of them in carriages, most wearing silk hats, whether they styled themselves Liberal or Conservative. They nodded politely to each other: after all, it made no difference whether a chap was Liberal or Conservative, he was still a member of the Best Club in the World.

And suddenly into this scene, like a Go-Kart sputtering on to the course at Ascot, came Keir Hardie.

The noise of his arrival was at first so deafening, so upsetting, that no one took notice of its appearance. The loudest trumpet in Christendom was playing, at the top of its owner's lungs, a tremendous, home-made fanfare. Then, as the vehicle came to a halt, the trumpeting stopped.

The stunned audience noticed now that it was a large, two-horse wagon—the horsed equivalent of our Utility trucks, and less than fashionable outside the Palace of Westminster. As it stopped at the gate, a bearded man, stocky, near middle-age, and dressed in tweed suit with cloth cap, hopped nimbly down and went in. The wagon with its load of cheering workers, its trumpeter, drove off.

So entered history's first "Labour" Member of Parliament—a number of years before that Party came into existence. Many, but by no means all, M.P.s were affronted by this "blatant self-advertisement" of a man with a trumpet and wearing, of all things, a *cap*. Anyone. even this chap, could have borrowed or hired the right rig.

In fact, had the soft hat he ordered arrived in time, the cap which caused such a stir would never have been seen.

He was a man without a Party—but by 1893 he had formed one: the Independent Labour Party of all men, inside or outside Parliament, who believed in the idea of labour being independently represented, being kept clear of the two major parties. He was the first Chairman of this ILP: one of the first members to attend meetings was George Bernard Shaw.

He lost his seat in the election of 1895, but a year later was returned for Merthyr in Wales—and this community went right on electing him throughout the rest of his life. By 1900 it had become obvious that though people in Parliament listened and sometimes took action when he spoke or asked questions there must be more than one solitary Labour man in Parliament. The Trades Union Council called a meeting to devise means of getting more of them in, and the Labour Representation Committee which was born at that meeting was the real ancestor of what we know as the Labour Party.

The Committee did its work well, and in 1906 no fewer than twenty-nine Labour members—one of them, of course, Keir Hardie—entered Parliament. The Labour Representation Committee proudly changed its name to the Parliamentary Labour Party. It has never looked back— and all the good or evil, depending on your political views, which that Party has brought mankind, dates from that day in 1906.

But what of Keir Hardie, its founder?

He went on doing exactly what he thought was right. History may prove some of this to have been very wrong, but he never budged an inch from his principles. He was the, virtually unique, entirely honest politician. To this extent he treated political opponents as personal enemies; could never see—or never saw—that one could be friendly with a man whose principles one deplored. He agitated for working-class rights, votes for women, Home Rule for Ireland. He went on publishing *The Labour Leader*, which remained the vehicle for his most biting comments. With it he fought the slippery Horatio Bottomley, just acquitted, for the third time, of fraud. When Bottomley wrote angrily that he would not have his honesty brought in question, *The Labour Leader* wrote: "It must be a source of the greatest satisfaction to a man that he has the verdicts of three juries to certify that he is not dishonest."

At this point Bottomley conceded the argument by default.

The South African War came, and Hardie lost sympathy in the country by his vigorous objection to it. He had forgotten that Britain is a country ruled by Fashion, and that while a fashionably large minority will declare for Pacifism (or Nuclear Disarmament, or the Abolition of the Royal Family, or what you will) under favourable circumstances, a change of circumstance—like war—which reduces that minority by a large percentage, will result, overnight, in its baffling disappearance. Hardie advocated Pacifism—and many agreed—but when the time came to implement it he found himself quite alone, with Press, Public, snarling. He refused to alter his point of view.

Unlike Ramsay MacDonald, he remained through life a Pacifist; there was no question, ever, of supporting a war, just because, like Mount Everest, it was there. He fought war, and the idea of war, with every means at his disposal, and he was—not without reason—branded a traitor. To Keir Hardie the most beautiful thing in years had been the scene he witnessed during the Russo-Japanese war, when fraternal delegates from Russia and Japan to the new Socialist International had embraced in public. The fact that, even as they hugged, a few thousand on each side were being slaughtered, and both huggers knew and cheerfully accepted the situation, was far too Machiavellian for Keir Hardie to understand. The Socialist International made no difference, the war went on. And as the years went by, and he aged prematurely through overwork, Keir Hardie grew bitter.

He believed, unlike MacDonald, that Marxism would prevent war. It was simple: the workers of the world would go on strike, the war would end.

The 1914 war came, and nobody, at least at first, went on strike.

But this was incredible. Surely with the Weapon to Stop All Wars right at hand it would be used?

It was not—and the shock, the disillusionment, killed Keir Hardie. He protested feebly, angrily, about "the roar and song of a war-maddened people", and these very people, his ardent supporters of a week before, booed at him, screamed at him. He was a traitor, an enemy of his country.

On 26 September, 1915, he died.

He had done great things—and perhaps some harm. He had founded a Labour movement, a long-overdue Labour Party. Had he lived another nine years he would have seen what he so long dreamed of, a Labour Prime Minister of Great Britain.

And, because he was a saint and a simple one, it was easy for others less saintly to follow cynically in his footsteps, to organize, to destroy. It has been said that Keir Hardie unwittingly lit the fuse which was to destroy Scotland's shipbuilding industry. For a start.

Only time will tell if he did.

SIR JAMES BARRIE, BART.

The Scots work hard, play hard (when there's time), strive more than most, perhaps, for success. Every one of them in this book achieved it, though success may have been short-lived or sown with the seeds of disaster, like that brief happiness of Queen Mary, or the self-imposed death sentence of Sir Walter Scott. But, surprisingly, the successful authors among them were, almost all of them, brilliant amateurs. In other words, they regarded themselves as essentially something quite different, and writing as their hobby. That they beat the full-time professionals at it is beside the point: Scott was a lawyer, Buchan a lawyer, Burns a farmer and exciseman; Byron—just being Byron, which was a career in itself.

But one was the most dedicated of professionals. He made up his mind at an age when most of us are struggling to spell out one-syllable words (and hating it), that he would be a writer of words. And absolutely full-time, to the exclusion of all else.

So he was. Not just a struggler in a garret, but the proverbial household word, who at one time was pulling in almost fifty thousand pounds a year, entirely from his literary exertions—and in a period of time when that sum was worth far, far more than it is now.

And this was without assistance from the film industry. There wasn't a film industry.

His reputation, as well as the real value of his earnings, has depreciated in the years since his death. Earnest Scotsmen—and there is nothing so earnest as an earnest Scotsman—have derided the sentimental Kailyard School of which he may be regarded a founder (and which we touch on, as indeed Buchan did, with venom, in the Tweedsmuir article). But literary fashions change and there seems no reason at all why J. M. Barrie should not one day be rehabilitated, as Dickens has been.

To millions of now-grown-up children he is still the father of Peter Pan. For real, nineteen-sixties' children his position is less assured; the whole idea of a magic boy standing at the front of a stage and getting the audience to agree it believes in fairies is far removed from the world of the telly. Not that Barrie didn't people his world with all sorts of terrifying creatures, fully as frightening as the wickedest bad-man in a Western. It was this that captured the children; their parents wept over Peter.

But one doesn't go on making fifty thousand pounds a year just on the strength of one good play. James Barrie's output was very large indeed, and much of it is well worth our attention today.

If Barrie had been only a lovable little man, devoted to children, a man with an uncanny knack of writing for them, there would be little point in including him here. But he was more and less than this; an exceedingly complex creature.

He was born, more than a century ago, in the small town of Kirriemuir, Forfarshire, some twenty miles in from the east coast of Scotland, and north of the Firth of Tay. And Kirriemuir, of course, is the Thrums of his novels. He was born in an absurdly small cottage, and was the ninth child to be born there, though two, by the time of his arrival, were already dead, and the eldest away at Aberdeen University. The date was 9 May, 1860.

David Barrie was a weaver who worked at home, on a piecework basis, and how he found space to work, to say nothing of earning sufficient to keep his large family, is still a mystery. But he did, and with his wife was able to instil a love of learning and a zeal for education into all of them, so that Alexander, the eldest, not only won his bursary to Aberdeen University, but went on afterward to a distinguished career in education.

Like some others in this book, the Barries had long seceded from the Established Church of Scotland. They were members of the Original Seceders or Auld Lichts (lights of purity, no less), and young James's uncle had risen from the same artisan stock to be Doctor of Divinity.

There was tragedy, too, in those early years. To get some idea of what life was like in The Tenements, Kirriemuir, we can do no better than look through James Barrie's book about his mother, *Margaret Ogilvy*. It is a sentimentalized account, but even in this cynical age it isn't hard to shed a tear over it.

But back to the boy. With everyone in the family helping, including free board with the eldest brother, Alec, who was conveniently teaching there, James went on to Glasgow Academy. The fees at this excellent school were less than £5 a year, but still a great sacrifice for a father with other children for whom he planned the same thing. James did well at the Academy, but he had to move from it when his brother changed jobs.

By this time their father had become a clerk and been able to buy a larger house, *Strath View,* still in Kirriemuir. Alec had got a better job in Dumfries and the arrangement was renewed so that Jamie now went to Dumfries Academy and boarded with him there. Probably these school years really *were* the best years of his life, the only time when he was entirely happy: he liked writing stories; he liked being a boy. Dumfries was the last time he was able to indulge both simultaneously.

Peter Pan was still thirty years off. In the meantime, Jamie contributed to a school magazine and acted strenuously in a drama group. "I came out strongly as a young lady, with my hair tied to my hat." He even wrote several plays for it, in one of which "I played all my favourite characters in fiction, artfully rolled into one".

There were girls, too, in Dumfries Academy, and as time went by Jamie found them attractive. (For some odd reason they were not allowed into the drama group, and boys still had to tie their hair to their hats.) As for the girls from other schools in the town, whom he met at tea-parties, some of them "looked so soft that you wanted all at once to take care of them".

He did, too. And this attractive quality about him was almost to destroy him, many years later.

It has nothing to do with that prognosis—but James Barrie was now sixteen years old and five feet one inch in height. He went on from sixteen, but his height remained constant. Perhaps this was the closest he could get to staying a child.

To Edinburgh University, aged eighteen. He worked hard (unlike Stevenson who had been there a year or two earlier) and emerged as James M. Barrie, M.A.—still determined to enter one of the few professions where this distinction would be of no use.

He began to bombard the press with articles, suggestions for articles, suggestions for books. Just as one wonders how Buchan the story-teller managed to produce his tome on *Taxation*, one finds it hard to reconcile the author of *Peter Pan*—or *Dear Brutus*, or *The Admirable Crichton*—with his suggested *Early Satyrical Poetry of Great Britain with some Account of the Manner in which it illustrates History*. Nor, for that matter, *A Queen Dowager in Love*. Neither was ever written.

It was his sister, Jane, who turned the tide of rejection slips. She was the only member of the family who believed in the wisdom of setting out to become a writer pure and simple. To the rest he was only "wasting an M.A.". And it was Jane who saw the tiny advertisement in the *Scotsman* for a leader writer on the *Nottingham Journal*.

He got the job: he was twenty-three.

The *Nottingham Journal* was one of three local morning dailies at the time, and, like the Three Little Nigger Boys, soon there'd be two. It was owned by a pair of brothers who knew nothing of running a newspaper, but had private means, and within a few years it had sunk without trace. (Though the name has been revived since.) But for two of those years it was a splendid training ground for young Mr. Barrie, who wrote profusely for it, in different styles on different subjects. Sometimes he was anonymous, sometimes *Hippomenes*, sometimes *A Modern Peripatetic*. Always he was readable.

He also fell in love, in a hopeless way, for the first of many times. He wanted to "look after her", but probably he was more in need of that assistance himself. She vanished.

By 1884 he had had quite a few articles accepted by London journals. After some had been taken by the *St. James's Gazette*, he seized time by the forelock and wrote to Frederick Greenwood, the editor. He enclosed an article with the unpromising title of *The Rooks in Dumfries* and suggested that he might move to London: all he would need was a little encouragement.

Stony silence; followed, many days later, with curt advice to stay where he was.

At which point James Barrie bought his single ticket south. On the night of 28 March, 1885, he took the train to London.

His impertinence—there seems no other word, so let us make a fine haggis of our metaphors—his impertinence bore fruit. In a remarkably short time, having calculated he could live on £1 a week, he was making two or three times that amount. In later years a pink haze of sentiment obscured those first months in London, and he wrote that he lived near starvation on penny buns. He pointed out that this young and foolish J. M. Barrie had—instantly on

Ramsay MacDonald, *left*, and Keir Hardie, *below*, were men from similar humble backgrounds and with the same dedication to the cause of Socialism. They found their separate ways into politics, by different means, and went on to develop a Labour Party. MacDonald ultimately became its first Prime Minister. These two pictures give an indication of their differences: MacDonald was the astute politician, aware that his craft was the art of the possible; Hardie, the passionate, silver-tongued, orator.

Harry Lauder, *left,* was near the start of his career when this unfamiliar picture was taken shortly after his journey south to London and fame. A few years later he had become the stocky little middle-aged man with the infectious grin, who had never been young and would never grow old. Mary Garden, *below left,* the little girl from Aberdeen who emigrated to the States with her parents, amazed Americans with her lovely, untrained, voice, then they sent her to Paris for lessons with the finest teachers in the world. There she found international fame. Sir James Barrie, *below right,* was already making a handsome living from his pen when this picture was taken in 1896, but real fame was to start some eight years later with his immortal *Peter Pan.*

disembarking at St. Pancras—bought himself a silk hat, with which to impress editors, though it cleaned him out of money. Other evidence from himself and his friends contradicts all this (in any case, he arrived on a Sunday) and it seems a fact that he made a reasonable living from the day he arrived. He had already given himself a flying start because *The Rooks Begin to Build* appeared on Saturday, 28 March, in the *St. James's Gazette.*

Soon he was making a good living out of journalism alone, and finding time to begin the longer work on which his heart was set. He had found with Greenwood and the *St James's Gazette* that anything with a Scotch setting usually sold (and to the end of his days he refused to use the newfangled word Scots). His first long works, blending family and Scotland in a fairly thick gravy of sentiment, were *The Little Minister* and *A Window in Thrums.* Before this he had produced and sold *When a Man's Single* and *Auld Licht Idylls.* Always he worked on a number of projects at the same time—and by no means all of them were sentimental or even respectable. It was years before he published it, but he wrote and re-wrote a mock-serious attack on various personalities of the day, *The Case for Doing Without Some People,* which annoyed them all.

He had met, on the *Nottingham Journal,* a fellow-Scot, Thomas Gilmour, who had preceded him to London and done well for himself straight away by not only remaining a journalist but becoming Lord Rosebery's secretary as well. Gilmour was probably the greatest friend Barrie ever had, though they quarrelled often. He was certainly a good friend, with infinite patience, for Barrie steadfastly refused to open a bank account for himself and for years demanded that Gilmour cash all his cheques, which he sent to him in bundles every few weeks. ("Do not trouble about the odd pennies——") Eventually Gilmour could stand this no longer (or perhaps it was his wife, for the showdown took place soon after his marriage). Barrie was taken firmly to a branch of Barclay's Bank and made to open his own account.

(But Barrie's lack of interest in money matters was notorious. Once he was embezzled out of £16,000 by a theatre manager and never noticed it until others took legal action on his behalf. There is a sad sequel to that story, for while Barrie was prepared to forget the whole thing, didn't want his money back, the others pressed the case, and the man committed suicide.)

In 1892—catastrophe. Not, perhaps, for a different sort of man—but what seemed catastrophe, the end of everything, for James Barrie.

His much-beloved younger sister Maggie was engaged to be married to a young clergyman in Caithness. Barrie had gone up to Kirriemuir on holiday with her, and was almost as excited as Maggie about the approaching wedding. They went for long walks together, chatting about the way Maggie would decorate her manse, how often Jamie could come up and visit. He had a bit of a proprietorial interest as he had given the young minister, Jim Winter, a horse to help him get round his far-flung parish.

They got back to the house in Kirriemuir to find a telegram. Jim Winter had been killed instantly, flung from the horse Barrie gave him.

Barrie was appalled; he was entirely responsible for the tragedy; he had presented the horse. Maggie collapsed.

And now for weeks they sat together in this darkened room in Kirriemuir, both of them in an agony of grief, and Barrie "looking after" his sister. He took her completely under his wing, sat with her day after day, making sure no one came in to interfere with her grief. There would be no question now of his ever marrying: he would give up his life for Maggie.

Six weeks of this at Kirriemuir, guarding his sister, comforting her—and then he decided they must move. He got the loan of a cottage, near Guildford, and took her there.

At this point, mercifully in time to take his mind off his troubles, he got the first, thrilling letter from Samoa. Robert Louis Stevenson, the great R.L.S., had written from all those thousands of miles away, written to comment on a somewhat impertinent essay about himself which Barrie had included in the book he wrote on leaving Edinburgh University, *An Edinburgh Eleven*. Good-humouredly, Stevenson wrote that he had just discovered the work and read it: he had "a great mind to write a parody and give you all your sauce back again——"

Barrie was as excited as a schoolboy. Grief was forgotten. (Which was as well, for as soon as he stopped reminding her of her sorrow, Maggie made a fine recovery.) He wrote back immediately, and the correspondence between the two, R.L.S. and J.M.B., went on until Stevenson's death. In the course of it, Barrie looked up Stevenson's relatives in Scotland; Stevenson urged him to come and stay in Samoa.

When he was thirty-four, Barrie married an actress, Mary Ansell. It was, on the surface at least, a happy marriage for a number of years. There wasn't a great deal of "looking after" to do, for Mary had a mind of her own and plenty of resource. They moved to Kensington and she set to work making her house and garden the height of fashion. Already people turned to look at them in the street; and now the house in Kensington was pointed out in awe, for Barrie's first full-length play, *Walker, London*, had appeared and been a success.

The novels of Scottish life poured forth: *Margaret Ogilvy* (about his mother); *Sentimental Tommy; Tommy and Grizel*. His *Little Minister* was dramatized (eventually bringing in no less than £80,000). He was an assured success, and rich.

He turned full-time to writing plays. This is hardly surprising, for, as we have seen, he was fascinated by drama at Dumfries Academy and after; he had fallen in love with many, many actresses; and succeeded in marrying one for himself.

And then, over the Christmas season of 1897, the Barries met the Davieses. No one knew it at the time, but the pattern of all their lives was changing.

Sylvia Davies was beautiful and talented. She was the daughter of George du Maurier, the artist and writer. She was happily married to a struggling barrister husband, and when the two families met, she and Arthur Davies had three small sons, the youngest of whom was called Peter. The Barries had only an enormous Newfoundland dog.

The parents grew ever friendlier, and at the same time the Davies boys became fascinated by the little man, this friend of their parents, and particularly of their mother, whom they met each day with his Newfoundland dog in Kensington Gardens. Sometimes his wife was with him, more often not. He was a tiny little man and lots of fun.

As for the three boys, they were eager youngsters, full of life, and they wore unusual little square-necked blouses which their mother made for them. (Soon these blouses would be seen on the London stage and copied all over the world.) The little man told them exciting stories as they strolled by the Round Pond, and even Nanny listened.

This friendship heightened that of the parents and soon the Barries and the Davieses were in and out of each other's houses, on opposite sides of the park, almost every day. Or to be more accurate, Mr. Barrie was in and out of the Davies house, dragged there by the adoring boys.

Arthur Davies seemed to tire of this: he knew that Barrie was far richer than himself, that the boys loved him, that his wife thought him amusing. He, of course, trusted his wife, but it was only too obvious that, once again, James Barrie had fallen under the spell of a beautiful woman. Of course, there was nothing serious, but it was irritating, just the same.

And at this point we leave this promising parallelogram to note that *Peter Pan* was produced in 1904 and was, as everyone knows, a staggering success. The American producer Charles Frohman had been offered two plays by Barrie on his visit to London and accepted both. One had been still untitled, just *A Play*, the other was called *Alice Sit by the Fire*. Frohman liked them both, proposed putting on *Alice* first. But the theatre he needed was booked for the autumn and he plumped for *A Play*, a thing about fairies and pirates which obviously must be a Christmas production.

The first night was 27 December, 1904. By this time, *A Play* had been named *Peter Pan, or the Boy who Wouldn't Grow Up*—and there can hardly ever have been a more instant success. The first shrieks of delight were heard when Nana the Newfoundland (so like Barrie's) picked up

Nicholas Darling's nightclothes: the shrieks, the applause and the laughter kept up until long after the closing curtain.

The critics liked it, too. But there was one dissentient voice among them. A critic, confronted by this stage-full of children, had muttered, "Oh, for an hour of Herod——"

All that is history. The play went to America, did just as well there. The sort of money that started rolling in made it possible, as we have seen, for a theatre manager to fiddle the books for many thousands of the playwright's money, without his noticing. Apart from this, the years went by happily, prosperously.

And one morning something delightful and odd happened. A statue of Peter Pan was unveiled in Kensington Gardens, very close to where, as half the world now knew, James Barrie and his big Newfoundland dog had strolled with the three Davies boys, one of whom was Peter. What a charming idea, that a lover of Peter Pan should have erected this memorial to the boy who never grew up!

But when it was discovered that the statue had been erected by Barrie himself, eyebrows rose.

He made a great friend now, Robert Falcon Scott, who was as fascinated by the genius of the playwright as Barrie was by the bravery of the explorer. Barrie and his wife introduced Scott to his future wife, a sculptress, and later J.M.B. became godfather to Peter Scott—today's naturalist —the only child of that marriage.

And, still later, a tragic letter from Scott to this dearest friend gave details of the South Pole expedition in which he perished.

But now, back to our parallelogram, our Davieses and Barries. Much had been happening. Arthur Davies, just becoming successful and wealthy as a barrister, died of a terrible cancer of the face, leaving Sylvia and the boys destitute. (And there were now *five* boys, not three.) So Barrie, much as he had done with his sister Maggie, began to "take care" of the family. He had sat bravely—and lovingly—by the dying man's bedside: now he adopted the survivors.

It was a selfless act, but a foolish one. He cheerfully took on a heavy financial burden, helping educate the boys, keep them all in the manner to which they had been accustomed. He did his best to comfort and cheer the widow (and this is not said with sarcasm or innuendo: he did just that).

But Mrs. Barrie fell suddenly in love with a much younger man. Why? Because her foolish, kindly husband had planned and taken a holiday on the Continent: two Barries, six Davieses, plus a young man he had recently met to even up the sexes of the adults. The holiday took place, seemed successful. Everyone returned happy and healthy to England and their respective homes.

Barrie was told the truth a few months later by his gardener; and Mary Barrie, who might have been planning to run away with her lover, was suddenly confronted by a distraught husband. He would forgive adultery, forgive anything, but she must not leave him.

She did and he was forced to grant her a divorce. The shock and the scandal nearly killed him. He moved, a completely broken man, to the Adelphi (built by Robert Adam and his brothers, on another page of this book), and had as his neighbour George Bernard Shaw.

Slowly he recovered from the shock, the disgrace. He went on, of course, subsidizing the Davies family as before, getting one son into Eton, another (recommended by Scott) into the navy, and so on. Perhaps he and Sylvia considered marriage, but that future now ended with Sylvia's death, as tragic as her husband's.

James Barrie was in charge of five growing boys and minus a wife to help him: he shouldered the burden without complaint. It told on him; the lines on his narrow face grew deeper and deeper as he worried more, worked harder. But that work never faltered, and a stream of successful writing poured from his pen over these years: *What Every Woman Knows, The Twelve Pound Look, Dear Brutus.*

In 1909 he refused the offer of a knighthood—and his public were impressed that here was a simple man who wished to remain plain Mr. Barrie to the end of his life. But, rather as with the discovery of the donor of the Peter Pan statue, the public was disappointed in 1913 to find that the higher offer of a baronetcy had been accepted.

The work went on—and with it fame mounted. In 1922 he got the Order of Merit, that proudest of all British honours, with a total membership of only twenty-four. In 1930, to his great joy, he was made Chancellor of his old University.

On the other hand, old friends were dying. This grieved him terribly; each death was a personal tragedy. His own health began to fail, slowly but steadily, until in 1936 there came a triple shock. His biblical play, *The Boy David,* flopped disastrously; his life-long friend, the casher of cheques, Thomas Gilmour, died; and he himself, for the first time in his life, was seriously ill.

There is one touching and attractive episode to brighten the last sad months. He had been one of the great for years, had come in contact with the Royal Family and in particular had struck up a friendship with little Princess Margaret, still a child. He had slipped into the mouth of Elisabeth Bergner, star of his ill-omened *The Boy David,* some felicitous phrase which Margaret had spoken when they met: later he told her of it, gleefully confessed his plagiarism, promised a royalty. Perhaps the idea of Royalties-for-Royalty amused him: at any rate, Princess Margaret's would be a penny a performance.

There were, alas, not many performances. The abdication of Edward VIII more or less coinciding with the first night of *David* was partly responsible for its death. But now the new king, George VI, did something imaginative and kind, exactly tailored to the idiosyncrasies of the dying playwright. He professed to be angry that no royalty had been paid, and a tongue-in-cheek missive came from the Palace. If Sir James Barrie did not immediately honour his agreement, he would be hearing from His Majesty's Solicitors. It was quite possible that His Head Would Be Chopped Off.

This—as George VI knew—was exactly what was needed to kindle the spark of life. Barrie got better immediately, arranged for a proper legal settlement to be drawn up by his solicitor, and for the—very small—royalty to be handed over by himself in newly minted pennies. He would, of course, require a Royal Receipt.

The game went on, the preparation of the Document took him out of himself, and for a while it seemed he might recover. Then, when his secretary sensed he might not, the Document was sent to be signed at Buckingham Palace: the bag of pennies would follow, just as soon as the Debtor was well enough to deliver them.

He never was. The Document came back, signed and with many kind messages. But Barrie was never well enough to complete the transaction, and he was determined no one else should. He died, after a long illness, on 19 June, 1937.

To the world Westminster Abbey seemed the obvious resting place, but Barrie had been definite about this. His body was taken north to be buried beside the rest of his family at Kirriemuir.

It had been a long life and—perhaps—a happy one. James Barrie left behind many, many things for which we have cause to be grateful. He died before that second great war which would change the life he had known, sweep it away and substitute something quite different.

Which he would never have liked or understood.

RAMSAY MACDONALD

He was the most unpopular man in his country: hated, despised, by all political parties and most people. He was a turncoat, a Socialist who had "yielded to the temptations of the aristocratic embrace", a bolshevik, enemy agent, tool in the pay of foreign governments. The lot.

His almost unbelievable rise from rags to riches, from the humblest of childhoods, of which he very naturally made good use in politics, is quite true. Rather more remarkable, if we look at it, than other climbs up the ladder of life in this book.

Time has thrown the man, and what he did, into some sort of perspective. Not only is his a famous life: it is in many ways a great one.

Unfortunately for the biographer, almost all Ramsay MacDonald's achievements were political, and politics, even if the performer is alternately a "bolshevik" or "yielding to the temptations of the aristocratic embrace", can be deadly dull.

We will try to see the man as he was. With Ramsay MacDonald. I think the man is more important than the politician.

Hard up against the Moray Firth, not too far from Inverness, where as the inhabitants know the only perfect English in the world is spoken, there lies the small town of Lossiemouth. Those of us who live in, or visit, the hills to the south of Huntly tend to view Lossie askance. For one can be terrified out of one's wits by the sudden explosive arrival of a Buccaneer supersonic jet from behind a grouse butt or belting up the roadway like an airborne cow. Yes, the Vale of Huntly is in the Low Flying Area of the Royal Naval Air Station, Lossiemouth, and men have been known to collapse in ditches, the word "Lossie!" on foam-specked lips.

But a hundred years ago, Lossiemouth, and the whole of that chunk of northern Scotland, was at peace.

In one household, however, as summer slithered into autumn, the heather blossom faded and the first days of October passed, there was trouble. Isabella Ramsay, middle-aged, work-weary, deserted these years past by a shiftless husband, had brought up four young children in this two-roomed cottage. Now, all too soon, another mouth would come to be fed. Isabella's youngest daughter Anne had worked at a farm outside Elgin and been seduced. She was now with child by the head ploughman and in a few days' time that child would be born.

They regulate most things well in Scotland, and, of course, the father—though Anne refused to marry him—would give his name to the child. The kirk might frown upon fornication, but it happened, and often. There was no question of young Anne being flung out, metaphorically, into the snow. She would deliver her child with all the help and care her family could provide. And they would help her look after it.

The boy was born on 12 October. The year was 1866.

Later in life he was to remark—and some would think it boastful, many would think it untrue—that extreme poverty of the kind he had been born into tended to "breed the aristocratic virtues". Certainly the normal Scottish urge to learn, be educated, succeed, flowered to an unusual degree with young James Ramsay MacDonald. His mother was able to provide the eightpence a month needed for him to attend the village school at Drainie, and here he swallowed learning at a prodigious rate. Anything, as long as he could understand it: arithmetic, history, all the usual subjects, plus the unusual choice for a small boy in a village school: literature in Latin and Greek.

Partly this may have been an hereditary urge, for his grandmother had books, a surprising number of them, in her cottage. And her daughter, James Ramsay's mother, had been acknowledged the most intelligent of her four intelligent children.

There was another man of letters in the neighbourhood: the watchmaker had his library, which Ramsay devoured in slices, like cake. It goes without saying that he was the star pupil of the Drainie School. In fact, when the time came to leave, the dominie urged him to stay on as pupil teacher. There would be a salary of seven and a half pounds a year.

During the two years that Ramsay MacDonald held down that job he read and absorbed more than most men do in a lifetime.

Perhaps it was just the sort of books the dominie had: MacDonald seems to have read every social history in print and to have decided, then and there, that he must be a social worker. The term is a portmanteau one, of course, and every Member of the House of Commons (and of the Lords) is as much a social worker as the youth club leader. For Ramsay MacDonald it would be social work of one sort or another for the rest of his life.

At the end of two years' teaching and reading he headed for England. He had read an advertisement for the "right sort of man" to organize a young people's club in Bristol.

Here, quite by chance, for this was just about the only city in England with such a thing, he found a Socialist organization. There was no such thing as a Labour Party in those days and he eagerly joined this Social Democratic Federation in Bristol. At the same time he developed his latent taste for geology: in the intervals of running his youth club and attending meetings of the S.D.F. he took up the serious study of this science.

This included the purchase of books about it. Within a few months Ramsay MacDonald had returned to Lossiemouth, poorer than he had ever been—and armed with a totally useless knowledge of geology.

Another suitable-seeming job was advertised, in London: he made haste to get there. Unfortunately, this one had gone by the time he got there, and unlike James Barrie, who was able to start earning a living immediately, MacDonald very nearly, and literally, starved. No one was interested in an uncouth lad from the north. However well-read he might be, no one could understand a word he said, for a start. In order to keep himself alive he got his family to send down oatmeal (for which he paid, when he had the money), and with hot water he made porridge.

Sometime the only water available was cold: then it was sawdust in the mouth, but he ate it.

At last he got a job. A little later he got a better one. Neither had any bearing on social work—or even science, which had now become an obsession. Once again he spent his available money, after sending some to Mother, on science books. Once again he had to creep back to Scotland, half-starved, health and finances apparently ruined.

But now his fortune changes. He recovers his health and a little later is back in London, doing a job he really enjoys, being Private Secretary to a Parliamentary candidate. He is with him for three years, coming in contact with all sorts of people, all sorts of political thinking. At the end of the period he is able to keep himself in some comfort by writing for Liberal newspapers. There are no Labour papers.

Suddenly, Ramsay MacDonald discovered a new and

civilized form of Socialism. He became a Fabian—and his attitude to social reform changed accordingly.

The Fabian Society—named after the Roman general, Fabius, The Delayer, and therefore pledged to fulfil its aims gradually—had been founded two years before, in 1884, for "the advancement of Socialism by democratic means". It was against all forms of "revolutionary heroics" —and young MacDonald found this a novel and pleasing point of view. Not only this: the Fabians, like MacDonald, were dead against the various irrelevant cults, from free-love to theosophy, which had slipped in under the umbrella of Socialism. They—and he—wanted justice, fair play, for the poor and less fortunate: anything else was a distraction.

On the other hand, though Fabians might demand a rational approach to Socialism, though the man-in-the-street was beginning to think he might want Socialism, there was no hope of Fabian egg-heads—like Bernard Shaw —converting the proletariat. However worthy their motives, no one would listen to them.

Had it not been for the birth in 1893 of the Independent Labour Party (not independent of the Labour Party, which didn't yet exist, but independent of the other two big parties with which, perforce, the labouring man had been allied) Socialism would probably never have come to Britain: it was all too remote, too silly.

And so we have MacDonald as an avowed, even accredited, Labour supporter, growing steadily in the estimation of others like himself, so that in 1895 he is even allowed to contest a Parliamentary seat as I.L.P. candidate at the general election. Catastrophic defeat—which was all he expected—but marvellous experience.

Another landmark: he now married a girl from a different, very different, social background. She was a great-niece of Lord Kelvin, and her name was Margaret Gladstone. No relative of the politician Gladstone; but her father, as well as being a scientist, was a social worker. As these were Ramsay's chief interests, the two men must have been drawn to each other.

Margaret had become attracted to Socialism—no doubt

this is the reason she married him—and she became a devoted, loyal wife: MacDonald would need that, in the years ahead: though, alas, they would share very few of them together.

His wife also had an income of her own: from now on he need not scribble away for newspapers whose policy he disliked. From now on the pair of them would do what they could for mankind—through the Labour movement.

A house in Lincoln's Inn Fields, and quite a new social horizon. Sherry parties of Fabians, tea-parties of trade unionists, the constant planning of Utopia By Democratic Means. He was able now to travel, and over the next few years he wrote thoughtful books on what he had seen and thought. Two of these were *The Awakening of India*, and *What I Saw in South Africa*. The former is one of the best books ever written about India.

Nearer at home, he dealt knowledgeably, provocatively, with *Socialism and Society*.

And in 1906—Member of Parliament for Leicester. The Labour Party was born this year. Whatever MacDonald might have styled himself before, he was now the Labour Party Member for his constituency. Most of the twenty-nine Labour successes in this election came as a result of a pact with the Liberal Party—and this fact must be borne in mind when screams of "turncoat!" and "renegade!" are heard in a few years' time. He was soon risking a great deal: in 1911 he became leader of the Labour Party and three years later had enraged the whole country by opposing Britain's entry into the First World War.

By this time personal tragedy had struck. His youngest son died and, a little later, his wife. He wrote a tribute to her and this was later published, as *Margaret Ethel MacDonald*—a moving and revealing piece of writing.

But now, in 1914, because of his supposed attitude to the war (in fact, now it had been declared he wanted it fought hard, and finished), he was the most hated man in Britain: a pro-German and a pacifist (he was neither). At the end of that year he joined an ambulance unit and got as far as Belgium before being brought home.

Unfortunately for Britain, and in particular for Mac-Donald, the Germans were able to make good propaganda of what he had once said. This distortion of his views made certain that he would be hated by everyone in Britain. He was.

A next opportunity for getting himself hated came in 1917. In March of that year the first Russian revolution took place, under the moderate, Kerensky. MacDonald loudly applauded this. (And had the aid which he so shockingly wanted to offer Kerensky been permitted, that mild and beneficent regime might have been able to stay in power, not be obliterated by the Bolsheviks.)

At the General Election in 1918 he was defeated at Leicester by a staggering margin.

After having worked four years behind the scenes—but sometimes very much on stage, as Labour Party representative at conferences abroad—he got back into Parliament in 1922. He was now Member for Aberavon, in Wales; and he was immediately elected chairman of the Parliamentary Labour Party. Two years later he made history—with Liberal support again, let us not forget that important fact —made history by forming the first Labour Government.

Probably he should never have allowed himself to become Prime Minister, for he now made the great mistake of trying to couple the duties with those of Foreign Secretary. Without doubt he was better at the latter. Domestic affairs, and therefore the future of himself and his Party, got steadily out of hand.

1926—the General Strike. MacDonald, having failed to avert it, fell in with the aims of the strikers, though hotly repudiating both violence and Communism.

Three years later, as a result of a marathon speaking campaign in which he travelled to every part of the country and held meetings, Labour was returned, with an absolute majority for the first time. He himself was returned for Seaham, in County Durham.

Still his main interest lay in foreign affairs. He was a great believer in personal contact between Heads of State, and in the same year he made the first visit of a British Prime

Minister to a President of the United States. (I was eight at the time, living in America, and I clearly remember the excitement I thought I felt at having our Prime Minister over: the pictures of lantern-jawed Mac and pie-faced Hoover standing affably together.) MacDonald was no longer allotting himself the role of Foreign Secretary, only devoting most of his attention to that job. Understandably his hold on the Party and the electorate began to loosen again.

And now, in 1931, still more disgrace. Recession—depression—had come and there was so much disagreement within the Parliamentary Labour Party over steps to combat it that MacDonald had to rush to the King and say his colleagues just couldn't agree: they were thus not an effective government. He tendered the Labour Government's resignation.

At his Sovereign's request, MacDonald now formed an all-party coalition government—and while a large slice of his own Parliamentary Party were in hot disagreement over its policy, he yet chose to remain Prime Minister, supervising his hybrid. Lord Passfield angrily accused him of having "succumbed to the aristocratic embrace" and MacDonald was firmly deposed as head of his Party. But, of course, he was still Prime Minister.

There seems little doubt now that he had one chain of thought in his head: he must stay in office to solve the vexed constitutional crisis; and he must steam-roller through the urgent legislation needed to "end the depression". There was no intention in his mind that these strange and kicking bedfellows, the Libs, the Labs and the Conservatives, should stay more than a week or two between the sheets.

Circumstances demanded that they did. And still, while all sides cursed him, he stayed Prime Minister.

Yet in October, when his coalition government appealed to the electorate for a "doctor's mandate" to do what it thought best for an ailing Britain, and risked itself at a General Election, it was returned by a very handsome majority. And MacDonald himself, rejected by his own

Labour Party, was yet returned by Seaham, which had been as solid a Labour seat as any in Britain.

This new Government (still, of course, a coalition) was MacDonald's fourth administration, and although many still complained vociferously that he was a turncoat, should be shot, and the rest of it, the fact remained that he was the chosen head of an administration overwhelmingly returned by the electorate (it had all but fifty-nine of the seats in the House of Commons). MacDonald seems to have handled all members of it with tact and skill, aware, as many Labour people were not, that politics is the art of the possible: that if there were not this hybrid government in charge the country would be in total anarchy.

The threat of Hitler soon appeared on the horizon, growing bigger every month. The British Government set itself to trying to appease the lunatic house-painter—and at the same time getting its own defences in order. MacDonald is often dismissed as an "appeaser" (and who wasn't, in Britain between 1935 and 1938?), but the important White Paper on National Defence which gave the green light to rearmament was very obviously his own brainchild. It also bore, and still bears, his initials.

But now he was tired, ill, disillusioned. On 7 June, 1935, he resigned the Premiership, handed over to Stanley Baldwin. In November of that year there was another General Election and this time his popularity had waned yet again. He was heavily defeated at Seaham. He had been fully aware that he would be, and in fact regarded his political life as over, but he had courageously agreed to stand to ensure the survival of the coalition government he had originally formed and of the small national Labour group. (He might no longer be P.M.—but he must not leave altogether and imply the ship was sinking.)

Two months later he was returned at a by-election for the Scottish Universities seat, but his career was over. A sick man, he was not involved in the various alarms and excursions of 1936 and 1937—like the king's abdication— and at the end of 1937 he embarked on a sea voyage to South America in an attempt to recover his health.

He failed. On 9 November, 1937, Ramsay MacDonald died at sea. The body was brought home, and he was buried beside his wife, near Lossiemouth.

Full circle. It is hard to do justice to this outstanding Scotsman, simply because he was so involved all his life with politics—and politics is not the red blood of life. He was, above all, a brave man. (He was dragged back, as we said, from his unauthorized service with British ambulances in 1914, but in fact he got back again a fortnight later as an "official visitor". His coolness under fire much alarmed those who were responsible for conducting him, had to stay with him.) His last years as coalition Prime Minister can hardly have been enjoyable, but he stuck it out, to the accompaniment of such abuse as few P.M.s have endured before or since.

He was also a remarkable ambassador. Perhaps he set a bad example, for though he did this superbly (often to the detriment of his political job at home) he led the way for the hordes of little prime ministers, presidents, kings and the like who now scurry from capital to capital doing "diplomacy", for which few are fitted and fewer trained.

He wrote delightfully, and his two travel collections, *Wanderings and Excursions* and *At Home or Abroad,* are a joy to read. There is little doubt that he might have made a career for himself in diplomacy, literature, or science. Possibly even on the stage, for he had the distinction (within an admittedly poor field) of having been Britain's best-looking prime minister of the twentieth century.

One thing seems certain: he was too good to be a politician.

SIR HARRY LAUDER

It is axiomatic that Scotsmen do best for themselves when they leave Scotland—if only to cross the border into England. Like all axioms, it is only partly true; we have but to glance at Sir James Lithgow. But there are several examples in these pages of those who went much farther afield than England and made great names for themselves. One of these is wee Harry Lauder from Portobello.

In all history there was never a Scotsman who looked or sounded like him—but to the world he was Scotland incarnate.

Certainly he was for me. Fate had decreed that I be brought up, as a child, some three thousand miles away from the Aberdeenshire I regarded as my home. I was happy in New York, but very conscious of being a Scot, eager to clutch at anything which would bring it back to me, take

243

me, if only for a moment, to the land I loved, the land of my fathers.

Which, of course, was a load of codswallop. At the time of which I write—I was ten—I had no recollection of Scotland at all. But these things are of the mind and of the blood, and during those early 'thirties, in New York (and in Auckland, Sydney, Vancouver and Capetown), there must have been plenty of Scotsmen who knew as little of their native land, and were prepared to weep as hard over it, as I.

There still are.

I listened to Harry Lauder on our big Stromberg-Carlson, with its loudspeaker yards away at the end of a flex, crouching on its little table and echoing round the room. He sang from WJZ—or maybe WOR or WABC—and the tears oozed down my face like steam down a haggis. This was music, real music, and the stuff Dr. Walter Damrosch talked about in his Music Appreciation programmes, Mozart and all that stuff, couldn't hold a candle to it. We Scots were a musical race.

What was more, *I*—because I was Scotch—I *understood* what he sang. Thousands wouldn't, over here in the U.S.A., but I was Scotch, and I did.

But, of course, everyone else did, too, from Broken Hill to Boston, Pietermaritzburg to Pike's Peak. There might have been difficulty in the remoter parts of Scotland.

And so the world was fooled—and loved it. This was a real, unspoiled Scotchman, dressed in his native tartan, singing his native songs in his own, artless way. Why, he even couldn't stop laughing at the funny bits; he broke down so helplessly that you felt sorry for him, you loved him. Somewhere along the line the King must have felt that way too, given him a knighthood, for the little wee man was a Sir.

It was one of the most professional, most rehearsed, acts in the world. Every chuckle, every syllable of patter, every catch in the throat, had been rehearsed a thousand times—and it was perfect.

He was born on 4 August, 1870, at Portobello, Edinburgh, the son of a potter who made the stone marmalade jars and gingerbeer bottles which have almost disappeared today. Soon the Lauders moved to Musselburgh to be nearer the pottery, and here, aged five, Harry began his schooling. Unlike others in these pages he took little interest in studies, only in the active world outside the classroom. By the time his father had been offered a better job in the north of England, Harry had picked fruit, been a golf caddie, a feeder of pigs. All this ceased and the family packed to go south with father.

And within weeks John Lauder was dead, of pneumonia. The grief-stricken family, with twelve-year-old Harry as breadwinner, was back in Scotland, in Arbroath, where Mrs. Lauder had relatives.

Harry, when he got over the loss of his father, enjoyed being a half-timer in a flax mill—doing one day in the mill and the next at school. He was a towie who collected the tow or thread, after it had passed through the machinery, and got it into a bag. For this work he was paid a little over two shillings a week; not enough, even in those days, to support a mother and six brothers and sisters, but with mother herself going out to mind families, or do other people's washing, they got by.

It was while the family lived in Arbroath that he started to sing. His mother had insisted he join the teetotal organization, The Band of Hope, and he cheerfully agreed because of the music: every meeting ended in song. Now and then boys and girls might be asked to sing or recite something they knew. Harry, suddenly faced with the demand, promptly forgot all the hymns he knew and blurted out a maudlin ditty called "I'm a Gentleman Still".

Barefoot, ragged, he was applauded to the echo.

From that moment he seizes every opportunity to perform. At first it is only in competitions (though in the very first one he collects a "real Abyssinian gold watch" which works for a week and which he cherishes for the rest of his life), but eventually he begins to be paid a few shillings for his services.

There were two years in Arbroath. School was ended now, and life divided itself between the flax mill and whatever village concert might present itself. Opportunities, platforms, were few. Then an uncle urged the family to join him on the west coast, in the mining district of Hamilton. There was plenty of work to be had there, and wages down the mine were better than those above ground. The Lauders moved.

And it was here, down the mine, that Harry Lauder came to the conclusion, quoted in the Keir Hardie article, that mining wasn't a bad job at all. As it happened, both Lauder and Hardie started off in the same jobs: first, as a trapper, opening and shutting a trapdoor to control ventilation; then, as driver of a pit pony. For his work with the pony Lauder got a pound a week.

He got married—to Nance, the pretty daughter of a pit manager. By this time he was suplementing his income regularly with four shillings here, six shillings there, as singer and comic. He had carefully mastered a dozen jokes, rehearsed the telling of them with even more care than the singing of the songs that came between; and financially he was not a bad catch at all. The wedding was the standard Black Country festival of the period and rather gayer than the nuptials of today, for all non-family guests had to buy tickets. For the sum of rather less than ten shillings, a couple could—and obviously *did*—dance, eat and drink till buttons burst, and dawn broke. The happy couple—in this case, Mr. and Mrs. Harry Lauder—stole away at three in the morning and were never missed. A few hours later they were catching the first train to Glasgow and their one-day honeymoon.

Local concerts abounded in the west, and in most of these Harry Lauder put in an appearance; in most of them —for there was always an element of competition—he won a money prize. Sometimes the prizes were medals, clocks, or vases—even moustache-cups—and these, too, he eagerly competed for. The future was getting clearer: it was all good experience, the chance to learn new songs, new jokes, practise one's patter. Soon Harry Lauder would be a Professional Entertainer.

His biggest engagement of those early days was at the old Scotia Music Hall in Glasgow. Once again there was competition, for if old Mrs. Baylis or her patrons didn't like the turn, off you came, usually encouraged by a long crooked stick which emerged from the wings and grabbed you round the neck. One furious artist—this was the start of the Boer War—screamed at the audience, "I hope the bloody Boers win!" But Harry, trembling with fright in the largest auditorium he had ever seen, was allowed to get through two songs, and asked to come back later. Success at last.

A brief sally into the risky business of being a full-time professional. He took the risk, left the mine, and worked a few months with concert parties. Then the summer season ended, there was suddenly no work, and he crept back to Hamilton. Ashamed, cursing himself for taking a risk with his family's future, he resolved to be a miner for the rest of his life.

The decision didn't last long. Out of the blue came an offer which just could not be refused—a month's tour of the Moss & Thornton Music Halls in the north of England, finishing up with two weeks in Glasgow. It was the last chance, and he took it.

This time there was no doubt at all about it, he was a huge success. He had been practising for hours each evening—as he did for most of his life—and for the English tour he made the wise decision of singing his songs in "English with a Scotch accent". To a Sassenach this may seem a contradiction in terms; surely "Scotch", unless we mean the Gaelic, is "English with a Scotch accent"? But, of course, it is not, and the songs which Lauder had been singing, many of which he made up himself, were stuffed full of words which were meaningless south of the border, indeed meaningless after he had travelled a few miles within Scotland, though he carefully switched some of them around as he travelled from county to county.

From now on—even in Scotland—Scots words were out. The accent itself had to be made clear to the Tynesider, the Londoner, to be clear to men and women in whichever part of the world Harry Lauder might travel. Already he was thinking big.

Later, Harry Lauder described for the benefit of Sassenachs the linguistic complications of travel in Scotland. Like all southern Scots, he points out that the Aberdeenshire way of speech is all but incomprehensible south of that county—a fact which, though from constant reiteration I now believe it, I find strange. To me the language spoken north of the Dee is picturesque and crystal clear, whereas after an aggregate of many months spent in and around Glasgow I can still find myself occasionally unhorsed by the speech of the south-west. But Lauder tells a story of the Aberdonian visiting London for the first time and being fascinated by the lights of Piccadilly Circus. One of the characteristics of broad Aberdeenshire is the substitution of "f" for both "v" and "w", and the question our northern visitor addresses to a newsboy is "Fat's a'them reed and fite and blue lichties bobbinootaninowerheresee?" The question is repeated several times, with both parties getting more exasperated, until the newsboy shouts, "Get aht, yer bloody Portugee!" and the interview is at an end.

The red and white and blue lights, bobbing in and out, have fascinated other visitors, too. One of them was Harry Lauder, who bought his third-class single (like half the people in this book) to London. It was March, 1900, and he had gone to considerable trouble to select a wardrobe which would evince both prosperity and talent. He wore, travelling south, a pair of tartan trousers above yellow spats and brown boots. Above this he sported a frock coat and coloured waistcoat. He duly arrived, and such is the *sang-froid* of England that few people stared. Memories have clouded over, and the various people who recalled meeting him on that eventful day disagree with the wee man and each other as to what he wore, or where he went in it, but one fact is certain. He met Tom Tinsley, manager of Gatti's Music Hall, and was signed up for a turn—just a song or two—that very night.

He was in the dressing-room an hour and a half before he was due on stage. Carefully he did and re-did his make-up, adjusted his highland dress, nervously fingered his stick. When the moment came, he dashed on stage, thumping the floor as he always did with the stick, to give the orchestra the beat, and sailed into "Tobermory".

Success. Within a day offers flooded in and Lauder— grasping at security now; whatever happened he wouldn't go down the mine again—signed himself away to various theatre managers for a total of three hundred weeks, at £10 a week.

Soon he was to regret this—but he carried out each one of the engagements at the agreed fee, even though he requested a few of the dates be altered a bit to allow him to fit in others at ten or fifteen times the rate.

Not too far distant was the time when he would be making £1,000 a week. Perhaps he suspected this—but there was no time to lose. New songs had to be composed— "Stop Yer Ticklin', Jock", "Roamin' in the Gloamin' ", "I Love a Lassie", and, of course, "Keep Right on Till the End of the Road", which has probably given rise to more heartfelt emotion than anything Burns—or Beethoven—ever wrote.

On to America, sailing from Liverpool on the old *Lucania* at the end of 1907, with his son, John, now sixteen. A disastrous press conference; a suddenly truculent and suspicious Scotsman descending a foreign, seemingly hostile gangway; but it was completely forgotten in the thundering success of that first-night success at the theatre in Times Square.

An unbroken tale of success from here on. Tours over much of the world, to whom this little man with the creaking, emotional voice, the infectious—epidemic—laugh, the easily-understood way of speaking and singing, was symbol of all that was best in Scotland. And in a way it was, for this was professionalism at its zenith, with even the manic laugh in "Stop Yer Ticklin', Jock" being rehearsed daily for ten weeks, every gesture worked out, refined, so that any audience anywhere could instantly be made prisoner. Every community he performed to dredged up its Scots ancestry, found a tartan. There were Scotch Finkel-baums, Scotch di Maggios, Scotch Joneses, all suddenly awash with haggis, chappit tatties and sentiment: every night was Burns night.

It can't go on—but it does. The years rush by, with ever-increasing success. War comes, and with it personal tragedy: John, the Lauders' only son, a captain in the Argyll and Sutherland, is killed, and the news arrives in London, where he is starring in the revue "Three Cheers", on New Year's Day 1917. He is heartbroken, considers giving up his career altogether, but is persuaded not to. Visits to the front to entertain the troops, and in 1919 a knighthood.

Much of the rest of Lauder's working life was spent in America or touring the world and, long before the end, these tours were announced, in all sincerity, as "The Farewell Appearance of Harry Lauder". But the storms of protest, the urge to keep going anyway, made these farewell appearances an annual affair.

But at last the time came to settle down. He was alone now—his wife had died—and he settled into his large home in Lanarkshire. An earlier attempt to settle at another spot, to be a farming laird, had ended in financial disaster, but here he was happy. His niece Greta joined him in this final home, Lauder Ha'.

Sir Harry lived there until 1950 when he died after the busiest of long lives. His niece died in 1966, still living in Lauder Ha', and as I write, in early 1967, the house has just been sold. While it remained in the Lauder family's hand it bulged with curios, keepsakes, mementos.

Now that chapter has ended. Whatever lights—whether they be reed-and-fite-and-blue, or just feeble—may burst over the horizon of the entertainment world, there can never be another Harry Lauder.

MARY GARDEN

She was vain and often petty. Perhaps it would be fairer just to say she was very feminine.

And she sang like an angel—but more than that: Debussy, Charpentier and others less renowned, swooned when she came on stage.

She came from Aberdeen.

She is commonly believed to have given its name to the gardenia, but as that attractive plant has been around for many, many years, it seems more likely that she gave her name only to a gardenia perfume—and we know she did this.

Her sudden, instant rise to fame, her Cinderella-night, must have been one of the great moments of musical history. The year was 1900, the scene Paris, and the *Opéra-Comique*. Gustave Charpentier's opera *Louise*, with some of the most moving, melodious music ever sung, had opened two months earlier. Among the audience tonight was a young Scots girl, Mary Garden, studying to be a singer. She had had the good fortune to be allowed to sing before Albert Carré, Director of the *Opéra-Comique,* had begged a copy of the *Louise* score from him.

And on today, Friday, 13 April, two months after the opera began, she got an urgent message from him: "Come now and see me."

She did, tearing down the five flights of stairs like a mad thing, up the street like a greyhound.

There he was. What did Monsieur the Director want?

"I want you to be prepared to sing *Louise.*"

"But—but——"

"You have been studying it—my score—haven't you?"

"Yes, Monsieur Carré——"

Then, going to his desk and taking out a theatre ticket— "Please sit there, tonight, in the audience. And if Mlle Rioton is taken ill—you take over her part. The lead, Mlle Garden."

And so she did. The star got through the first two acts, and then, during the second interval, a messenger came to Mary's seat, Number 113, and led her backstage.

She would sing the role: Mlle Rioton had left, plunged out into the street with hysterics, and there was no understudy.

Feverishly, they pinned her into some sort of costume. Not the right one, for there was nothing of the sort that would fit, but a long, blue dress that could be tucked into place around a tiny, seven-stone girl.

The conductor, André Messager—who nevertheless would soon be professing violent love for her—was incensed that his orchestra's performance be made a vehicle for this untried nonentity. It would be better, far better, to give the audience back its money and cancel the rest of the opera.

Carré refused to listen, and the third act began. Mary was led to her spot in the wings and from there she began to study the audience. Everyone was so beautifully dressed:

the men, with light glinting off their stiff white shirt-fronts, looked like penguins.

And then she came on. Slowly she walked up to the spot on the stage where she was to sing her aria, *Depuis le Jour* —and she sang it.

At the end, André Messager rapped loudly with his baton, made his orchestra stand up and bow to her. The audience thundered its applause, minute after minute.

From then on she sang *Louise* every night. "I began my career at the top, I stayed at the top, and I left at the top. When, many years later, the time came to leave it all, I did so without any hesitation."

No false modesty about that. And absolutely, exasperatingly, true. It was the secret of the Cinderella success, of the girl who took over the star's part and succeeded. "I have never been nervous in all my life and I have no patience with people who are. If you know what you're going to do, you have no reason to be nervous."

Many singers, most of the best ones, might disagree with her. But for Mary Garden it was true.

How did this diminutive Aberdonian find herself in Paris?

She was born, of quite prosperous parents, in 1874. Not 1877, as she let it be known. When she died, on Tuesday, 3 January, 1967, she was just short of her *ninety-third* birthday, and more active than many of us half her age. Her first contact with music, apart from the nursery rhymes she sang with her sisters, was when her parents took her to the Aberdeen Music Hall to hear a statuesque and rather terrifying woman sing "Ocean, thou Mighty Monster". It was thrilling—and the seed was sown.

Mr. Garden was offered a better job in America, and accepted. He went ahead, then sent for the rest of the family. Mrs. Garden, Mary, Agnes and Amy set sail on the *Anchoria*.

Their first address in a strange land was President Street, Brooklyn. A little later they had moved with father's job to Chicopee, Massachusetts, where a fourth daughter was born. And it was in this town that Mary had a first chance to sing in public. There was a church fête, and during it she was ushered to the front of a platform and asked to perform: someone had heard that Mrs. Garden's little girl Mary could sing.

The song, with simpler melody, easier sentiment, than *Depuis le Jour* (which had yet to be written) was, "The Birds Were Singing in Every Tree, at Five o'Clock in the Morning".

Great success. And now a musical career, not necessarily as a singer, began to beckon. She took violin lessons.

They returned for a visit to Scotland and Aberdeen. Mary began the piano, worked hard at it, largely because she was in love with Mr. Smith. Mr. Smith taught the piano in Aberdeen. He didn't know, didn't care, that his protégée loved him—but his physical presence hastened study, and soon she became a skilled performer. The skill would be invaluable to her later, when she began to learn operatic roles.

Back again to America, this time to Chicago, where Mr. Garden had transferred to the Pope Company which made bicycles. It was a friendly company under the benevolent rule of old Colonel Pope; and when the boss came to dinner and the meal had been successfully ended, he turned to Mary, asked her to sing.

She did—and a few days later, at the Colonel's insistence, she had been bundled off to a teacher. Mrs. Duff was astounded at the Scots girl's voice, eagerly took her on. Some months later she made the startling request that she be allowed to take Mary to Paris, arrange for her to study there.

What did one use for money?

Mrs. Duff would arrange that. She knew rich people, people who would be eager to have a stake in a new, exciting talent. She would get all the backing they needed.

She did, and a little later we find the two of them sailing bravely into the unknown, at the same moment that the Garden family moves yet again, to Connecticut.

Mrs. Duff stayed long enough in Paris to find lodgings and a teacher for her pupil, then sailed home. Mary would stay with the Chaigneau family, musicians all, and she would study with one Trapadello.

The singing, and the French, progressed steadily, and after eighteen months had passed our young singer was wondering what chance there was of professional work, however humble. And then, disaster struck. Or so, at the time, it seemed. Her American sponsor refused to go on sending money. No reason was given; it just stopped. And by now she was studying under two teachers, Trapadello and Fugere.

Shaken, she went to each in turn, announced she would be giving up lessons: she had no more money. And both teachers, without hesitation, insisted they carry on, without payment.

Both of these, as in all good fairy-tales, would live to have their gesture rewarded. But an odd, un-fairylike note now intrudes. Mary did everything she could to find why the money had stopped. Free lessons or no, she could not continue indefinitely, even with the sums of money her father now sent, could not go on paying the landlady. But she refused to grovel. When it became clear the money had been stopped deliberately, that there was no question of a mistake, she wrote firmly and told her erstwhile sponsors they could keep the money. Some day she would repay all she'd already had.

The tale is no longer Cinderella's: real human emotions are involved. And in no time at all these are roused to a pitch of rage when a messenger, a woman, arrives from the Chicago sponsors.

" 'We have been hearing stories about you——'"

" 'What sort of stories?' I asked, beginning to sense something ugly.

" 'About your private life.'

" 'Please go on,' I said coldly.

" 'We have been getting anonymous letters about what you are doing in Paris.'

" 'And what have I been doing in Paris?'

" 'Just about everything—except work.'

" 'Will you be more specific, please?'

" 'They said you had a lover.'

" 'So that's it,' I flung at her. 'You can see for yourself the way I am living. Does it look to you as if I have lovers, or that I am not serious about my work?'

" 'Also, that you've had a child——' "

So *this* Cinderella has her troubles.

We have no reason to doubt the letters were false, and inspired by jealousy—or straightforward dislike. For here was a girl who was going to get on, and it must have been obvious not only to Mary, but to all who met her. The happy accident over *Louise* would accelerate the process, make possible the boast, "I started at the top——", but if ever anything in the arts were inevitable—but, of course, nothing is—Mary Garden was booked for stardom the moment her first teacher heard her sing.

Coupled with talent, a Scots urge to succeed, was a gift for friendship. Men and women simply fell in love with her (though not all of them) and it is easy to see how this would trigger off an avalanche of anonymous letters. Within weeks of losing one sponsor's support she had another, far better. Singers are not as a rule overkind to singers, particularly of the same sex, but the American, Sybil Anderson, was a splendid exception. She was assured and successful (Massenet had just written his opera *Thaïs* for her) and when she recognized the young Scots girl in the street she invited her into her carriage. What was the reason for that woe-begone look?

By the end of the day the outstanding rent on Mary's lodging had been settled, and she had moved, complete with piano, to a room in Mrs. Sanderson's huge house.

And it was there that she met Albert Carré. He told her he was producing a new opera, loaned her a copy of the score. When he found time he even, at Mrs. Sanderson's request, heard her sing. So perhaps it is less than surprising that a waif of a girl — ninety-eight pounds all up — the epitome of all sad little *midinettes* in Paris, who also interested herself in the score of a new opera about a *midinette*; less than surprising than Mary Garden should find herself singing the lead role in *Louise*.

From now on her future was assured. But there were storms ahead. The composer Debussy became hynotized by her voice—strangely so, because he first heard it in *Louise,* an opera which to the end of his life he loathed. He had collaborated with the writer, Maurice Maeterlinck, over a new and unusual opera, *Pelleas & Melisande.* Maeterlinck wanted his own wife, Georgette Leblanc, to sing the part of Melisande, and according to Mlle Leblanc, writing years afterward about the affair, Debussy agreed that she would.

Rehearsals began. And it was only as Maeterlinck scanned his *Figaro* paper, weeks later, that he saw Debussy had signed up Mary Garden for the part.

Was it true? It was. Was it legal? It was. The law gave no protection to the author of an opera; the composer had the last word.

Maeterlinck—if we are to believe his wife—then dashed round to Debussy's house, brandishing a cane. Debussy collapsed, was revived by smelling salts, and his wife implored the stick-toting Maeterlinck to go home. And the writer "who did not like musicians any more than music" laughed and did so.

Perhaps that last sentence from Mlle Leblanc gives us the clue.

Mary Garden's story is a little different. The *Opéra-Comique* had taken the opera under its wing, and the director, Carré, handed out parts himself. One afternoon all the chosen were assembled in a rehearsal room while the composer played and sang the opera to them, from start to finish. A few days later, individual singers were sent one by one into a smaller room at *Opéra-Comique* to sing their parts to Debussy. So far there has been no suggestion that the roles as handed out by Carré met with Debussy's disapproval, no hint that he has someone else (like Georgette Leblanc) in mind. And at the end of Mary Garden's rendition of Melisande — to which he sings Pelleas in a thin, reedy voice—he suddenly gets up, leaves the room.

Puzzled, distressed, she is preparing to leave the building, when she is summoned to the Director's office. She enters and Debussy gets up from a chair.

" 'Where were you born?' he asked.

" 'Aberdeen, Scotland.'

" 'To think that you had to come from the cold far north to create my Melisande—because that's what you're going to do, Mademoiselle.'

"Then he turned to M. Carré, and I remember he put his hands up and said, '*Je n'ai rien a lui dire.*' 'I have noth-to tell her'."

But complications lay ahead. Maeterlinck wrote a bitter letter to the paper *Figaro*, pointing out that not only had "they" imposed upon him a singer he did not want, but "arbitrary and absurd cuts" had made nonsense of his story. He ended bitterly with, "I can only wish for its immediate and decided failure."

Somebody — perhaps Maeterlinck — printed a pro-gramme, with obscene drawings purporting to clarify the misty plot of this impressionist opera. On the night of the dress rehearsal these were distributed among the audi-ence. It rocked with laughter throughout most of the opera, including a death scene over which Debussy had lavished so much care.

The first night, however, went well, but now even Debussy began to have doubts about his work. He explained these by noting that as soon as a composer's work is on the stage, "nothing remains of the old dream".

But he had no fault to pick with the young girl who sang it. "Here indeed was the gentle voice I had heard in my inmost soul, with its faltering tenderness, the cap-tivating charm which I had hardly dared to hope for."

And Lalo, severest of all French critics, wrote, "She is Melisande herself".

For eight years Mary Garden held Paris in the palm of her little hand. Debussy wrote one of his loveliest songs for her, *Extase,* while adding that in any case he had written a whole opera for her before he realized the fact. The American impressario Oscar Hammerstein came over and heard her. He insisted she sign a four-year contract with him. On the understanding that he bring over the entire *Opéra-Comique* company as well, for a season, she agreed.

Her New York début, as it happened, was not a success. It was in 1907, and with the opera *Thaïs*. The critics hated the opera so much that they had few kind words for its star. To someone who had been the darling of a sophisticated audience three thousand miles away, the urge to get up, fly back to Paris, must have been overwhelming. But Mary Garden resisted. The public ignored the critics, began to flock in.

Louise came six weeks later. This time her success was as great as it had been eight years before, when the role of that little *midinette* launched her to fame.

A virtually unbroken success of twenty years followed, in America. The Scots girl seized the heart and imagination of the country, as she had in France. Wherever she sang, houses sold out long in advance.

Not that she didn't occasionally have to fight. On one of these occasions Hammerstein got the idea of booking the Italian singer Lina Cavalieri for *Thaïs* in the Manhattan Opera House. Mary was wild with anger, swore that if Cavalieri sang the role on Friday, she, Mary Garden, would be on a ship to France by Saturday. She bought her ticket, waved it.

Hammerstein backed down. And here, in Mary Garden's own words, is the footnote: "Cavalieri finally made her début with us in *Carmen*. I was in the front box, and my, was it awful! She wasn't Carmen at all. Hammerstein never gave her the role again. Then she was given *Tales of Hoffman* to do, and in that she was radiant, full of diamonds and beauty. After that season she never sang for Hammerstein again."

There's always room at the top and Mary Garden deserved her place: but it's a tough life at that altitude. Perhaps when she decided to leave, still at the top, and go back to Aberdeen, she felt an inward relief.

What was she really like, as a singer?

Sadly she made very few records, and those long ago. But they are absolutely thrilling, even one I have heard which goes back to the very beginnings of sound recording, long before an electrical system was invented. She is singing Melisande—and Debussy himself is at the piano. Another of her rare recordings was made in 1912—also before the electrical system—but the high D in that *Depuis le Jour* is liquid—and thrilling. She recorded the same aria years later, in 1926: now, because she was fifty-two (and not the forty-nine she claimed) she transposed it down a tone, so that the feat is less acrobatic, but with the higher standard of recording, more satisfying to the listener.

She was a very great singer. But her reputation, paradoxically, has suffered because she was, at the same time, a superb actress. And opera singers who can really act may be counted on the black notes of the key of C. Her misfortune, then, has been to be remembered in some quarters as a singing actress, rather than a singer. But this would not have upset Mary Garden: either one got under the skin of the part, lived it as wholly and utterly as any present-day Method actor—or one did something else for a living.

Her farewell season was with her beloved *Opéra-Comique,* in 1934, when she was sixty. As she had always maintained she would, she retired at the top of her profession. She never gave up her love of singing throughout the more than thirty years of life which remained. To the end she was an encouragement to younger singers, to whom she gave unsparingly of her time—and, on occasion, the rasp of her tongue.

One of those who was helped tells me she remembers Mary Garden, aged eighty, as kind, with a wonderful, ready smile—"and a loud, *very loud,* speaking voice". She wore, as she always did, a huge and startling hat, and every move was a picture of grace, theatricality.

The Singing Actress with the thrilling voice died, still unmarried, in Aberdeen. She was almost ninety-three.

JOHN BUCHAN, 1st BARON
TWEEDSMUIR OF ELSFIELD

Two Scottish authors have given me more joy than most writers, and although this volume of Lives contains the compressed, papered shapes of James Barrie, Walter Scott, and Robert Burns, all of whom I admire, I mean none of them. Nor, for that matter, Byron.

One of my two I am forced to leave out, in a book of this size; though if ever I have opportunity to write a sequel, he will take an honoured place within its pages. I refer to Mr. Eric Linklater—who started me reading books at the age of nineteen.

Not that I hadn't read before. But somehow, the experience of moving, as a fifteen-year-old adolescent, from one country to another, for keeps, had submerged all desire to read. I put down a book in Boston, Massachusettes, *en route* to catch the boat to England; I never read another—for pleasure, that is—until the age of twenty. Then, in an orgy of delight and discovery, I read everything Mr. Linklater had written.

Linklater, alas, did not keep up with my consumption, and I was forced to keep up the habit by reading the work of other folk.

And what was I reading before this self-imposed embargo on the written word?

Needless to say—or we would not have mentioned it here —the tales of Mr. Buchan. And Buchan runs neck and neck with Linklater, not in a sober estimate of their worth, which I am not qualified to give, but for the sheer joy they gave me at the time. I was extremely fortunate as a Little-Scotch-Boy at school in America to have the wisest, most understanding of English masters, who led our reading with a gift of insight, so that one was taken from *Twelfth Night* to the *Forsyte Saga* via the enchanting cat Mehitabel and her overworked amanuensis Archie, who bounced out her blank verse for her each night on Mr. Don Marquis's typewriter. Never, of course, using capitals; for though a cat may look at a king, no cockroach can hold down a shift key while he jumps on a letter.

And, of course, this rich and nutritious diet included the red meat of John Buchan. At the time, no bard or cockroach could hold a candle to him.

He was, as it happened, a name well-remembered at my American school. His name is there—somewhere, I remember it clearly—in large letters which proclaim that he gave the Alumni War Memorial Address in 1924. The War Memorial Foundation was intended to provide lectures by the great to inspire the young: it did, and I think still does. Great men were somehow persuaded to travel great distances in order to give the annual talk. Franklin Roosevelt, battling with the cruel paralysis which had seemed to nip off a political career in the bud, came and gave it two years later, in 1926. And others as famous, or about to become so.

But it was not because of the name on the wall that I read

John Buchan. I had been interested in him as a fellow Scot and I knew all about him, as people so often do, long before I'd read a line of his work. It was not until I came to *The Thirty-Nine Steps* (fell deliriously, joyously to the bottom) that I was hooked.

He was a man of many parts. Who among us has read his *The Law Relating to the Taxation of Foreign Income*? Not I, but in its day, and perhaps now, it was the definitive text-book on the subject. There is no space here to outline the plot of any of Buchan's books (even *The Law Relating*——), but if by this short re-telling of his life one person is persuaded to go out and borrow something of his from the library, something will have been achieved.

Like Byron—but only in this way, for two men could scarcely have been less alike—he was a brilliantly gifted amateur, and regarded himself as an amateur all his life. This, of course, is meant in the sense of being a lover of many things; for there was not one of them that Buchan did in an amateurish way. Everything he touched he did well. And he touched many, many things.

Apart from the tax book which was a succinct and superb setting out of dismal facts, not intended to bear any relationship with literature, he wrote on two quite different levels. On one shelf of his bookcase were his scholarly, readable biographical and historical works; on another, the rumbustious, blood-and-thunder tales of adventure. But despite the size of both shelves—and his output was enormous—he never regarded himself as a professional writer.

What was he then? For this sort of amateur approach quite understandably sends Americans, Germans and others stark, staring mad. There are, they shout, too many amateurs: captains of industry who play at being farmers and neither captain nor farm; non-writing writers; and so on. Yet everything Buchan put his hand to throve.

A superhuman? No—a very human human. He worshipped success, enjoyed snobbery and caused endless mirth among his friends—and enemies—by attempting to be on first-name terms with everyone from the butler to the Cabinet minister. The late John Strachey told with a smile how the only person in his life who had ever addressed him as Jack—and unfailingly did—was Buchan.

He was born in Perth on 26 August, 1875, the eldest son of the Rev. John Buchan, whose father before him, and also a John Buchan, had combined the offices of lawyer and bank manager in the town of Peebles. The second John Buchan was ordained to the ministry of the Free Church of Scotland, and it was while he was in charge of the Knox Church in Perth that his wife gave birth to her first child, the third John Buchan, and subject of this article.

Before the infant was a year old the family had moved to the manse of the Free Church in Fife, near Kirkcaldy. It was there, four years later, that the future author had an experience which may subconsciously have influenced his choice of the adventure story as chief medium of expression: he fell from a carriage and one of the rear wheels went over his head, fracturing his skull. Yet, always seeing the best in life, he maintained to the end that the long months in bed which followed this so nearly fatal accident permanently improved his health.

Yet in fact it endowed him with a fierce scar and permanently damaged eyesight.

He was thirteen and the family moved again. This time it was the Gorbals, and the manse of the John Knox Free Church—a very different surround to the one at Pathhead. To Sassenachs who believe all Scotsmen talk more or less the same way, it may be hard to realize that the teenage Buchan had difficulty in understanding the Glasgow lilt and in turn being understood himself.

But life was pleasant for the children—there were now four others, all younger than John—and no one objected too strongly when they gave wicked imitations at the dinner table. Imitations of visiting preachers—or even of the old man who made a point of visiting religious meetings, one after the other, and listening politely to confessions of sin. He would then stand up to admit that he, too, would have liked to oblige with a similar recital. Alas, modesty compelled him to admit that his own life for the past few years had been "humanly speaking pairfect".

From this stimulating good-humoured home John Buchan went to Glasgow University. It had only recently moved from its ancient home in the old High Street to its present western one near Kelvingrove Park. He had developed a taste for literature, and with it, a considerable ability at fashioning it himself. Already, at the age of nineteen, he had persuaded a London publisher to let him edit an edition of Bacon's essays. He enjoyed the work, but made no bones about the fact that he was doing it because he needed the money. Like Dr. Johnson and Sir Walter Scott, he believed no honest man writes a book except to make money.

From Glasgow he was able to get a scholarship to Oxford. By this time he was doing a great deal of writing—simply, he admitted, because he needed a great deal of money. Certainly he could never have got himself through that University, even with his scholarship, without profit from his pen. It goes without saying that the Reverend John Buchan and his wife were far from well off, unable to do much to help their son financially—though they had given him what was far more important; a liberal, and moral, upbringing in a highly intelligent family. (This had even included the chance for young John to take Sunday School classes of his own and entertain the younger generation of the Gorbals by his own, highly dramatized versions of Old Testament adventure.)

In the summer of 1899 he got a First in Greats at Brasenose—and failed to get a Fellowship to All Souls. The next best thing for a young man with his abilities and needs was to become a barrister. (For Scots, the law and medicine have always ranked highest as careers.)

He established himself in London, in the Temple, and subsequently in 1901 was called to the Bar. He was now writing regularly and profitably for the *Spectator*, concealing the fact from his large and rapidly swelling public that they were reading the words of a barrister—much as Walter Scott, respected lawyer, had denied authorship of the *Waverley Novels*. He was also writing for *Blackwoods*. He had become a perceptive critic of other men's writing, and approached it with as great an armoury of knowledge, technique and sheer ability as any critic can have mustered in this century. "Those Who Can, Do: Those Who Can't, Criticize." Buchan was cheerfully disposing of this old half-truth. He could write in different styles himself, as need or fancy dictated; he knew what made writers tick, could laugh at his own or their foibles. Already, he had made up his mind that he would never be a full-time author. He would always have some other, *serious,* employment, to which he would give the lion's share of his energy. When one considers the vast quantity of literature which he turned out, on several, carefully-surveyed, levels, and the money he made from it, the decision seems hypocritical; but, of course, it was not. Throughout an unbelievably active life Buchan gave himself to his real job, whether it be helping Lord Milner in Africa or being Governor-General of Canada. The sixty-four-dollar question has always seemed to be—how did he find time and mental stamina to write all he did?

Always, from the days of quietly mocking the "pairfect", John Buchan had hated the bogus, the hypocritical. As a critic he inveighed noisily and happily against The Kailyard School, that peculiarly Scottish manifestation of sentimentality. (The title, for those not familiar with our Scottishisms, comes from the first line of a Jacobite song: "There grows a bonny brier bush in our kailyard", from which one member of the as-yet-unnamed School had taken a title for his novel. *Beside the Bonnie Brier Bush* he called it, and a great success it was, too). James Barrie must be considered a member of the School: but it extended to other fields, and Harry Lauder, towards the close of his career, was frequently upbraided, because of his dress, his sentimentality, for being a Kailyarder.

As for the self-righteous, particularly in politics, John Buchan had no time at all for them. One well-known Scots politician was thinly disguised in his description of the Home Secretary in a fictitiously awful Liberal Government. The vivid, painful description is in Buchan's *A Lucid Interval.*

But writing this sort of thing for money and fun was all very well: Buchan had to be doing something else. South Africa now swung into focus; the war was drawing to a close and Alfred Milner, as the new High Commissioner out there, had the task of reconstructing the country in a just and enlightened way, particularly the new colonies of the Transvaal and Orange Free State. He wanted, he said, men of brains and character on his staff—and in a hurry. Experience was secondary, for he knew "first-class men of experience are not to be got, they are too busy already". Buchan was suggested to him. Very soon the young man was on his way, signed up as Milner's private secretary.

On Buchan's side there was hard-headed realism in this: he gave it much thought before agreeing to go. It was the consideration that he might in the process acquire South African clients for his law practice that convinced him.

Whether he got them is another matter, but he certainly did his work well, and built up, if not an eager clientele, a huge storehouse of experience which was to serve him handsomely in other fields. He admired the Boer fighters immensely, but deplored their "unlovely kirk", despite a certain similarity to his own. They were, he decided, "shocking liars" and they used their religion to "buttress self-sufficiency and mastery over weaker neighbours". Some years later he was to write *Prester John*, which with all its references to "blacks" and "niggers" now offends people all over the world. Yet it is packed with a compassion and real understanding of the black man's dilemma, lacking among some of its critics.

In 1903, his South African work done, he was back in London. Now his energies led him to accept a hard-working directorship with the publishing firm of Nelson. As a barrister he surprisingly dealt with taxation, and it was in this role that he wrote the dauntingly-titled volume on Foreign Income. By this time—though *The Thirty-Nine Steps* was a decade off—he had written much successful fiction on many subjects. He had also produced *The African Colony*, a work of massive scholarship; and on quite a different level—was mapping out *Prester John*.

He was also missing the open-air life of South Africa. As a substitute, he became enthusiastic about mountain climbing. He tried it in Scotland, tried it in Switzerland, and, though his experience was comparatively limited, was elected to the Alpine Club in 1906, because of his writings on the subject. By now, as we can see, he was a man with a foot in many camps. Not the least of these was the social whirl of London. He complained of the time-wasting necessity of going out, but he went, and in particular enjoyed his country-house weekends. He was beginning to consider a political career—which he would run in tandem with careers as barrister, publisher and writer.

And in 1905 something happened which, though it did not deflect by so much as one degree the purpose of his life to achieve great things in several spheres and become rich in the process, affected it greatly.

Someone took him to dine in London with the rich and well-connected Mrs. Norman Grosvenor. A little later, he was energetically courting Susan Grosvenor.

He married Susan—on 15 July, 1907—and as Winston Churchill wrote of his own marriage the following year, "lived happily ever after". Susan adapted herself easily to this most un-English of men, even to old Mrs. Buchan in Scotland. On their first visits north she understood not a word of what her mother-in-law was saying.

Buchan at the same time was doing well with Nelson's, sending ever larger sums home to his mother and sister, paying for holidays, clothes. He was also doing a lot, in secret, for friends he had made, for descendants of those less fortunate with whom he had worked, for other personal causes.

An example of the energy and ability he poured into everything he did was the Nelson decision to do a Spanish Encyclopedia. Buchan settled down and learnt the language at speed simply in order to edit it. It sold well, became a valuable addition to the Nelson list.

But Nelson's at the time was doing far more than encyclopedias. Under his guidance, they began the famous Nelson Sixpenny Classics, also a Sevenpenny Series of fiction still in copyright, and a Shilling non-fiction series.

The very first of the Sevenpennies, Mrs. Humphrey Ward's *The Marriage of the Ashe,* was exhibited a few years ago at the National Library in Edinburgh.

Still restless, anxious to tilt a lance at everything, he became parliamentary candidate for Peebles. He failed to get in. His health, for the first time since the accident with the carriage wheel, had been causing him trouble. His digestion took a disastrous turn from which it never recovered, and he was forced throughout the remainder of his life to adhere—when he could—to a diet.

He was ill when war broke out in 1914. A few weeks later he had his thirty-ninth birthday and began, in bed, writing *The Thirty-Nine Steps.*

He was not recumbent long. His firm decided to do a *History of the War,* written by John Buchan, and would require from him fifty thousand words a fortnight. He settled into this daunting task, and the *History,* published in instalments, was a huge success. All profits from its sale went to war charities.

He finished *The Thirty-Nine Steps,* during another bout of illness, and sent it off to George Blackwood. "I have amused myself in bed writing a shocker—it has amused me to write, but whether it will amuse you to read is another matter."

The Times now asked him to visit the front as its correspondent for the Second Battle of Ypres, and he cheerfully accepted. His despatches in the spring of 1915 brought home, as no others did, to the ordinary people of Britain, just what it was like to live in a battle zone. "In another room is a sewing machine, from which the owner has fled in the middle of a piece of work——" Hardly surprising, then, that this world-renowned war correspondent should have ended the conflict as Director of the Department of Information, the man who perhaps better than any other Briton could tell the world what was happening, and enlist its help. He wrote and wrote, travelled and lectured. He admitted privately that the job was "the toughest I ever took on".

But the adventure stories, the thrillers, were coming out now, one a year, sometimes more, and being seized from booksellers by the avid public. They were easy to write, for he based them firmly on the experiences of himself and his friends: the formula, if we may use the term, was to set exciting, often improbably exciting, action against an accurate, factual, background. And by this time John Buchan had seen plenty of background, and plenty of action, in South Africa and France.

He was Colonel Buchan now—and suddenly decided he should have a knighthood. His point of view was backed by his mother.

This desire may seem shocking in the eyes of innocents (like me) who have always fondly believed that honours come tumbling, undemanded, down the chimney. But it is only one more facet of the Buchan character. He worshipped success—but it had to be earned. And success should be rewarded. He was disappointed—but not as much as old Mrs. Buchan, writing furiously from Scotland —at not receiving the recognition he felt he deserved.

But the urge to be noted, rewarded, did not prevent him from doing what his conscience told him was right. He took the unpopular line of backing conscientious objectors who had been imprisoned for their pacifist beliefs, and fought hard for their release.

A few years ago—and it seemed a lifetime—he had loved Oxford. Now, though his spiritual home would ever be Scotland, he planned to move near that English town. He would have his twentieth-century equivalent of Scott's Abbotsford, of Stevenson's Vailima. He had admired a large house at Elsfield, four miles to the north-east, way back in those undergraduate days, and now he and Susan moved in. He began commuting five days a week to Nelson's in London, and loving it.

His family was growing and—a fact for which some in Scotland have never forgiven him—he sent the boys to Eton. He was proud of his Scotland, stayed there, would always stay there, on every possible holiday occasion, but his mind was not closed to the complementary merits of

England, and its way of life, of thinking. No doubt the idea of Eton was Susan's, for all the male members of her family had been there, but he cheerfully agreed to his own boys going there. Though, of course, they would spend school holidays in the north, learning to love it.

So life roared past. The verb may not be quite apposite, but nothing in John Buchan's life moved slowly, however convincing an air he gave of calm deliberation. The thrillers poured out, at least one a year; he wrote incessantly for the weekly press, he wrote historical works. (And re-wrote them, almost in the Soviet Russian sense: he completely re-wrote his *Montrose* in 1928, fifteen years after the original, because of new material and new thinking.)

The honours, at last, began to come. He was Lord High Commissioner to the Assembly of the Church of Scotland in 1933, a particular honour for a son of the manse. It involved residence for a short time in the Palace of Holyroodhouse, which was not only the chief Scottish residence of the British monarchy but sanctified as the Holy Rood from its connection, hundreds of years before, with Scotland's queen, Saint Margaret.

And in 1927 his urge to enter Parliament was gratified: he became Member for the Scottish Universities.

Eight years later: a far greater distinction. He was raised to the peerage as Baron Tweedsmuir and sent to Canada as Governor-General.

In this role, as indeed in every other he filled throughout one of the twentieth-century's busiest lives, he was highly successful. Popularity is not the sole criterion, but he achieved this and much more besides. Never before had a Governor-General travelled so extensively, got to know his Dominion so minutely. On the other hand, he disappointed Canada's Prime Minister, Mackenzie King: Buchan—or rather, Tweedsmuir—felt himself unable to work with him on the terms of intimacy King had hoped for.

Mackenzie King, though, was one of history's more complex characters, and deserves a chapter to himself.

Before going to Canada, Tweedsmuir had asked King

George V's permission to publish literary work during his term of office. Permission was granted, on the condition that it would not be currently controversial. And so, almost incredibly, in view of the other work he now had to do, more books came from his pen: *The King's Grace, The House of the Four Winds, The Island of Sheep, Augustus*——

And, more notable than these, his autobiography, *Memory Hold the Door,* and, posthumously, a sad little semi-autobiographical novel, *Sick Heart River.*

He suffered from grave ill-health during these Canadian years, ill-health made worse by his constant travelling, travels which included the United States and an official visit to President Roosevelt. During 1937 he made a journey of *ten thousand miles* into the Arctic and the north of British Columbia.

In the next year, on home leave, he was made Chancellor of Edinburgh University. Perhaps he regarded this as a culmination, the greatest of all his honours.

On 11 February, 1940, while he was shaving—and exactly like Robert Louis Stevenson—he had a stroke and died.

Sixty-four years is not a long life these days. But John Buchan packed into it more than four ordinary mortals could have done in the same time.

SIR ALEXANDER FLEMING

He picked up a small piece of mould with his spatula, put it carefully into a test tube. Then he scooped out the rest of the fungus, put that carefully into another.

He had without knowing it taken the first active step towards preparing penicillin. For the moment there was other more pressing work in that laboratory, and he put the test tubes into their rack and got on with it.

But all the while he was thinking, turning over in his mind the implications of what he had seen, what he had done. It had, in a way, been a most ordinary, humdrum occurrence. There were the usual colonies of plump bacteria ripening for examination under the microscope, the usual collection of lab equipment, Bunsen burners, crucibles, pipettes, test tubes. During the day he had taken the lids off several Petri dishes and studied the development of the bacteria within them. Often the bacteria were contaminated by mould—it flew in through the window, or merely spent the day floating about the laboratory, waiting to tumble into an open dish. Then, in no time, the tiny organism, the spore, put out shoots in every direction, grew bigger. It was a nuisance but nothing more: one merely had to dig the thing out and throw it away.

He had found one, been about to clean the dish, when he stopped.

He brought the Petri dish up closer, squinted at it.

Yes—very odd. Very odd indeed. The dish was breeding a colony of staphylococci and the mould, the fungus, had spread from one side and come into contact. But the colony, that part of it which the fungus had spread to, was dead. The staphylococci had been dissolved, and instead of being a yellow clump they had lost their colour, become simply drops of water.

Yes, it had been interesting—and for that reason he had set the mould aside to examine later. To minimize the chance of some mischance, a dirty test tube, a broken one, damaging it, he had divided the thing in two.

And the next day he began to cultivate it. It was still growing slowly when he removed it from the two tubes and spread it on a large bowl of the nutritive broth the lab used for breeding bacteria. Then he covered the bowl with a glass top to prevent further contamination.

The fungus grew, day by day. This, of course, was perfectly natural and it would have been puzzling if anything else had happened. He would just leave it there, let it grow, till there was enough of it to experiment with. Each day he looked in, saw the thick, soft, pock-marked mass change colour from white to green to black, and back again.

Then, without warning, the nutritive broth on which it had been feeding changed suddenly from a clear liquid to a vivid, opaque yellow.

Trembling slightly, Alexander Fleming took a drop of this yellow liquid and placed it carefully at the exact centre of a dish on which he had arranged, like the arms of a star-fish, six different colonies of bacteria, all radiating from the middle. He watched and waited.

Nothing happened.

And then, to his delight, it happened. Slowly, agonizingly slowly, the streptococci, the staphylococci, the gonococci and the rest of them began to vanish.

This was it. Somehow, he had made a discovery of the very greatest importance. There had been no method at all of killing these bacteria before, only by vicious acids, cruel disinfectants, which would kill the patient as well. Something told him the substance before his eyes was harmless to man, and to prove it to himself he gulped down half a glassful. Then, a trifle apprehensively, he waited for an effect.

None came. The germ-killing substance was harmless to man.

He diluted it, first to a half-and-half solution, then gradually to one part in five hundred. The action was less rapid, but it went on killing bacteria.

The next move was to discover what the substance was— what fungus it had been which found its way into that first Petri dish, a week ago. Frantically he thumbed through books of mycology, the science of fungi, trying to recognize the shape of the growing mould, but to a man, however brilliant, who is not a student of that esoteric branch of science, one mould is much like the next.

But at last, with help, he found it. Penicillium notatum —that was it: a penicillium, or fungus, of the notatum variety. The main problem was to get more of it, for the slow breeding of that original spore would not produce a large enough quantity in a short enough time. He needed the penicillium, and lots of it, right now.

There was another problem. How did one get that yellow liquid into a form stable enough to be stored, to be used when necessary? Already he had seen that the germ-killing quality lasted only a short time before the mould degenerated and turned into an inert, useless liquid.

These two problems were to hold up the development of Fleming's wonder drug for ten years. But as we know, the breakthrough came—and mankind will ever be in Alexander Fleming's debt. The first patient to be treated by the wonder drug, penicillin, was an Oxford policeman, dying of septicaemia from a small scratch which had infected his blood stream. The date was 20 February, 1941.

There was very, very little of the drug in existence. An intravenous injection was given; another after three hours. At the end of twenty-four hours the improvement was absolutely incredible: the patient had almost recovered, was sitting up, taking notice, laughing.

And then, what Fleming and his helpers had most feared: the penicillin, the whole world's supply, ran out before the treatment was over. The bacteria fought back and slowly got the upper hand. There was nothing to do, nothing at all, but stand by and watch the patient die.

But now the sceptics, or at least many of them, had been convinced. Efforts to produce the stuff in quantity were doubled, re-doubled. It took years—but now there is enough of Fleming's penicillin to treat any man, woman or child in need of it.

Alexander Fleming, son of a hill farmer in Ayr, was born in 1881. There are many Flemings in Scotland and probably the name stems from the weavers and small farmers who fled to England and Scotland from their own Low Countries, at a time of religious persecution. Hugh Fleming, Alexander's father, had an eight-hundred-acre farm called Lockfield, right on the boundary between Ayr and Renfrew and Lanark, though it was just inside Ayrshire. Alec Fleming, subject of this article, was born of his father's second marriage, when the old man was over sixty.

He began going to school when he was five. It was a fine, small, country school, and to the end of his days Fleming maintained that the best, most valuable part of his education had been achieved there, only a mile from Lockfield. Life was pleasant and soon the boy showed an interest in all sorts of sport—an interest which would some day alter the course of his life. He and his brothers, too poor to buy a gun between them, would yet go on rabbiting expeditions through the heather, stalking the little animals, catching them in bare hands. They swam, they ran, they played football, climbed trees: they were happy.

From the little country school Alec Fleming went on to a bigger one in Darvel, the nearest town. This was fun, too, and part of the joy was the walk through the countryside to get there each day, four miles in the morning and four miles back at night. And from the Darvel school to another at Kilmarnock, where the final two years of his schooling took place: he left Kilmarnock, aged fourteen, and headed for London and a job.

The year was 1895, and he was fortunate—as in many ways he remained throughout life. Four of the Fleming brothers had teamed up to rent an old house in the Marylebone Road, and their sister Mary went south to look after the lot of them. Alec's first job was as clerk to a shipping firm and, surprisingly perhaps, he enjoyed the work and might well have stayed on to become an industrial tycoon. But a sudden, unexpected legacy from an uncle made him heed his older brother's advice. "Don't waste it," said Tom Fleming. "Use it to further your education."

A thoroughly Scottish bit of advice—and Alec took it. A bit of swotting and he sat for the entrance exam to medical school. He passed and selected St. Mary's Hospital in Paddington.

Why did he choose St. Mary's? Because he had only recently played water polo against them, thought they were a nice lot of chaps.

And so, as a man of the world who had earned his own living in a quite different field of endeavour and was older than his fellow students Alec Fleming settled down to his studies. We may feel that the years he had spent as shipping clerk were wasted, but Fleming himself said, "I gained much general knowledge, and when I went to medical school I had a great advantage over my fellow students who were straight from school and had never got away from their books into the school of life".

At St. Mary's he found himself working in the lab of a very great bacteriologist, Sir Almroth Wright.

Why when in fact his bent was for surgery did he change

his mind and go on working with Sir Almroth in quite a different field, a field which should have necessitated his leaving St. Mary's? Because the great bacteriologist was persuaded to offer the young man the chance of working with him, in order that he stay at St. Mary's and support the rifle team.

He passed his finals in 1908, coming top and winning the Gold Medal of the University of London. He also wrote a thesis on "Acute Bacterial Infections" and won another medal. The thesis showed the line of research he would follow for the rest of his life. He outlined ammunition at the doctor's disposal in the fight against bacterial disease: there were surgery, when the infection could be reached in that way; antiseptics; general methods of increasing the patient's resistance; the few drugs which had effect on certain specific diseases, like quinine against malaria; ways of increasing the flow of lymph into the infection; and finally serums and vaccines.

An impressive enough list. But something was missing, and it became Alec Fleming's job to find it.

Working in London, he rather surprisingly joined the Chelsea Arts Club, an odd-seeming home-from-home for a country lad from Scotland, but he loved the atmosphere and the conversation, and for the rest of his life this institution remained The Club. He also joined the T.A.—the London Scottish—where there was a chance for sport and a bit of open-air life. His friends were mystified that Fleming, as a trained and unusually well-qualified bacteriologist, should choose to become a private soldier in the Territorial infantry, but Fleming spent several happy years in that friendly avocation, doing his summer camps with six or seven other men sharing a tent. He only left when the training periods began to conflict with his work at the hospital.

A few months after his resignation in 1914, war broke out. He rejoined the army, but now in his proper role, and almost immediately he found himself as a lieutenant in the medical research centre in Boulogne.

Very soon Fleming was forced to re-think his thesis on

bacterial infection. Wounded men, dying men, were brought in on stretchers, their wounds crawling with bacteria, and he found out only too soon that his antiseptics were useless. Not only did they not prevent, for example, gangrene: they actually seemed to promote its development. If a wound were near the surface the antiseptic could be useful, for a strong enough dose of it would indeed kill germs—and all the surrounding tissue at the same time. For a surface wound, some types of surface wound, this was acceptable. But, of course, most wounds were the reverse of superficial and here the antiseptics were either useless or destroyed vital tissue, or somehow destroyed the body's ability to fight back.

He realized that only one sort of antiseptic would be of real value—and that hadn't been discovered. A substance which would help the body's natural defences, that was the only solution.

For years he would search for that substance.

The war ended and Fleming went back to civilian research, with an eye open for his wonder drug. He felt it might have to be something from the body itself, and in 1921, after three years of research into the matter, he found that human tears had a startling effect on bacteria. If one dropped them into a culture, they dissolved the germs as if by magic. He analysed the tear drop, found it contained a substance which he christened lysozyme and which he isolated in hair, skin, nail-parings and certain leaves. It seemed a dramatic discovery.

Then he found that lysozyme, though dramatically effective against certain bacteria, was almost useless against any of the dangerous ones. He had come up against a wall —but it would not discourage him.

Eight years went by, from 1921 to 1929, and Fleming worked ceaselessly on the theory that something from the human body would be the answer to bacterial infection. Lysozyme was no good—but it had pointed the way.

And then, in 1929, through the window of his laboratory in St. Mary's Hospital, Paddington, the answer literally blew in. The fungus, penicillium notatum, fluttered down and settled in Alexander Fleming's Petri dish of cultures.

As we have seen, it provided the answer. It might not be a substance from the human body, but it occurred naturally and it dramatically inhibited the growth of micro-organisms. How, though, did one get enough of it, and stabilize it so that it could be stored, used when wanted?

Fleming had the patience of Job. For, having struggled eight years to get from lysozyme to penicillin (he coined both names himself), he was to labour another twelve before penicillin could be stabilized. Even then the quantities made available were minute. It was at this point, in February, 1941, that treatment was carried out on the Oxford policeman, treatment which ended in personal tragedy, but marked a further step in the development of the drug.

By this time the Australian Howard Florey had become interested in the work and assembled about himself a team of able chemists. They found, after months of frustrating work, that they were able to purify small quantities of the mould by a complicated method of evaporation—freeze-drying—and in this condition it could be stored for a short time. But, of course, far greater quantities had to be made, and a new source of the mould had to be found, for Fleming's original two test tubes of the notatum just wouldn't yield enough. To this end help was sought in America, and at last a laboratory in Peoria, Illinois, came to the rescue. The lab had been working on uses for the organic by-products of farming, and although they had not obtained any of Fleming's mould in the course of their work, they had discovered that corn-steep liquor, made from maize, was an ideal medium for the growth of fungi —far better than the usual broth that chemists used. Some of Fleming's original fungus was accordingly rushed to the United States where it began proliferating.

At the same time the research team, in England and America, was on the look-out for mould-strains which might give a bigger yield of penicillin. All of it now in existence had descended from the spore that landed on Fleming's bench in 1929.

Then, in 1943, another break-through. The Peoria lab

was already, thanks to its corn-steep liquor, producing twenty times as much as Howard Florey's team in Oxford. And one of its employees, a young woman employed to go round the markets of Illinois looking for rotten fruit, brought back a melon. It was in a splendid state of decay, and the usual tests on it produced the welcome discovery that its penicillium chrysogenum provided a mould of the pencillin type, which reproduced itself at great speed.

Success at last, and with it a realization by scientists in England and America that a wonder-drug was in reach. Production mounted rapidly in both countries, and, with it, technique for stabilizing the product. At first almost all of the penicillin was earmarked for the Services, and during the next two years thousands of lives would be saved on the battlefields by it.

By the end of the war enough could be made available for civilian patients as well. And now honours began to shower down on the shy and sensitive Alexander Fleming. He had already been knighted—in the basement of Buckingham Palace—during 1944. He had received the freedom of Paddington, the home of St. Mary's, where he had made the discovery; had received, too, the freedom of the little Scots town of Darvel where he had been at school. Now, in 1945, he was invited to the United States, to be fêted, and at the same time see how his brain-child was being developed, produced, in ever increasing quantity.

He was delighted to find that none of the firms—in America or in Britain—which were manufacturing the drug were making an attempt at monopoly. He had set the example himself by refusing to patent it, thereby passing up the opportunity of becoming a very rich man, and now the manufacture of penicillin, as he had long hoped, was public property. All firms, all research teams, shared their knowledge.

At the end of that triumphant year Alexander Fleming learnt he had been awarded the Nobel Prize for Medicine.

There was sadness ahead: throughout the long and lonely years in which Fleming had battled to make peni-cillin and to interest others in trying to help him, he had been wonderfully buoyed up by his wife, Sareen. She had been his constant companion for thirty-four years. When she died, in October, 1949, he was heartbroken. The tragedy was heightened by the fact that penicillin could do nothing for her—and by the sad remembrance of his brother's death, which penicillin, had he been able to use it in those days, would have averted.

To one of his oldest friends, he said, "My life is broken". Work was his only refuge and he plunged into it, devoting day and night, his entire life, to research. One of his team was a brilliant young Greek biologist, Amalia Voureka, who had received a British Council bursary, and been working in Fleming's laboratory since 1946. He had admired her work, begun to feel an affection for her, and in April, 1953, four years after the death of his wife, he married Amalia Voureka.

Their happiness was to be short-lived. He was an old man now, and illness struck at him frequently. On one occasion he diagnosed his high temperature as pneumonia, the disease which had killed his brother John. He sent for the doctor, who confirmed that it was, and immediately injected penicillin. The improvement was so sudden and so marked that Fleming laughed like a child and said, "I never knew it was so good!" But his health failed gradually, and in 1955 he died of a disease his drug was powerless to control, coronary thrombosis.

There can have been few great men so modest and few who did more for mankind. It may be argued in a decade or two from now that Alexander Fleming, by saving so many millions of lives and ensuring the survival of millions more down our succeeding generations, has, alone, created the population explosion which will ultimately destroy us.

But if it does, we have only ourselves to blame.

No one who has seen a friend or dear one brought back from the very brink of death by one of the antibiotics which Fleming's penicillin triggered off, could feel that the shy, retiring Scotsman was anything but one of the greatest men the world has ever known.

SIR JAMES LITHGOW

His is probably the least familiar name in this book, to the general reader.

But it is one of the most important. Perhaps, for Scotland, the most important of all. Barrie, for all the good it did his native land, need not have bothered to write *Peter Pan*, Spence to design an English cathedral. Mary Garden to captivate audiences in Paris and Chicago. Thomas Telford did wonders in opening up his country, but if he hadn't it would have been done, somehow, later—and Scotland would have survived.

But James Lithgow, with ideas so old-fashioned any self-respecting egg-head would die laughing if he heard them; with his soup-strainer moustache and his narrowed, suspicious eyes—*and* the gun dog he insisted Oswald Birley fit into his portrait—this red-haired anachronism of our century can take as much credit as most for having saved not only Scotland but Britain from disaster.

He was a Lord of the Admiralty during the Second World War, a comic title which no doubt amused him when they insisted he take the job. In it he controlled all British shipbuilding and ship-repairing; and without a keen and practical brain in charge of that, Britain would have foundered even more surely than if the British forgot how to build aeroplanes.

And yet, to Scotland, Lithgow's importance goes back way before 1939.

He was an engineer, and his ancestors for generations had been that, too. Their name is for ever linked with Port Glasgow. No, not Glasgow, but the far smaller new town planted on the bank of the Clyde long before New Towns had been heard of. The Clyde was too shallow to allow big craft to get to Glasgow: throughout the middle ages and up till the seventeenth century Glasgow was famous, not as a port, for it stood, in effect, miles inland, but as the seat of an archbishop and the home of a University. The town's trade overseas was done through the port of Irvine, thirty miles away.

Then Irvine started to silt up. The dramatic decision was taken, in 1667 to build a new port way up the Clyde, where goods could be transferred to lighters for the last few miles up to Glasgow. They built it, with docks and also shipyards, and they called it Port Glasgow.

The Lithgow family, long settled in this part of Scotland, became connected with the new town from the beginning. William Lithgow, born in the middle of the nineteenth century, became a shipbuilder there. He started off as apprentice at that exciting time when all the world had suddenly realized it needed Clyde-built ships of iron—and the Clyde was building them. He became partner of a firm which later he would control; married and produced a son, James, in 1883. Later the Lithgows had a second son, Henry.

By the time James and Henry were sent to Glasgow Academy the Lithgow family was enormously wealthier than the Barrie family which had recently pinched and scraped to send their son, James, to the same establishment. And though J. M. Barrie—on another page—became a very rich man, there is no comparison between that sort of wealth and the reward of a really successful man in Industry. Industry, that is, with a capital I, for Barrie knew all about the other sort. The Lithgows, any way you looked at it, were loaded.

Other pupils of the same period were John Reith and "James Bridie" (Osborne Mavor), as well as Walter Elliot, the future politician. (The last-named two were signatories to Reith's "Testimonial".) The Academy was, and is, one of the finest schools in the land, catering for the ambitious sons of professional and commercial men and turning out, as we can see, many of the most remarkable and successful men in Britain. It was a day school and the Lithgow boys travelled daily to it from their country home, *Drums*, six miles out of Port Glasgow. It was in those days completely rural, with all manner of wild life hopping and swimming and flying about the policies, and though young James Lithgow soon became a good shot, he was a naturalist in his approach to animals. To the end of his life he studied their behaviour, their habits, wrote long and informative letters about them to his children, letters full of foxes and badgers and buzzards.

When he was sixteen his father made him a proposition: the family was now so rich that he and his brother could live to the end of their days as country gentlemen, doing nothing. They could, if they preferred, go to any University in the world and take up any profession.

But, having embarked on either of these courses, "You will not ask later to come into my shipyards. That business is for men who know their trade thoroughly. If you wish to join it, you will serve an apprenticeship as I did, and devote your life to it, putting more into it than you take out."

Plain words, plainly spoken. And both boys resolved to follow in their father's footsteps and put more into life than they took out. As we shall see, they did. But before young James's apprenticeship began in the shipyard he was sent to Paris; which seems a delightfully imaginative prelude for a life to be spent among steam hammers, work-men and high finance. Not for nothing the Auld Alliance. He got everything an intelligent, very human seventeen-year-old could get from that lovely city; and yet there was nostalgia. A fortnight before Christmas there is this entry in James Lithgow's diary:

"Encore quinze jours. O bonheur, O Ecosse! O famille! O chasse aux canards!"

(Very little has been written about James Lithgow; no doubt because this most interesting of men was the least obtrusive. For that reason I have been greatly helped by the one excellent biography, *James Lithgow, Master of Work*, written by J. M. Reid, from which these extracts are taken.)

From 1901 the hard work began, back in Port Glasgow. Though James Lithgow's zone of operations would shift during his lifetime between the plumbers' shop of a Scottish shipyard and the Admiralty in London—and back again—it would be hard work all the way along the line; and all of it work he enjoyed. True to his word, the older Lithgow had put him through every trade in ship-building, with months spent working in each craftsmen's shop. Plumbing seems to have been his especial joy, and J. M. Reid tells the story of the naval officer, invited to Sir James's country estate for a day's shooting in the 1940s, who was surprised to be greeted by his host with a bag of tools in his hand. Would they please start off without him? He would join them on the hill when he'd fixed a burst pipe.

In 1908 his father died. By this time the craft apprentice-ship was over, for the two boys were twenty-five and twenty-one. James had already travelled about the Continent soliciting orders and been successful, at a time when work, all over the ship-building industry, had fallen off. Now, with his younger brother, he was in charge of a huge firm specializing in the manufacture of cargo ships, and with the task of holding its position as one of the greatest yards in the world. He did this and more, with the firm expanding steadily up until the outbreak of war in 1914.

Many people were caught with trousers down, and worse,

in 1914—but not James Lithgow. His firm, thanks to his uncanny ability at labour relations, his ability to do every job in a shipyard at least as well as the man who was paid to do it, and his knowledge of industry at home and abroad, was in apple-pie order and ready for work. So that, in his other role as Captain James Lithgow of the Clyde Royal Garrison Artillery (Territorial Force), he could delegate his ship-building responsibilities and get off to France just as soon as the War Office would have him. It would be a different France to the one he remembered, thirteen years ago; and shooting with a six-inch howitzer would bear little resemblance to *la chasse aux canards*; but he looked forward to it, as to every new task he undertook, with excitement.

Not that he knew he wouldn't be more valuable looking after his business at home. Henry was left behind to do this, but it was a heavy and often thankless task. Government policy towards ships and ship replacements veered drunkenly, first in one direction, then the other. There is a revealing letter James wrote to Henry, from the front, at the end of 1916:

"What you say about the present position of shipbuilding, and also the future, impresses me much and rather confirms the conclusions which I have been coming to lately with considerable reluctance.

"My views of the awful waste by the Admiralty of the productive capacity of the country at the expense primarily of the business I am now in (which now seems to have got over it) and secondly of our *own* line, which has now landed where you and I expected it—in the soup—are well known to you. Put bluntly, it does not matter a damn to us selfishly how deep in the soup it gets, as it will be all the more profitable to pull it out, but both of us can lay definite claim to having been guided by better motives in all we have done since this trouble arose.

"You are aware that I joined up in the Volunteers because I thought it was up to one of us to show an example in that line. I did not chuck it in 1908 nor since, when it was a decided tax on my time, and I did all I could to get out here last year for the very same reason. Conditions have entirely altered now. The authorities can claim whom they like for military service; three of the four juniors who came out with us are now considered fit to do my job here and the supply of such fellows is ample. I am therefore forced to the conclusion that I would be more useful helping you in our own business than messing about out here.

'I should have very much preferred that this decision should have been forced upon me by an omniscient Govt., which after all ought to know the relative value of a practical trained cargo shipbuilder who has made and intends to make the building of 'Standard' ships his life work, and a siege gunner of 18 months, or really only 9 months, standing. The trouble is, they don't——"

But it was well into 1917 before James Lithgow left the army. By that time he had been Mentioned in Despatches and awarded the Military Cross. As the varnish tends to come off all men under active service conditions, I think we may get a fairly clear picture of this Scotsman who was to become (in fact, already was) a tycoon, by two comments from men who served with him.. A staff sergeant describes an evening in France:

"There were just our lads there, and one fellow with a clarinet, and all of us singing, and Major Lithgow sitting cross-legged over a barrel of beer conducting the proceedings with a pig's trotter. We were all calling for our favourite tunes, and then somebody shouted, 'Come on, sir, what's your favourite?' The Major hesitated, and while he was making up his mind a lad at the back imitated his voice and shouted: 'Get on with the *work*!'

"There was a roar from the lot of us. 'Get on with the work' was his favourite all right! He had more energy than any officer I ever saw——"

Lithgow's departure from the army was accelerated by a wound: not a severe one, and described by himself as "a dust with a bit of a brick". The man who now left the army to sort out Britain's shipbuilding was described by a brother officer as a man who knew his own men intimately: "He usually addressed them by their christian or nickname, quite unlike anything done by the orthodox Regular. . . . As an instance of his force and ingenuity there is the story of the inherited German dugouts, with their entrances

This picture of Sir Alexander Fleming, *left*, was taken at St. Mary's Hospital, Paddington, where he discovered penicillin. Without Fleming's passion for sport — he joined St. Mary's to play water polo with them—the wonder drug might never have been discovered. Sir Robert Watson-Watt, *below left*, here addressing a wartime meeting, used his brain and rare ability to weld men into a team, to develop radar. John Buchan, *below right*, was one of the most prolific and successful of writers, yet he believed, like Sir Walter Scott, that no honest man can be only a writer. So Buchan was barrister, editor, translator, diplomat and statesman, as well as best-seller.

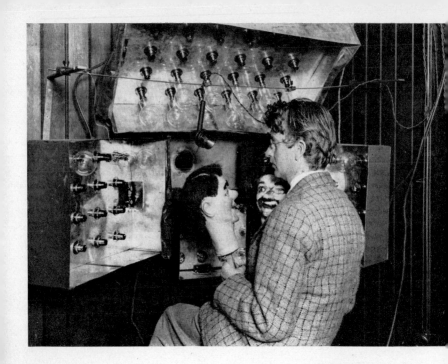

John Logie Baird, *above*, discovered television one winter's evening in late 1925 when he suddenly transmitted a perfect image of his dummy, "Bill", from one room to the next. A few months later he proudly invited the whole of the Royal Institute to come and see. To his dismay, most of them did, far more than his tiny Soho premises would hold at one time. This picture of him was taken then, with Baird seated in front of his transmitter, holding "Bill" in his hand. Although the system Baird developed was superseded by another, he rightly deserves the credit for making television possible. Sir John Reith, *right*, later Lord Reith, was one of the pioneers of broadcasting, who showed what the miracle of radio could be made to do.

pointing the wrong way, from our point of view. One day, on return from a long observation-post job, I found the mess servants and batmen sweating profusely, covered in chalky earth, but with the mess dugout re-oriented, and a demon, whiter and hotter than any there, driving them on in a manner to which by this time they had become accustomed. My principal objection to the proceedings was that I was immediately press-ganged. However, J.L. would never ask others to do what he was not prepared to do, and this always helped in our understanding of the man. . . . For quite a long time after our meeting I had no idea of the importance of J.L. in what is called the Industrial World. He was just another officer who had the ability to get a lot out of his men and yet keep them together, and who tried very hard to learn a new job. . . He had a terse way; quite an irregular one, in dealing with some of our correspondence (for which he had another word). I hesitate to repeat in writing his observation across a demand note from the Ordnance Corps which reached us on the Somme, relating to blankets lost or damaged at a time when we were training at Lydd or Portsmouth, but the matter was never heard of again——"

From the army James Lithgow went back home, but not to Port Glasgow. He had been made Director of Merchant Shipbuilding. A lifetime of public service had begun.

Shipyards which had been allowed to contract now had to expand, and rapidly: Germany's campaign of un-restricted submarine warfare had made this a matter of the first priority. The expansion duly took place, much as dugouts in France had been re-shaped, but there were far more problems than mere man-management to cope with. There were armies of Civil Servants, avalanches of official documents—and, as it turned out, so little time. The war ended, the Department of Merchant Shipbuilding closed down, and Lithgow headed for Port Glasgow. By this time his firm, which from the name of its original founder had been Russell & Company, was officially Lithgows Limited and many times the size of the original. There was more work than the firm—or any firm—could handle, with so many skilled workers still being demobbed from the forces.

But the writing which Lithgow read clearly on the wall was the hard, indeed perilous, times were ahead. The demand for ships would tail off, and the British industry which had been allowed to wither until the last year of the war, when Lithgow was able to do something to stop the process, would get only a small share of the work that was available. Fifteen million gross tons had been lost during that war (of which more than eight million were British), and although the British shipbuilding industry was smaller than it had been at the start of 1913 the world had four million tons more shipping than it had possessed in that year. Obviously, it had not been made in Britain: the American industry had multiplied its output no less than fourteen times, and other countries, Japan in particular, had expanded enormously. As soon as the bubble broke, and the sellers' market ended, Britain would feel it.

There was another factor, an important one, involved. Pneumatic tools had been invented, converting many highly skilled shipbuilding jobs into unskilled ones. Armed with such tools, the unskilled workmen of other countries who had entered the race were every bit as good as the British craftsman. During the war, with a shortage of labour in all industries, the power of workers' organizations had grown greatly, particularly in shipbuilding. A situation had now arisen where men were being paid craftsmen's wages for doing unskilled labour—wages far higher than the same tasks commanded in other countries—and refusing to step up their output. Lithgow's highly unpopular suggestion was that the job, which was far easier now than it had been, should be paid at a lower rate. The workman, *if* he paid as much attention to the new task, did it with the same care and attention as he had expended on the old one, would easily compensate himself by a greater output.

In many parts of the shipbuilding industry this advice fell on deaf ears. Within Lithgows, however, the example and leadership of the two Lithgow brothers maintained some realism: when the slump happened, it was Lithgows which not only kept going, but was able, by large injections of capital, to keep many other firms alive.

In 1920, James Lithgow became President of the Shipbuilding Employers' Federation: he was thirty-seven. His forthright views shocked almost everyone. Some of his ideas shock us still, though the motives behind them were sound and even altruistic. When the slump which he had predicted took place he was against unemployment pay, on the grounds that it killed the desire to work. He maintained, not without reason, that if men were prepared to do something different within their industry (and most jobs had now become unskilled labour, easy to learn) there would be far less unemployment. To actual cases of hardship his attitude was too paternalistic for these more enlightened days, but he expended vast sums on private, and usually anonymous, relief. He set up one of the country's first schemes to provide milk and meals for the needy.

When shipbuilding orders reached an all-time low in Port Glasgow, his firm took up shipbreaking, purely in order to keep men employed. In fact, it was impossible to keep any man employed continuously, and James Lithgow got the local authorities to draw up a rota, so that every man— or as many as humanly possible—had a spell of employment. All profits from this work went to local charity.

At forty-one, James Lithgow married, built himself a house. Like *Drums,* his previous home, it was very near his work.

At forty-two, having rejected the offer previously, he accepted a baronetcy. It coincided with a stunning blow to the morale of British shipbuilding. A shipping company— and a British one at that—had placed an order in Germany for five vessels at a price less than three-quarters of the lowest British tender. And apart from the price, it was now becoming commonplace that British shipbuilding took too long.

An opportunity to disprove this came late in 1925. James Lithgow heard that the Red Cross Shipping Line would have liked a cruise ship by the next summer, but had omitted to place the order in time and would now do without. Lithgows would show them: James offered to do the work in seven months.

For a passenger ship of 6,000 tons this was an incredibly tall order, but the contract was signed on 3 November, and under James and Henry Lithgow's example of working all hours the vessel was launched the following March. By the first week in June the *Nerissa* had completed trials and been delivered to the Line.

The Clyde was proud of itself, and of Lithgows. But in a few years' time James Lithgow would be highly unpopular.

The slump had continued and it became clear that one reason Britain was uncompetitive in world markets was that shipbuilders were trying to keep open too many uneconomic yards. Lithgows closed down some of their own, and now, in charge of the new National Shipbuilders Security, it became James Lithgow's task to suggest that other yards should suffer the same fate in order that the industry survive at all.

He pointed out that a few yards working to capacity would employ at least as many men as more yards working at less than half pressure. The task of the new N.S.S. would be to buy these uneconomic yards, close them down, allow labour to re-deploy.

But inevitably there was hardship, for many towns lived by shipbuilding alone, and were isolated from other centres. One of these was Jarrow on Tyneside. When its shipyard was closed by the N.S.S. in 1933 there was understandably great bitterness. Its Member of Parliament, Ellen Wilkinson, wrote a bitter book about it, *The Town that was Murdered*. The murderer, at least in the book, was Sir James Lithgow, Bart.

It did not go unnoticed that Lithgows had been quite busy with orders throughout all this. (Though they, too, had closed some yards.) Between 1919 and 1929 they had been building nearly two per cent of all shipping in the world. Later, in the depths of depression, Lithgows were building five per cent of world tonnage, and nearly sixty-two per cent of the Clyde's output.

He became interested in the new Scottish National Development Council, agreed to be chairman of its executive committee. As probably the most successful industrialist in Scotland he took a very important part in its work. He was insistent that those who had made their money in Scotland had an obligation to keep it there. The Council, under his guidance, set itself to encouraging Scotsmen and others to set up new industries in the country, to undertaking research into Scottish industrial problems, to simply inspiring Scotsmen with a belief in their own future. It did, and still does, remarkable work.

The great Glasgow firm of Beardmores, with its various forms of engineering activity and its vast steel foundry, fell on hard times and the Bank of England stepped in to prevent it going bankrupt. The Bank then asked that James Lithgow buy control of the firm and become its active head: otherwise it would collapse.

Lithgow left his shipyards in Port Glasgow, moved to Glasgow itself from where he could control his latest, unwanted acquisition. He had risked his personal fortune and there seemed little hope of ever making profit on the deal. It would, however—and that was the reason for his agreeing to the request—it would keep men in work.

He was now fifty-three: he set himself to learning another new job, the manufacture of steel.

A little later he took over Fairfields, in the same condition, and met all its dishonoured bills. By now the entire fortune of himself and his brother was involved in these two risky enterprises, and, if both had collapsed, James and Henry Lithgow would have joined the ranks of the unemployed. But, for these, the same quiet, anonymous schemes of welfare went on: a children's convalescent home was given to Port Glasgow, a boys' club as well. A hospital clinic went to Glasgow, and the stream of minor but individually all-important bequests continued. A man whose living depended on his barrow had it flung in the Clyde by hooligans: James Lithgow made sure he got another one and made equally sure its donor was never discovered. A church was in need of repair: Lithgow would match every pound the congregation could raise. He did, to the tune of well over a thousand pounds.

The new Iona Community was mooted. Here, in the

home of St. Columba, a new religious organization would spring up, a community of craftsmen with students of divinity, whose members would be continually replaced to go out and live in Scottish communities, and help them.

The plan was Dr. George MacLeod's and he approached Lithgow for £5,000.

"Will you give up your damned pacifism if I do?"

"Not on your life."

MacLeod got the £5,000—and the Iona Community, as we all know, has been a profound influence on religious and community life in Scotland.

The Scottish Development Council, still guided by Lithgow, staged its great Glasgow Exhibition in 1938 (with much of its design done by a new and promising architect, Basil Spence). In the concert hall of the exhibition he gave what turned out to be one of his last public speeches before that Second World War which would involve him even more deeply than the First. It was the usual hard-headed, hard-hitting setting out of facts, and it prophesied a new economic crisis as a result of Government policy:

"In industrial economics there are two schools of thought. One of these emphasizes the fact that industrial prosperity must be based on the spending power of the people. The other emphasizes the necessity for cheap production to stimulate purchasing power, not only at home, but also abroad. The fact that Britain has in recent years followed the first school of thought is clearly brought out by certain official figures——"

Perhaps the economic crisis would have come. War came instead.

And this time there was no fooling about in the trenches. Sir James Lithgow became Controller of Merchant Shipbuilding and Repairs—and a Lord of the Admiralty. Once again he moved to London, and this time there was desperate work to be done. 150,000 shipworkers had been employed in 1913. Now, in 1939, the number had shrunk to 26,000.

The first thing was to use the existing capacity in the most intelligent way, and to this end it was divided into three sectors. Yards most suited for the work would build naval craft; others, standard merchant vessels; others would deal with repairs. And very soon it became necessary to strengthen the repairs sector. An extra ten thousand men were brought into the repair yards, and new techniques increased the output per man. With a labour force smaller than in the First World War, the rate of ship-repairing in the Second was higher.

There is a characteristic remark of Lithgow's which I think is worth quoting. He had a team at the Admiralty, and sometimes, when he was busy, these younger men would have to take his place at important meetings. One of them suggested that, really, they weren't senior enough to make important decisions.

"You're representing me," came the reply. "And that means you're on a high enough level to decide anything. The whole bunch of you are on a low enough level to know what the hell you're talking about."

He held down this vitally important job till the end of the war, combining other functions from time to time, like heading the Tank Division of the Ministry of Supply at a time of grave and sudden shortage. And throughout he refused to take any salary from the Government.

He refused, too, to be recommended for a peerage: a man who accepted one ought to attend the House of Lords and do something constructive there: James Lithgow was a builder of ships.

He went back to it.

A great sorrow in 1948: his brother Henry died. And within a week of the funeral the Inland Revenue in Edinburgh were startled to receive the largest cheque it had ever seen: £2,000,000 of death duty.

James Lithgow's life had less than another four years to run. He died, still in harness, on 23 February, 1952.

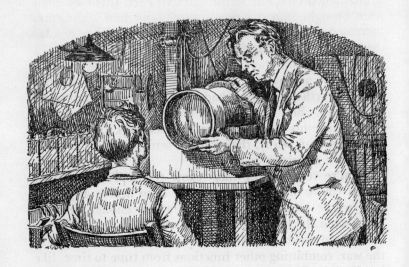

JOHN LOGIE BAIRD

In May, 1941, the B B C organ *Radio Times* ran an article on television. "A week or two ago, we made a mention of colour television. Now we have seen it for ourselves. John Logie Baird gave us a demonstration of the system on which he is now working; he has been using colour television in one form or another since 1928. He is now using 600 lines, which is very much higher than the standard officially fixed for black-and-white television at Alexandra Palace before the service was closed down by the outbreak of war."

And now, twenty-odd years later, how much farther have we got?

But John Logie Baird, inventor-by-necessity (it was the only job his health would permit, and he set himself to it as another man might become a writer), Baird has received very little credit for the fact that he showed the world's first colour television. And—far more important—that he showed the first moving television picture of any sort.

He was—obviously—a remarkable man. Without him, television, though it might exist in a practical form today, would almost certainly be less developed, less efficient. He gave it a head-start, for like Marconi he was able to sift out the ideas of other men, improve and expand them into something remarkable and worthwhile.

Unfortunately for Baird, his mind, his inventor's, innovator's, mind was far too active. Stages in the development of his telly brainchild (and no one west of the Iron Curtain is likely to deny him paternity) which he should have followed up himself, or at least kept under the closest personal control, were often left to subordinates, while the brilliant J. L. Baird rushed on with newer, better ideas. We do not know which of these it was that the *Radio Times* raved over in 1941, but a year previous to that Baird himself described his new "Deluxe Superscreen Teleradiogram". It showed a picture two feet six inches square, and was fitted with push-buttons. These brought into action an all-wave radio set; an automatic record-changing gramophone, the BBC Television Programme, the "Baird Colour Television Programme" *and* the "Baird Stereoscopic Television Programme". We are still many years short of this sort of thing, at least as a commercial proposition. But had Baird settled for a little bit less, like cutting out his Stereoscopic programme, we might well have been seeing colour television in Britain for many years.

But Baird, though he liked money and what it could buy at least as much as the rest of us, was the least commercial of men. With a lot more business acumen, coupled with a realization that first things, in commerce, come first, he would have died a very rich man. He would almost certainly have become a peer, too. Though I like to think of him as the shy and brilliant Mr. Baird, with the short sight which occasioned that first, terrifying, meeting with John Reith—on another page—I cannot think of him as Lord Baird of Gogglebox.

He died in 1946—neither a rich man nor a very famous one. He might have been amused to see how famous he then became.

But back to the beginning. He was born in 1888, and like a surprising number of those in these pages, Reith included, he was a son of the manse. Sometimes that seems almost a first ticket towards fame. His father was minister of the West Parish Church of Helensburgh on the Clyde. Young John seems to have been a normal lad with a slightly precocious interest in technology; with another boy he made a life-size aeroplane, or at least, in his own words, "a weird contraption, two box kites joined in the centre". It was only a year or two after the thrilling first exploits of the Wright brothers, and like them John and his friend Godfrey planned to glide first, then attach an engine and really fly.

But here we get an insight into Baird's character; the frankness, the modesty—which gives more than a clue to his failure in later life. For frankness and modesty, as distinct from an appearance of both these attractive attributes, are, sadly, two qualities least wanted in the tough, twentieth-century world of commerce, or most other worlds. Did Baird fly, taking his life in both hands, and of his own free will? Not likely; he'd had no intention of risking his neck, he tells us; that was for young Godfrey. Baird just happened to be on board their wondercraft when "Godfrey gave the machine one terrific push and I was launched, shouting, into the air. I had a very few nauseating seconds while the machine rocked wildly and then broke in half and deposited me with a terrific bump on the lawn."

And he never, ever, had any further desire to fly.

From local school to the Royal Technical College, Glasgow. Here, though he worked extremely hard, for he was poor and desperately needed a good job at the far end of the tunnel, he did badly. This was largely owing to the ill-health which dogged him throughout his life—and to which, in a way, we owe television. He eventually completed the course and persuaded his parents to let him use the Associateship of the Technical College he had thus acquired to go and work for a B.Sc. at Glasgow University.

This was 1912. Two years later, the First World War broke out. Urged by a sense of duty and what he described later as "possibly the desire to appear well in the eyes of my friends", he offered himself to the army and was smartly rejected. The army had no time to waste on someone who was so obviously a candidate for the sick-bay.

He completed his University course and took a job as electrical supply engineer. It was miserable work, rushing out to deal with mains failures and the like, at all hours of the day and night, and his health suffered. But it was a vicious circle, which his boss summed up in a memo: "We cannot give Baird a better job: he's always ill."

So he left. Anything must be better than this—and the "anything" which John Logie Baird chose was to be a professional inventor. He would start by improving and marketing other people's ideas and the first one he selected was a formula for easing the discomfort of haemorrhoids. No doubt it is as well for posterity's legend of John Logie Baird that his cure was a flop and was hastily withdrawn

But the pattern is emerging.

From pile cures to diamonds, which would be home-made from carbon. His idea, though chemically sound, was another failure, so he rushed on to make and market "The Baird Undersock". This would be "Medicated, Absorbent and Soft, keeping the Feet Warm in Winter and Cool in Summer. Ninepence per pair, Post free."

After a shaky start (the newspaper advertisement cost thirty shillings and it sold one pair of socks for ninepence), he actually began to make a success of the idea. But once again ill-health struck him down: he suffered so long and so severely from a cold, with the one-man business vanishing behind his back, that he gave it up. When he recovered from the cold he realized it was time for another dramatic interference with his own destiny. He spent all his sock-profit on a one-way ticket to Trinidad. Here at least he would be warm and well.

Like an early explorer, he took with him cases full of trinkets to sell to the natives. We have no space to go into his performance as a businessman in the Caribbean paradise, but we must register that as a trader Baird was a flop. He sold his stock at a thumping loss—and then rushed on, with the same youthful enthusiasm, to start a jam factory.

Here everything possible went wrong: enormous ants stormed in and made off with a hundredweight of sugar overnight; the jam (and the chutney and the syrup and the jelly) filled up with loathsome insects. Small wonder that he had the greatest difficulty in selling any.

Ill-health again and on his recovery he decided to set sail for England, bearing tins of his product, to sell in Britain.

We need not consider what happened. After some more disasters—and one or two very near misses in which he *almost* laid his hands on a fortune—Baird found himself in 1923, aged thirty-five, in Hastings, on the south coast. Here, even without much money, he would have fresh air and sunlight. And here he would settle down and really be an inventor, not just a marketer of other people's ideas.

He sat down and started inventing.

Glass razor-blades were among the earliest of his inventions. They were a disastrous precursor of today's blades of stainless steel, and they were quickly followed up by pneumatic shoes like car tyres and intended for the same purpose, to give a smooth ride; but they had the unfortunate result of making the pedestrian seem very drunk indeed.

And then suddenly he remembered an idea which had popped in and out of his fertile mind many times since childhood: pictures by radio.

And this—as we now all know—worked. Somehow Baird seems to have known it would, and he put all his energies into this one exciting idea, forgot all about razor-blades and socks and jam: he would send a picture by wire—and soon.

But although Baird made something practical out of it, the idea of sending pictures along wires and even through the air had been in the minds of others for years, ever since Marconi had sent his first radio message. The German Paul Nipkow had produced his Nipkow disc by the time Baird turned his brain to the idea, and this disc was, in its crude way, the forerunner of all television. By punching holes in a certain way round the periphery of a cardboard disc, Nipkow found he could illuminate an object in front of the disc with a light from behind it; illuminate in a series of tiny points of light which scanned the object from top to bottom and from side to side. If this illumination of, say, a human head could be picked up by a light-sensitive device, a photo-electric cell, the consecutive points of light, each of varying intensity depending on the light and shade of each part of the face, could be sent along a wire as separate electric pulses, of different strength. If these pulses could then be converted back into light, through a bulb, and re-constituted by a similar disc, in the right order, flashing the points of light on a screen, the original object—the human head—would be reproduced on it. And if the two discs revolved fast enough, spattered their points of light fast enough to make use of the eyes' natural persistence of vision, the picture would seem complete, not just a series of dots.

Nipkow's apparatus was far too primitive to transmit anything recognizable, but the principle was sound, and it was this that Baird set out to develop. He worked out a plan of scanning so that the dots moved from left to right in horizontal lines, thirty of them, one line below the other, to fill up a frame. (The BBC now uses 625 lines, but in exactly this way.) The frame itself would be swept away to make room for another, many times a second, like successive pictures in a cine film.

Baird put immense concentration into the task: he experimented with different-size discs, with different numbers of holes, different speeds of rotation; and with different photo-electric devices. And at last, to his unspeakable joy, he was able to transmit along a pair of wires, the shadow of a small Maltese cross.

Others had been working along these lines in different parts of the world—but Baird was way out in front.

But now troubles began with Mr. Twigg, his landlord in Hastings. Mr. Twigg was shocked and alarmed at the dangerous nature of the experiments he believed were being carried on upstairs, and a fierce argument ended in Baird's removal to London. But there is now a plaque mounted on the wall of that little Hastings shop above which Baird had his lab. It reads: "Television, first demonstrated by John Logie Baird, from experiments started here in 1924."

These experiments were now continued in an attic at Number 22 Frith Street in Soho, while Baird himself lodged out at Ealing. So far he had little more than the transmission of a small cross to his credit, but he had an absolute faith in himself and knew, somehow, that the rest would follow. But he must have money. He canvassed prominent people and newspapers, most of whom dismissed him as a lunatic. But gradually interest grew, and some rash folk even invested a little money into his invention. He was helped by the enterprise of Gordon Selfridge, who wanted a demonstration of something exciting for his big London shop's Birthday Week. For the princely sum of £20 a week, for three weeks, Baird eagerly demonstrated his toy, and puzzled customers bent down to marvel over silhouettes transmitted a number of yards along a mere piece of flex.

Two far-sighted commercial firms now came to the rescue: one, having failed to sell the penniless inventor £200 worth of batteries, gave them to him; and another gave him valuable valves.

And on a winter's evening in 1925—break-through:

The evening before, he had run through a whole chain of experiments and tests. He had altered the equipment a dozen times, replaced almost all of it. The only survivor was Bill, the mute, sympathetic witness who had attended every experiment since the transmission, more than a year back, of the Maltese cross. Bill was a dummy.

He sat Bill up in his chair, switched on the apparatus and walked into the next room.

There he tuned in his receiver, got a pink rectangle in the viewing box, focused it. He ran back to the other room, adjusted the light over Bill's head.

Back to the receiver. Now the pink glow was streaked with black bars. There was always a few seconds of this, while receiver and transmitter got into sync. After this, if things went as usual, there would be Bill, just a black-and-white, fuzzy-sided silhouette. Not a picture at all.

Suddenly the picture locked, the bars vanished, and Baird gasped. There Bill was. Bill in his viewing box—but not just a black-and-white outline, a child's drawing: he was there, every feature recognizable, eyebrows thick and curving, head correctly rounded.

Baird tore down the steps to the floor below and burst in on William (whom we must not confuse with Bill), the office boy of the firm downstairs. William was sorting envelopes and he looked up in some surprise as the "mad Scotch inventor" from upstairs burst in.

In a few moments he had been persuaded to leave the envelopes, and shaking his head he followed Baird up the steps to his lab. A flick of the wrist and the dummy was on the floor, grinning at the ceiling. A moment later William was in his place. "Still still—that's all. Sit *still*——" Baird was off.

But this was dreadful. A moment ago there had been a picture. Now there was nothing. He tore back, ready to put the dummy back in his seat, send William back to his envelopes. Then he saw what was wrong.

"I *know* it's hot—but you've got to sit up, just where I put you. Look, here's half a crown——"

Back to the receiver, heart pounding.

And there, in that other room, was the office-boy's face: puzzled, indignant, but there, with every part of his round face clear and in focus, correctly shaded.

And William, this young man whose face was the first ever to be seen on television—and who, a moment later, when they reversed roles, became the second man in history to see television, went back, grumbling, to his envelopes.

So this was it! No need to go back to jam and undersocks now.

He worked harder still, for many weeks. Then, in

January 1926, he recklessly issued an invitation to the Royal Institute in London—all of it—urging it to come to a demonstration.

He was shocked at the large number which did so, and they were shocked at the smallness of his premises, but somehow the demonstration was shown to all of them. Bill's face and those of distinguished scientists were transmitted, time and again, from one room to the next.

Baird had demonstrated real television. The next step was to send these visual images over a distance, and now he received welcome help from the Chief Engineer of the BBC (still the infant British Broadcasting Company). They let him send his picture along telephone wires to a BBC studio and then put it out on the air for him. Baird himself picked it up on a receiver at 22 Frith Street, and was overjoyed to find his picture "practically unaltered" by what the BBC had done to it.

But he wouldn't be able to use BBC transmitters for ever: they had other things to do; and if he used them after late-night close-down someone would have to pay the staff that manned them. If Baird wanted to go on transmitting television signals into the air he would have to build his own transmitter, and get it licensed.

He did—and 2TV became the first licensed television station—indeed the first television station, licensed or no— in the world. He moved from Frith Street to slightly larger accommodation near Leicester Square, built his transmitter there and received the pictures on receiving apparatus in Harrow, ten miles away.

Flushed with excitement, he rounded up a few partners and formed Television Limited.

It seemed as if the whole world were at his feet. Early in 1928 he transmitted a picture across the Atlantic, and a little later to the liner *Berengaria* in mid-ocean.

But now his luck turned—and Baird's bitter words tell us why:

"If an inventor reads these pages, let him by this be admonished and do what Graham Bell, inventor of the telephone, did, and sell for cash. Inventors are no match for financiers where stocks and shares are concerned, and will, if they hold on, find that the financiers have the cash and they have the paper."

John Baird made little money out of his invention. Partly through his lack of business ability, partly through bad luck, he found others reaping the benefit of his work. When he died in 1946 he was not the rich man he had hoped to be. It has been said that he "sold himself to Mammon" too soon; if he had not allowed unsuitable people to take shares in his invention at too early a stage he would have retained greater control over it. He might have convinced John Reith, the daunting head of the BBC, that this was a discovery which needed to be used, and used soon, which wasn't a commercial stunt. As it was, the BBC, after taking years to work up a real interest in television, or agree to any system of transmission, finally settled on another one which had been developed after Baird's and yet which owed its very existence to those early experiments in Hastings and Soho.

He was disappointed, terribly disappointed—but he went right on inventing. Colour TV, stereoscopic TV (which we may never have a chance to see, but which worked well when Baird demonstrated it), large-screen TV, TV-on-your-telephone: all these things Baird worked on, made work.

Yet he died, if not exactly a poor man, a lot less rich than he might have been. In fact, at one stage, a very early stage, he had been offered £125,000 for his shares in his own Baird Television. This he characteristically refused by saying: "I just wouldn't know what to do with that sort of money; why, I'd not be able to sleep at night." So he hung on, hacking a way for others.

He died after yet another of the severe bronchial troubles which had plagued him from childhood (the trouble which had driven Alexander Graham Bell from Britain to invent the telephone in America). He was buried near where he had been born, in the little churchyard at Helensburgh, on the Clyde.

Five years went by.

And then, quite suddenly, another plaque in his memory went up. This man who had demonstrated television in black-and-white, in colour, in relief and—at the very end of his life—in the dark (using infra-red rays to transmit a picture of something the human eye could not see), John Logie Baird was acknowledged as the Man who Invented Television.

JOHN CHARLES REITH, FIRST BARON OF STONEHAVEN

"I met Reith for the first time in rather unfavourable circumstances. I was always very short-sighted, and at the beginning of one of the classes the Professor asked if those who were short-sighted and wanted front seats would hand in their names. When I went up to the platform to hand in my own, three large, impressive young students were talking to him. They were talking on terms of equality. As I did so, the heaviest and most overpowering of the three 'heavies' turned round and boomed at me, 'Ha! What is the matter with you?'"

The words are John Logie Baird's, and it would seem that throughout his life poor Baird, inventor of television, was in awe of the enormous fellow- countryman on whom—or so Baird thought—so much of his future depended.

So much has been said and written about Lord Reith;
he is such a part of life in Britain, such a national institution, that while one may not be able to add to the sum of
human knowledge on this sometimes controversial subject
one could no more omit such a towering twentieth-century
personality from a collection of Famous Scottish Lives than
leave out Robert Burns.

The BBC has had a number of chiefs since Reith's day,
some of them providing almost as much material for staff
humour and "In" jokes as the First of All. The Reith legend
were often built around the presumed piety of the great
man, and like all good legends—though this is not to question that piety—they were largely untrue. I suppose my
favourite is of the occasion he descended on Broadcasting
House late one evening and was taken round the studios.
A play was going out, and the Continuity Announcer, who
therefore had nothing to do till the end, when he would
intone "That was——", seemed to have vanished.

Suddenly, to the horror of the middle-man who was conducting his Director-General, the announcer was discovered behind an acoustic screen in the arms of a young
woman.

Middle-man and Reith—so legend runs—turned around
with dignity and left the studio. They walked in terrifying
silence for hundreds of yards through the battleship interior of B.H., and then the middle-man turned, pale and
trembling, and said to his superior:

"Sorry about that, sir. Very bad show."

"Indeed, yes. And just who *was* that—er—young man?"

The middle-man told him.

"I see." Reith turned on his heel. "Well, he must *neverrrr
neverrrr* be permitted to read the Epilogue."

That was years ago. Nowadays reputations crumple more
easily, mean less in the first place. Nobody cares, and
nobody would bother to make up a story like that. Not long
ago I was on the third floor of Broadcasting House, where
an inches-thick blue carpet outside the lift signifies that one
is within yards of the present Director-General's office. It
was late at night and no one—not even the prowling shade

of that first D.G.—was about the passages. The very young man who was with me went up to a handsome bronze bust on a stand just outside the D.G.'s locked door. Of course, it was Reith. Suddenly he stuffed an arm up inside it. There was a sound like a distant dinner gong.

"The Head of Our Founder," he said with a grin. "Quite, quite, hollow."

In fact, no description of John Reith could be less apposite. If ever there was a man who never stopped thinking, or doing, it was Reith.

There are many contradictions about him. One is that he never appeared to give a damn what the other fellow thought, or did, as long as he, Reith did what he felt was right. And in the case of poor old Baird, to whom the terrifying meetings and negotiations with the then Director-General of the BBC seemed a matter almost of life and death, the little man seems scarcely to have registered at all. It was decided not to use his method of television transmission: that's all there was to it.

In Reith's fascinating autobiography, *Into the Wind*, there are 236 pages dealing almost exclusively with the BBC from its inception (when he took command) to the day in 1938 that he left. On not one of those pages is Baird mentioned: that name which was a household word when the BBC led the world in T.V., in the 'thirties, is not in the index, or anywhere else.

Baird obviously made no impression at all: Reith did what he thought was right.

But within the pages of that autobiography there are a surprising number of testimonials to the author, quoted at length. Things like "Even those not given to hero-worship can look upon Sir John Reith as one of the few really great men of our time——"; By your own efforts you have done more than tongue can tell——"; "Vehement, determined, aggressive, masterful, capable of thinking and administering on the big scale——". Example after example of this sort of thing, with the comments, as well, of two British Prime Ministers, Ramsay MacDonald and Stanley Baldwin, about the great difficulties of being Prime Minister. One is quoted as saying to Reith, "Maybe you'll find out for your-self one day"; the other, on a later occasion, remarks, "Perhaps *you'll* find that, some day".

There is also a rather baffling document, quoted in its entirety as a "Testimonial" from three Glasgow University students, fellow members of the Officers' Training Corps. One of them was O. H. Mavor, soon to become the play-wright James Bridie. They testify that Reith is the "only sergeant in the Corps with the smallest right to pretensions of honour, manliness or good fellowship . . . we could go further, but our pen is done". It is oddly reminiscent of what three other Glasgow University Students had done to William McGonagall, Poet and Tragedian, whose story is on another page.

So it seems the biographer is left with a man of intelligence, moral fibre, organising ability, refusing to suffer fools gladly or at all—and aware of all this. And probably no other man could have piloted the infant British Broadcasting Company, and the Corporation it became, piloted it through the shoals; could have dealt with little prime ministers, little kings, and got his way. This is no place for a write-up of the BBC, but few would deny that what it is today, from the accepted impartiality of its news to its often outrageous debunking programmes in which no person or institution is safe, it owes in some measure to John Reith. As a Canadian newspaper suggested not long ago, during a long article about the excitement for Canadians of short-wave listening: "Whizz round the dial and hear what's happening, from Washington, from Paris, Moscow, Peking, Bonn. And then, to find out what *really* happened, tune to London."

The first Baron Reith of Stonehaven could hardly ask for a more suitable scroll on his coat-of-arms.

But enough, for the moment, of the BBC. John Reith was there for rather less than sixteen years. What about the rest of him?

For what he looked like—still looks like—we can do no better than turn to John Logie Baird again. This is Reith, observed during a confrontation over the future of television: "A large gaunt frame surmounted by a grim, rugged visage, surmounted in turn by a domed forehead, rendered more impressive by a heavy scar."

He was born in 1889, son of a minister of the Church of Scotland. After eight years at Glasgow Academy he was sent for another two to an English public school, Gresham's School, in Norfolk. Thence to Glasgow Technical College, as prelude to what was intended to be a career in engineering. It was at the Tech that the class-room meeting with Baird took place, and as we know that he would have preferred to do almost anything else—preferably academic—than be pushed into engineering, he must have been unhappy at the time. His father had decreed that every man, whatever his inclinations, should learn a trade. At his English public school he had enjoyed being a member of the Corps, had become a sergeant. In Glasgow he kept up his military hobby with the University O.T.C.—where he received his Testimonial. Early in 1914, aged twenty-four, he travelled south to London in search of a job, and got it with Pearson's, the big civil engineers. This was pleasing, up to a point, for he was glad to be out of mechanical engineering, able to deal with bridges, not boiler-rooms.

In 1911 he had been commissioned in the Volunteers—the 5th Scottish Rifles—and on the outbreak of war in 1914 he eagerly reported to them. After the initial confusion of mobilization he was finally settled in as commander of the transport section with the privilege of "wearing spurs". And the little phrase has given a title to a delightful book he wrote about that military life.

He was transferred, because of his specialist knowledge and his inclinations, to the Royal Engineers, and it was with them in October, 1915, that he was badly wounded. He made an astonishing recovery from a head wound, demanded to be sent back to the front, but was invalided out of the service.

His senior at Pearson's, E. W. Moir, had been ordered to the United States to organize munitions supply, and now, at Moir's request, young Reith went along as his assistant. The job seems to have involved travelling about American munitions factories and checking on the suitability of what was being manufactured for the British services. He spent eighteen months in America and liked it enormously. Always in later life he welcomed opportunity to go back.

But he had his reservations about American big business —and these must have considerably influenced him when British broadcasting began.

War ended and he found himself, after some indecision, working as General Manager of a big engineering firm in Scotland—William Beardmore and Co. It was not what he had in mind as life's work, and in 1922 he resigned.

And it was in October of that year that he saw the advertisement for a General Manager to take charge of the new "British Broadcasting Company (In Formation)".

As everyone knows, he got the job, and he literally made the Company. The history of the BBC from Company in 1922 to Corporation in 1927, to its present position in the late 1960s, has already been well documented. We may sum up, if we wish, by saying that Reith, in the course of his fifteen and a half years in broadcasting, created and developed a broadcasting system for the British Isles which was to foreshadow the modern pattern of publicly owned but independent utility corporations, from the Tennessee Valley Authority to British Overseas Airways; he started an Empire broadcasting service on short waves; and he instituted the first regular service in the world of high-definition television—way back in 1936.

Reith fought not only for what he felt was right—and fought like a tiger—but for his employees (which is not always the same thing). He defended them to the hilt in their work; and workers in a monopoly system of broadcasting, completely surrounded by a Press which understandably wants to set up in opposition, with "a licence to print money", often need defence.

Early in 1936, John Reith cut out and kept a Buckingham Palace announcement of a dinner party at which "Mr. and Mrs. Ernest Simpson" had been present. At the end of the year he was making the arrangements for Edward VIII's Abdication Speech.

Those who heard that speech may recall a loud bump near the beginning. Reith, who announced the king himself, was accused of saying his piece and banging the door as he went out. But in fact the noise was caused by the royal knee coming in contact with the table-leg.

He had been knighted in 1927, when the original Company became a Corporation. The peerage, as Lord Reith, was to come thirteen years later, in 1940, some two years after he had left the BBC; so it is as Sir John that he is remembered; the idea of having a Baron-in-charge-of-Broadcasting is tempting and one wonders what the Press might have done with it.

In 1938, with his BBC running smoothly, he felt in need of new worlds to conquer. From a figure of 36,000 wireless licence holders, when he and another three men had set up their embryo Company, to 8,700,000 licences when he decided to leave, the expansion, the progress, had been almost continuous. It would be—and was—a great wrench to leave what he had come to regard as his life's work, but he did it. His description of going down to Droitwich on his last evening, driving in and asking to close down the big oil engines of the high-power transmitter, is moving. On he goes, to Daventry, driving through the night, dawn climbing up into the sky as he gets there; and the red lights on the aerial masts switch off. No need to ask how to deal with the mechanism, for this broadcaster started life dealing with it. "A new day was breaking for Daventry and the BBC. In it I was nothing and nobody to Daventry and the BBC."

Perhaps not—but the world would be hearing more from John Reith. He had accepted the post of Chairman of Imperial Airways, an organization badly in need of his help, and a little later he was responsible for its merging with British Airways to become B.O.A.C.

War came; with it more demand for his services. He became successively Minister of Information, Minister of Transport, Minister of Works and Buildings. The peerage came in 1940 and he chose his tiny East Coast birthplace for the title 1st Baron Reith of Stonehaven. In 1942—great disappointment. Churchill, with whom he never saw eye-to-eye, dismissed him from his ministry. Determined to keep working "at full stretch", he joined the R.N.V.R. For the first eight months he organized the desperately urgent business of repairing coastal craft. By 1944 he had become Director of Combined Operations Material.

In 1945 he became Chairman of the Commonwealth Telecommunications Conference, and from the next year until 1950 was Chairman of the Commonwealth Tele-communications Board, responsible for the re-ordering of all cable and wireless systems in the British Commonwealth, a job of the utmost complexity.

Since then, there have been many public appointments—and, from 1953, directorships in commerce. His auto-biography, *Into the Wind*, was published in 1949 and, in 1960, *Wearing Spurs*. At the close of 1966 he had the great satisfaction of becoming Lord Rector of Glasgow University.

During his years in the BBC he had found time to write his highly entertaining reminiscence, *Wearing Spurs*. It is typical of the man that he hid it in a drawer lest it cause embarrassment to the great institution of which he was Director-General, and only published it in 1960, after yet another war had come and gone. Perhaps he was right; for the image of stern rectitude which the BBC had somehow built up between wars might have been confused by the reminiscences of a founder who clearly loved "wearing spurs"—a man who would have made an unorthodox and highly successful general.

SIR ROBERT WATSON-WATT

To many of us born between the two World Wars, the battle of Britain remains not only one of the fixed points in history, but an event surpassing in importance Waterloo, Thermopylae, and the invention of the steam engine.

Odd, in fact, that the outcome of the Battle of Britain should have been so influenced by a direct descendant of the developer of that steam engine, James Watt—usually credited with being its inventor—whose story is on another page. Robert Watson-Watt, like his ancestor James, was not exactly the inventor of radar, but he did more than any other single man to develop it, make it effective.

Did, in short, more than any other single man to win that Battle of Britain.

As he himself has listed it, success in that battle is owed, first to the fighter pilots themselves whose courage and training outfought the Germans; second, to the Spitfire and Hurricane aircraft which gave them some small advantage over their opposite numbers in Messerschmitts; and thirdly to the effectiveness of what would some day be called radar.

Not that it was, at the time: by the time somebody thought up the word, the battle had been won.

Few of us, I imagine, who watched the vapour trails four and five miles above our heads in 1940 knew what part radar was playing in the battle we observed from down below, knew that a large number of that ragged-seeming German bomber formation had been intercepted and shot down over the English Channel, before entering English skies. We had little idea that the formation had been detected by some magic device which saw through mist and fog and darkness to pinpoint an enemy formation—or even a single aircraft—even before it had left the coast of France; and could direct the Spitfires on to it.

For that matter, hardly any of us knew that the aircraft alert at eleven a.m. on the Sunday, that Sunday, 3 September, of Mr. Chamberlain's declaration of war, had been caused by the effective functioning of this new device. Captain de Brantes, the Assistant French Military Attaché, was returning by air from France and had omitted to tell anyone of his plan. Radio-location (to give it the name it enjoyed at the time) picked up this one small aeroplane as it left the French coast—and the rest is history. Fortunately for the gallant captain and for Anglo-French relations, his identity was revealed before a flight of Hurricanes dropped him in the Channel.

Before we look at the father of radio-location, let us examine the child.

Radio waves—short ones, long ones, and those in between, all travel at the speed of light—to which, of course, they are close cousins. In our own archaic units of measurement this speed is 186,000 miles a second. In more enlightened lands, and in our own laboratories, this is shown more conveniently as 300 million metres a second. Furthermore, the speed is constant, so that when a radio voice says,

"Here is the news"—we know that those words are flying through space at this very great speed; they are not slowing down as they travel, like a cricket ball, or a bullet. And therefore, if by some means we can measure the time it takes for the words to reach us, we can easily calculate just how far away the radio station is.

We can, too, by the simple expedient of turning our portable radio to face in different directions till we hear the News at its loudest, get a reasonably accurate idea of the direction the waves are coming from. This latter principle had been in use for many years before real radio-location put in an appearance. A ship, without getting involved in the computer-arithmetic of micro-seconds which would tell it how far it was steaming from a shore trans-mitting station, could still plot its own position on a chart by taking bearings on two or more such stations. Where the lines drawn along the appropriate bearings from, say, Cardiff and Bristol, crossed on the chart—that was the ship's position.

So we can see that the theory behind this distance-and-direction-finding by radio was not exactly new.

But this, of course, is not to belittle the remarkable experi-mental physicist who had the vision, the drive, and above all, the patience, to make something out of it. A part of the secret of radio-location's success lies in the personality of the man himself. Robert Watson-Watt knew he was right, knew he was going to make it work and work well. He also knew he would be able to make others see his point, and do something about developing his brain child.

In this major respect Watson-Watt differs from Baird. He had the Scots pugnacity to go with his imagination. Without the combination he might well never have suc-ceeded in getting the all-out support of his government to make his brain-child grow—and earn its keep.

In the United States, men like Hoyt Taylor were work-ing along much the same lines, but the U.S. Government, on this occasion, made little effort to help them. Even despite the successes of British radio-location during the first two years of war, successes which were freely acknowledged by

American observers, Pearl Harbour, on its fatal day, was equipped with out-of-date and inadequate equipment, which was manned by unskilled operators. These in turn were mistrusted by those to whom they passed on their reports. A flight of about a dozen American B17 bombers was expected in from San Francisco: when something like ten times this number of aircraft were shown as coming from the opposite direction no one believed it. And so Pearl Harbour nearly died.

Robert Watson-Watt was born 13 April, 1892, at Brechin in the County of Angus, down in that eastern corner north of the Tay, where so many of our famous people seem to have been born. His father was a carpenter and by hard work the boy got himself via Brechin High School to University College, Dundee, a part of the University of St. Andrews. At the age of twenty, armed with his B.Sc., he was teaching physics at the same University College.

But shortly afterwards he was invited to join the Meteorological Office of the new Royal Aircraft Establishment at Farnborough: he accepted with some misgiving, though the prospects seemed good, for a study of wind and rain seemed at a far remove from the heavy engineering which had been his first love.

Fortunately for all of us, the job young Watson-Watt was given to do caught his imagination and, though he could hardly have spotted the similarity at first, was closely involved with the principles on which he would some day develop his radio-location. The Royal Aircraft Establishment wanted to be able to warn aircraft of thunderstorms, and to this end Watson-Watt began to experiment with atmospherics. As we all know, these are picked up by radio receivers and are at their worst during thunderstorms—for a flash of lightning is about the biggest atmospheric with which we have to deal.

The system of radio direction-finding, whereby, as we've seen, a ship can plot its position by taking bearings of two radio stations, can be adapted so that two receivers and aerials can take the bearings of a single radio station and plot its position. In the same way—at least in theory—the position of a flash of lightning could be found, however far away, or even out of sight.

There are obvious difficulties about this: lightning doesn't stay still, waiting to be measured. But now Robert Watson-Watt set about his strange new hobby of chasing these lightning flashes. It was a prospect that would have daunted most scientists because of the practical difficulties involved, but to Watson-Watt this was only a challenge to be met.

He thought about it—and wrote to the BBC. Would they let him have the text of a series of talks which were going to be given by Sir Walford Davies, Master of the King's Musick? They would be called "Music and the Ordinary Listener".

Obviously, you say, the man was mad.

But he was not. It *was* just this Ordinary Listener he wanted, and now Watson-Watt persuaded him—a whole army of him—to listen to the talks, script in hand. As he described it himself, each listener would mark on his copy of the script the "syllables which were mutilated by atmospherics as he listened; the relative intensity of the atmospheric was indicated by the number of lines he drew through the syllable; the duration of the disturbance was recorded by making the lines begin and end on the syllables on which audible disturbances began and ended. Disturbances falling between words were indicated by crosses, of size roughly proportional to intensity, in the appropriate places."

This strange team of co-opted scientists, all over Britain, listened for ten minutes on each of seven evenings during the summer of 1926. The information the team provided was so revealing that the net was then spread far wider, from North Africa to Norway, Ireland to Germany. The findings revealed that many of the atmospherics audible on ordinary broadcast receivers came from as far away as *4,500 miles.*

Not content with them, Watson-Watt embarked on a cruiser, H.M.S. *Yarmouth*, to pursue his lightning flashes round the world as far as the Bay of Bengal. On his return he disembarked in Egypt and went with his wife to Cairo and Khartoum to take observations from both these points.

The scientific work went on, and many developments in weather forecasting as well as aerial navigation stem from it, but now, in the start of 1935, he got a strange request from the British Government.

Did Mr. Watson-Watt have any ideas about a Death Ray?

Those of us who remember those 'tween-war years will remember that one of the many things which (like today's H-bomb) would "make war impossible, unthinkable" was the "Death Ray". Oh, it was a terrible thing, the Death Ray; not only had it "in secret trials" killed people at great distances (apparently they were condemned murderers who were given this splendid chance of serving king and country), but the Rays would ground the whole of an enemy air force, paralyse an army's transport, by short-circuiting ignition systems. As for the enemy's ammunition, if he still had the heart to want to use any after all these distressing setbacks, that could be exploded by Death Rays long before he got round to loading it up.

The only trouble with the Death Ray was that it did not exist. And now Robert Watson-Watt pointed out that it almost certainly never would.

Then, as an afterthought, he wrote in his report to the government that there was a good chance of using a "ray" to spot the position of enemy aircraft, a form of "radio-location", seeing through cloud or darkness. He added this rider merely in order to relieve some of the gloom of his report; the government had wanted its Death Ray; he could not produce one, but as a sop he offered a Detection Ray.

The result was a government request for enlightenment, preferably by demonstration. And this, at remarkably short notice, Watson-Watt arranged.

There are, at this very moment, many short-wave radio transmitters at Daventry and other places, beaming programmes from Britain in many languages to many parts of the world. In 1935 there were fewer of them, but Watson-

Two widely separated moments in a great life. Queen Elizabeth the Queen Mother on the steps of the Sydney Town Hall in 1958, as Australians in their thousands cheered a brave and gracious lady. *Below*, as the young Duchess of York, she had endeared herself to people with the same calm naturalness of manner—and in doing so had enormously helped her husband. Between these two pictures there is a career —unwanted, yet superbly carried out—as a queen.

"Harold Macmillan may be the last of the suave, almost courtly, British statesmen; the sort of man who can turn up in Moscow wearing an astra-khan hat, or sit cross-legged with a Middle - Eastern sheik without losing his dignity." Even here, *right*, where he is being mightily heckled and is showing the appropriate scorn, one sees a wise—and suave—man, completely under control.

The eighteenth-century architect Robert Adam, on another page left behind beautiful buildings last hundreds of years. But th twentieth-century architect, Ba Spence, *left*, will leave behin him one of the great cathedra of the world, built to last thousand years or more. He shown here when his contro versial design for the ne Coventry Cathedral was accept and work began on replacing t old one destroyed by Germ bombs in the Second World Wa Sir Basil Spence has design everything from military ba racks to airport buildings and university, and his aim h always been simply: "Will it the best and most beautiful f what it has to do?" So his stru tures differ widely: one cann "spot a Spence" by its shap

Watt decided to make use of one which transmitted a powerful signal on fifty metres.

He would work on the known fact that, as we have seen, the distance and direction of a radio transmitter can be fairly easily calculated. An enemy aircraft was not a radio transmitter, but if it could be persuaded to *reflect* the wave from that transmitter back to earth again, the same process could be adapted to discover its position in the air.

But would an aeroplane reflect a sufficiently powerful signal? Would the reflected signal be strong enough to detect, analyse?

It was—and at Daventry in the English midlands, in February, 1935, radio-location was born. Eight miles away the aircraft reflected sufficient of the Daventry short-wave station's signal to the home-made apparatus on the ground, for a clear indication to be shown on the visual indicator. When the old Heyford passed overhead, the little stub of vertical line on the screen grew to its maximum. Then it shrank, till at eight and a quarter miles it vanished.

At this point in his career, Watson-Watt was superintendent of the new Radio Division at the National Physical Laboratory in Teddington. He now left this important job in order to follow up the exciting new idea of radio-location —and many people thought he was throwing away his career in pursuit of a will-o'-the-wisp. But he was to write later that he was absolutely certain he and his team would succeed and he "never doubted for a moment that everything would work out, with many delays and a few blind alleys, to an effective warning system. I believe, too, that our predominant feeling was a lively anticipation of privileged fun in playing such a fascinating game to a win which was certain, although the final score could not be estimated."

The team set up its H.Q. on a remote part of the Suffolk coast, near Orfordness. The work had to be kept secret and all sorts of cloaks were patched together to explain what all these young men were doing with their instruments and their masts; they were making a "death ray"; they were prospecting for oil; doing a dozen other improbable things. A few service personnel now joined them, but these, of course, worked in civilian clothes.

A few months after starting at Orford the team moved a mile or so away to the stately Manor of Bawdsey, to complete the work in greater secrecy. By this time, held together by the forceful and brilliant Scot, it had solved many of the problems of radio-location. The time taken for a radio wave (not one borrowed from the BBC as before, but sent out by their own miniature transmitter) to travel to an aircraft and be reflected back again was represented visually on the face of a cathode-ray tube (the screen, in fact, of a television receiver) and the length of the fluorescent green line on the face showed the distance involved. The transmitter directed its radio signal along a narrow beam—not broadcast like a normal radio transmitter, which deliberately splashes Radios One, Two and Three in all directions more or less indiscriminately—and it was a fairly simple matter to note in which direction the movable transmitting aerial was pointing and from this to see in which direction the aircraft would be found. The altering length of the fluorescent line, the changed direction of the aerial, and the rate at which these changes took place, showed which direction the aircraft was travelling, and at what speed.

By December of this year, 1935, the system was so advanced that it was decided to set up five radio-location stations on the east coast. By March of the following year, aircraft were being plotted at distances of up to seventy-five miles. The signals were sent out from masts 240 feet in the air, and these same masts, some millionths of a second later, received their reflection.

During 1936 the training of R.A.F. personnel to man these stations began, and plans were laid for another twenty stations. As the process was refined, new developments became possible: Ground-Controlled Interception could direct defending aircraft right up to an approaching enemy; searchlights could be directed on to enemy aircraft before the light beam was switched on, and then be automatically locked to that aircraft so that it was unable to escape from the beam; aircraft themselves could carry equipment which would locate enemy warships; and so on.

In 1937, with the threat of war growing imminent, Watson-Watt and his wife were sent as tourists to Germany to investigate what progress, if any, the Germans had made along the same lines. They plodded from place to place, made sketches, took photographs, fooled everyone—and for this act of bravery they deserve our heartfelt gratitude. They reported that the Germans seemed to have very little in the way of radio-locating equipment—and the war, when it came two years later, proved this correct.

1938. And now, with Watson-Watt working directly for the Air Ministry, there was twenty-four-hour-day radio-location cover of the North Sea approaches. No plane was able to approach Britain from the east without being tracked. And yet the system was still top secret and hardly anyone—least of all the Germans—knew of it.

War came—and now we may abandon the cumbersome but accurate name under which it was developed, and adopt the American "radar", that sensible shortening of "radio detection and ranging". There had been considerable American work on a similar system, and when the Battle of Britain proved beyond all doubt the effectiveness of Watson-Watt's brainchild, American teams were sent over to study it. British scientists began to make regular visits to the United States to co-ordinate development.

With the Battle of Britain a disastrous German failure, the Luftwaffe took to night bombing. It is an indication of the development and expansion of radar that whereas in the whole of December, 1940, R.A.F. night fighters shot down only two German bombers, they destroyed, in May, 1941, over a hundred.

The research establishment now moved from Bawdsey to Swanage—where it was attacked by a desperate Luftwaffe. It went on, shaken but functioning, to Malvern College, where it stayed till the end of the war (while Malvern, as a school, moved to Harrow; the happy combination, to those inside, was simply "Marrow"). To the great mass of the British public its work was a baffling secret, and when Watson-Watt was given a knighthood in 1942 the citation only hinted at the service he had rendered his country.

The war ended and Sir Robert Watson-Watt stayed on as a government scientific adviser until 1949. By this time radar had become an indispensable adjunct of civil air navigation, blind landing for aircraft and their maritime equivalent, getting ships into port in a fog. Douglas in the Isle of Man was the first harbour in the world to be equipped with radar apparatus giving a complete picture of the approaches through any fog. Since then many other ports have followed suit.

Work on applications of the radar principle is still going on, and possibly always will, with the development of new, miniature components like transistors, and of new materials, new ideas. Navigational radar, directing aircraft over hundreds of miles to within a few yards of a target, was brought to a high pitch of development during the war, making possible 1,000-bomber raids on places like Cologne. Possibilities are limitless. It could be made impossible for aircraft to collide in the air or crash into hillsides (or for cars to crash into each other). It has already been found possible to land an aircraft in zero visibility without a pilot at all, and the pilotless aircraft is no longer a silly story ("Please fasten your seat-belts, your seat-belts, your seat-belts, your seat-belts——"), but a definite probability for the future.

An exciting new development is radio-astronomy, based on exactly the same principles. Scientists tried aiming radar at the moon to check its distance and its relative movement, and were surprised at getting back a great deal more, radio-wise, than they had given; there were literally hundreds of different signals coming from outer space. It was shown that these came from stars, many of them too far away to be seen by eye or telescope: from this discovery sprang the whole new field of radio-astronomy which not only reveals great unknown regions, but is just as effective by daylight as by night.

Sir Robert Watson-Watt has been described—by some

people—as a "difficult" man, ready to burst into print on almost any subject and rightly jealous of the part he played in the development of this amazing new branch of science. There was heated controversy after the war about whether the developer of radar and his team should receive some financial recognition of their work which had been handed over gratis to both the British and American governments. After considerable acrimony, and argument as to exactly who had invented radar, a sum of £87,950 was awarded (the sort of sum that only a British government could conceive, and one wonders why they omitted the odd shillings). The team had already agreed on the size of each man's share: Sir Robert got £52,000.

Not perhaps a very large sum, for saving his country.

HAROLD MACMILLAN

Few men could be more dissimilar than the two Prime Ministers in this book: Ramsay MacDonald and Harold Macmillan.

And—*en passant*—how exasperating it is, even for Scots, that the Gaelic "Mac", "The Son-Of", should sometimes be shown before a capital letter, at others before a small, lower-case one: should, too, be represented by the mock-Gaelic of "Mc". A digression—but sub-editors have wasted years of their lives keeping the record straight.

MacDonald was born in the deepest poverty, out of wedlock, and in a small Scots village. He was almost entirely self-educated; a "self-made man". He was a Socialist.

Macmillan—with the small m—was born in affluence, wedlock and London. To a great extent we make ourselves what we are, and educate ourselves, but Macmillan did have the considerable assistance of Eton and Balliol College, Oxford. He was, and is, a Conservative.

Not that it always seemed he would remain one. He was first elected to Parliament, as Conservative Member for Stockton-on-Tees, in October, 1924. His maiden speech, several months later in the April Budget Debate, though an attack on Ramsay MacDonald and the Labour Party, was yet a hint of the more radical way he intended to think and vote in the future. There was nothing wrong with *real* Socialism, he suggested, but if MacDonald and his party could only offer "as the true Socialism, a kind of mixture, a sort of horrible political cocktail, consisting partly of the dregs of exploded economic views of Karl Marx, mixed up with a little flavour of Cobdenism, well iced by the late Chancellor of the Exchequer, and with a little ginger from the Member for Gorbals—if he thinks that this is to be the draught given to our parched throats, and that we are ready to accept it, he is very much mistaken——"

He became accepted as a promising member of the Conservative Left. He approved of Planning, as against Laissez-Faire; he even wrote, some years later, a book called *Reconstruction—A Plea for a National Policy* with a chapter in it headed "The Case For Planning".

He was, it seems fair to say, at least halfway to being a Socialist, in what he regarded as the true sense of the word, right up until the outbreak of the Second World War. The year before that he published another book, *The Middle Way*, in which he advocated all sorts of things which, in those days, were not considered Conservative Policy. "It would do nothing but good to the children of every class if the early years of life were spent in the same school." Basic foods should be organized and distributed on a large-scale, national basis; he mentioned milk, butter, margarine, cheese, eggs, bread, flour, potatoes and sugar as suitable commodities to be handled by a non-profit-making organization, though he was "under no delusion that it will be an easy matter to overcome the resistance of vested interests in the undertakings now engaged in the retail distribution of these commodities".

And the important thing was that society "be organized in such a way as to bring the economic system under conscious direction, and control, and that the increased production should be directed towards raising the standard of comfort and security of all people".

So, though he would not have used the term about himself, Harold Macmillan in 1938 was an unofficial Socialist, considerably to the Left of Centre in his Party.

The easiest thing to accuse a man of is hypocrisy, of being a turn-coat—for the simple reason that only a very stubborn or unimaginative man could go through life without changing his mind. It was easy to leap upon Ramsay MacDonald, say it about him; it should be fairly easy to say it about any one of us, though fortunately our remarks are usually off the record; it was easy to say it about Harold Macmillan, when the interlude of war ended, and he was back as a politician.

But let us go back to the beginning.

And in the case of Macmillan this means going back rather farther than our usual jumping-off spot of log-cabin or castle. To see and understand the factors which have helped make the man what he is we must go back a hundred and fifty years, to 1813, and to that Island of Arran from which Robert Bruce had come, six hundred years before, to invade his own country and go on to conquer an English king. There, on 13 September, a remarkable Scotsman was born. Daniel Macmillan saw the light of day on a small croft—and went on to found one of the great publishing enterprises of the world. But it was a really hard struggle, via apprenticeship at one-and-six-pence a week to an Irvine bookbinder, work in bookshops in Stirling, Glasgow and London, to his own bookshop and then publishing business—to die at the age of forty-five.

The firm carried on, expanded, under his sons, and the family fortune grew. Daniel's second son, who was responsible for building up the famous Macmillan educational series, was called Maurice Crawford Macmillan. He married an American girl from Indiana and to this wealthy young couple was born Maurice Harold Macmillan in 1894.

As Harold Macmillan (he seldom used the Maurice) he was sent to Eton. In the holidays he often went to Arran, his grandfather's birthplace. He must have pondered, as he looked at the tumble-down ruin on the side of a hill, just what it meant to have come from an Arran cottage to a House at Eton. His family was rich, well-connected; and unlike some of his contempories who were also rich and even better-connected, he knew one could not take this for granted. He knew, too, of the grinding poverty which had driven not only Macmillans but boatloads of other families out of Arran, out of the highlands.

He did well at Eton, still better at Balliol. He went down from the University, and straight into the First World War.

A good record with the Grenadier Guards, a Military Cross and three wounds. According to an American biographer, "While lying wounded in No-Man's-Land, he read a pocket edition of Homer, in the original text". No doubt published by Macmillan.

War over, he became A.D.C. to the Duke of Devonshire on his appointment as Governor-General of Canada.

He married the boss's daughter; Lady Dorothy, the Duke's daughter, agreed to become his wife, and they married in London in 1920. Hardly surprisingly, it was one of the major events of the London season.

And now, perhaps, publishing seemed a little tame. All those text-books his father had worked on, books in Swahili, Arabic, Hindi, Afrikaans. He did, however, become a director of the family firm.

Then with a General Election on the way, Harold Macmillan was invited to become Conservative candidate for Stockton-on-Tees. The election took place in December, 1923, and he was narrowly beaten—by only seventy-three votes—in a three-cornered fight.

A Liberal had won the seat, but with Liberal support the first British Labour Government now took office. It lasted, under Ramsay MacDonald, only until November of 1924.

And it was in this next General Election, at the end of

1924, that Macmillan took his seat for Stockton-on-Tees. He would represent that northern constituency until 1929, then, after two years in the wilderness, would come back to represent it until the 1945 Labour landslide.

As we have seen, he had definite and sometimes unconventional views. His first notable venture into foreign affairs was in 1935 when he became a loud and outspoken critic of Stanley Baldwin (who had succeeded Ramsay MacDonald) over his handling of the Abyssinian crisis. Britain had talked boldly, bravely, about imposing sanctions against Italy when she invaded: and what had been done? Nothing.

The Labour Opposition moved a Vote of Censure Division on the matter. The only Conservative to vote against the Government was Harold Macmillan. In effect, he supported the Opposition motion that "His Majesty's Government, by their lack of a resolute and straightforward foreign policy, have lowered the prestige of the country, weakened the League of Nations, imperilled peace and thereby forfeited the confidence of this House".

He interested himself greatly in social reform and was generally regarded as a man with views ahead of his time. His book on the subject had only just come out when he once again caused a flutter in foreign relations. In October, 1938, there was a by-election in Oxford. Neville Chamberlain was now Prime Minister, and the Conservative candidate, Quintin Hogg, was standing for Chamberlain's policy of "peace by negotiation" with Hitler, a procedure which would soon be called "appeasement". The Labour candidate, Dr. Lindsay, opposed it—and Macmillan shocked many people by writing to Lindsay and ending his letter with these words:

"We are faced with the urgent need for a vital effort to ensure the freedom of our country and Empire and to preserve our conception of freedom and civilization. I hope therefore that progressive opinion in Oxford, whether Liberal, Labour or Conservative, will seize the opportunity of returning you to Parliament next Tuesday."

Nevertheless, the Conservative candidate got in. It says

something for the resilience of the Party that this act of open mutiny went unpunished. There is evidence that Neville Chamberlain found him insufferable, and this is hardly surprising, for Macmillan retained his independence in everything, from advocating a sort of British New Deal like Roosevelt's, to demanding fast rearmament and the end of any sort of appeasement.

The war came, and in the crisis months of 1940 Winston Churchill replaced Chamberlain, and gave Macmillan his first ministerial appointment, as Parliamentary Secretary to the Ministry of Supply. Two years later, aged forty-eight, he became Under-Secretary of State at the Colonial Office.

From this, and with his own personal attributes and background, he was a suitable choice to be given a brand-new post at the time of the Allied landings in North-west Africa: British Minister-Resident at Allied H.Q. He handled the extremely tricky job of uniting rival French factions with consummate skill, and it was said then, and has been said since, that he should have devoted his life to foreign affairs.

He watched the signing, in 1943, of the Italian Armistice: a little later he was Acting President of the Allied Commission in Greece. And somewhat later he was back in Greece, mediating in their Civil War.

For a short time in 1945 he was Secretary of State for Air. Then, in August, the defeat of Churchill and his Government—and of the Member for Stockton-on-Tees.

But three months later he was back at a by-election, representing the constituency with which he would remain till the end of his political career. On 20 November he took his seat as Member for Bromley.

From now on he was a member of the Conservative Front Bench and a thorn in the flesh of Labour, who complained—and not without reason—that many of the brave progressive ideas of the inter-war Macmillan had vanished by 1945. But, of course, it is a very different matter being a young, unworried junior Member working out one's political philosophy from being an elder statesman committed to getting one's party into power and keeping it there. And Macmillan was not the last to discover this.

All this is too recent history for us to dwell on: others could do it far better, and soon, one hopes, somebody will. But at present there is a remarkable shortage of writing about Harold Macmillan which is not hopelessly partisan —one way or the other.

After his party's six years in Opposition he was appointed Minister of Housing in the 1951 Conservative Government, a job in which he actually improved on the large Conservative target figure of 300,000 new houses a year. He was loudly applauded, while Labour spokesmen accused him of taking over the machinery they had set up themselves, and using it less efficiently. It will be many years before we know the truth—but lots of houses were built.

From Housing he was moved at the end of 1954 to Defence, an appointment overshadowed by the newly-tested Hydrogen Bomb. A few months later, when Anthony Eden became Prime Minister on Churchill's retirement from the office, he was made Foreign Secretary. In this capacity he was present at the long-delayed signing of the Austrian Peace Treaty in Vienna on 15 May, 1955. Two months later he accompanied Eden to the Summit Conference at Geneva, where the two of them struck up such a *rapport* with their Soviet opposite numbers, Krushchev and Bulganin, that the Russians were invited to visit London.

And now, surprisingly perhaps, Eden transferred this gifted Foreign Secretary to the post of Chancellor of the Exchequer. In this role he won fame—and notoriety—for the introduction of Premium Bonds as a means of encouraging saving through gambling.

The end of that year brought the short-lived Suez campaign in which Eden tried to regain control of a nationalized Canal by invading Egypt. International pressure forced him to call off the invasion halfway and then to retire from politics—though his decision was hastened by illness. Eleven years later, many of Eden's critics ate their words.

And so Macmillan was Prime Minister—though many objected within his Party, insisted that the choice of a leader had been too secret, and that it should have been

Mr. Butler. They would say the same thing a few years later when Macmillan himself retired as P.M., through illness, and Lord Home became his successor.

He has been described, by more than one knowledgeable observer, as Britain's best peace-time Prime Minister of the twentieth century. Perhaps, so far, he has been: it is too early to judge—quite apart from the fact that a large and ominous chunk of century still lies ahead.

We can, though, be absolutely certain of one thing. There will never, ever, again be a British statesman or Prime Minister like him: he was the last of the old school. To quote an American journalist who mourned his parting from the political arena: "Harold Macmillan may be the last of the suave, courtly British statesmen; the sort of man who can turn up in Moscow wearing an astrakhan hat, or sit cross-legged talking oil with a Middle-Eastern sheik, without losing his dignity."

QUEEN ELIZABETH
THE QUEEN MOTHER

Our book begins with a young girl who sailed from England
and became Queen of Scotland. It nears its close with the
story of a Scots girl who became Queen of England.

History may some day reveal that this Queen Elizabeth
did more for her country than even that saintly creature
of the eleventh century. It is hard, within the lifetime of
the great, to draw accurate conclusions about them. But
one dares predict that in a hundred years this gracious lady
with the common touch will have been acknowledged one
of the greatest Queens Consort—perhaps the greatest—in
British history.

Yet seldom can a girl have been more surprised—or
upset—on finding herself a queen. We know now that the

accident of fate which put her husband on the throne came as a deep shock to them both. Not only did Edward VIII's younger brother have no desire to be king (and a disability which made the prospect even more appalling than the fact): the circumstance of his attaining kingship seemed at the time to have dealt a crippling blow at the whole idea of monarchy.

But within a few years the monarchy was held in as great respect as ever in its history. The shy man with the stutter had—with the help and devotion of his wife—overcome these disabilities and more, to become a national figurehead.

He was to die, tragically early, in 1952, aged only fifty-six. The country was stunned. "But all I can say," said an old, wise friend of mine when we heard the news in London, "all I can say is, I thank God it wasn't her."

Elizabeth Bowes-Lyon was born on 4 August, 1900, the ninth child and fourth daughter of the 14th Earl and the Countess of Strathmore. They were a close, devoted family who divided their life between Glamis Castle, some dozen miles north of Dundee (made notorious by Shakespeare's *Macbeth*) and St. Paul's Walden Bury, only thirty miles from London. It was at this latter home that Lady Elizabeth was born. The First World War, arriving dramatically on her fourteenth birthday, ensured that she would spend more time in the north than might otherwise have been the case: just as, a generation later, her own two young daughters would spend much of the Second World War away from London, in Windsor Castle.

Glamis has been a part of recorded Scots history since the thirteenth century—long before Shakespeare laid hand on it—and although most of the present-day structure dates from later than that, it is reasonable to assume that Lady Elizabeth's childhood home had at least as much history and tradition behind it as the homes she would some day occupy as queen. Though Glamis appears in the pages of thirteenth-century history, we know that the kings of Scotland visited it in the eleventh. Quite probably Saint Margaret did so herself. Certainly Mary, the unhappy Queen of Scots, was familiar with the place.

But from all accounts the young twentieth-century family at Glamis was far from unhappy. Life was carefree and simple. Much of it was spent out of doors.

Elizabeth Bowes-Lyon's first public engagement, if we may use the term, was at the end of February, 1922. She had been invited, aged twenty-one, to be bridesmaid at the wedding in Westminster Abbey of Princess Mary with Viscount Lascelles. It was on this occasion that she met the young Duke of York.

She can hardly have guessed that the next royal wedding in the Abbey would be her own.

But a year later they were engaged, with the king's blessing—even though this projected marriage of a Duke of York, a king's son, with a commoner, would be a most unusual occurrence. Everyone agreed the young man had made an excellent choice: the king ("a pretty and charming girl and Bertie is a very lucky fellow") agreed with the man at the factory bench. And, after all, he was only a younger son, not heir to the throne: had he been, it is probable the marriage would not have been permitted.

All the same, it gave rise to problems. The Royal Marriage Act of 1722, drafted because of the embarrassing alliances contracted by the brothers of George III, prohibited the marriage of anyone in the Succession without the Sovereign's formal consent. This had been gladly given by George V, but there was doubt as to what precedence the Duke's wife would be given.

It was not until the glittering Abbey wedding itself that it became known the new Duchess of York would share her husband's style and title.

The honeymoon was spent in England and at Glamis—and there the young Duchess developed whooping cough. "Not," as she remarked later, "a very *romantic* disease."

Relations with the king and queen, when they returned and settled into the normal life of a royal family, were happy indeed. But it was very different from the gay informality of life among the Strathmores. Formal occasions were formal indeed. George V was a fanatic over punctuality, yet he dearly loved his daughter-in-law, who made great efforts but was sometimes late by a minute. Sometimes on these occasions he would say: "You are not late, my dear. We sat down two minutes too early."

The Duke of York had been born with a distressing impediment in his speech, which made it torture for him—and often for his listeners—when he spoke in public. It must on occasion have been agonizing for his wife, but she was always there with him, smiling bravely, lending him the support, the strength, he so desperately needed. He began to have treatment for the disability, tiring treatment with long exercises in front of a mirror, and she encouraged him, made him go on with it. Slowly he improved.

In 1926—great happiness. A daughter was born; and they can hardly have dreamed that one day she would be Queen of England. But Princess Elizabeth was only seven months old when duty compelled them into undertaking a state visit to Australia and New Zealand to represent the king at the first meeting of the Australian Parliament in Canberra, the new federal capital. We are told the Duchess of York was so upset at this parting from her young daughter that the royal car had to go twice round Grosvenor Gardens on its way to Victoria Station to give her time to recover herself, feel able to face the cheering crowds on the platform.

This was the first major duty since their marriage and it was one in which the young duchess proved her worth for all time. H.M.S. *Renown* sailed on 6 January, 1927, and began a leisurely progress towards the Panama Canal and the Pacific, but there would be no leisure when they reached their destination. They knew that there was no great interest in this disappointing visit of a younger son. The Prince of Wales had visited the two dominions seven years before and been worshipped wherever he went: why was the king fobbing them off with another son, a shy young man, from all accounts, with an embarrassing stutter? It was glumly predicted that the Duke and Duchess of York would receive a polite but unenthusiastic welcome.

But this was not so. There was great enthusiasm from almost the moment they arrived—and it was almost entirely owing to the young girl at the duke's side. Hardboiled, delighted journalists pointed out that "she smiled her way straight into the hearts of the people". And not once during the most lengthy and formal functions did her face lose its "look of alert interest".

They got home again at the end of June and their young daughter had changed: she was a lady of fourteen months. They purchased a London home, 145 Piccadilly.

Three years after this triumphant return from the Pacific, Princess Margaret was born, in 1930. But by this time they had undertaken other successful tours at home and abroad on behalf of the king.

The king died in January of 1936, full of years and honour, and the Prince of Wales became King Edward VIII.

And then, overnight, life changed. Edward VIII abdicated the throne. To the shock of such an incredible happening was added the realization, for the Duke of York, that he was now king. On the morning of Thursday, 10 December, 1936, he witnessed his brother's act of abdication—and the throne was his. Never can such an honour have been less welcome.

We may never know the degree of personal shock and distress involved. The lives of both the new king and queen were changed, utterly and forever. The shy man who had had to fight so hard to undertake the tasks of a younger royal brother was now king, and his wife, who had done so much to get him through these lesser tasks, was faced with others a hundred times harder. But as Lord Halifax said in moving the traditional Humble Address in the House of Lords: "No more than the King does her Majesty the Queen stand in any need of introduction to the people's love. Her name evokes great memories in the people's history and she has already won for herself a secure and distinctive place in their affections."

And yet despite this there was delay in public recognition of this new queen consort. No one was able to imagine any woman doing the job half as well as old Queen Mary: no one could look or behave so much a queen.

But it was Queen Mary's support for her daughter-in-law and her son which helped turn the tide.

Their coronation took place on 12 May, 1937, five months after the abdication—and not many months before the war which would so drastically affect the life of the king and all his subjects. The round of royal duties was enormously multiplied while at the same time the world rushed head-long down the slope. George VI launched a great battleship named after his father.

A few weeks after the launch, Italy invaded Albania and a shudder went round the globe. But British papers carried firm reassurance: there would be no change in plans for the visit of king and queen to Canada and the United States.

The tour was a huge success, with much of the same uncertainty of the earlier Australian one (at least in the United States), triumphantly resolved as it had been on that earlier occasion.

It was in Washington that the much-quoted—possibly apocryphal—remark was made by a senator: "I don't know what kind of a king you are—but you sure pick good queens."

Only weeks after the visit ended, in the summer of 1939, war broke out. And now it was that the king and queen really established their position in the hearts of their people. The two princesses were evacuated to Windsor, but the king and his wife refused to leave London. Tirelessly they toured bombed sites, raising fervent if exhausted cheers from the survivors, men and women who had lost their all in a night. And they knew only too well that they, the royal family, were in great personal danger. Not only was Buckingham Palace itself being hit by bombs, but the Nazis, now planning to invade Britain, intended to seize the royal family as hostage.

The war, though, was won, and in the grim days of "austerity" which followed, there was happiness in the marriage of their elder daughter, now heir to the throne.

The first sign that all was not well with the king came at the end of 1948. A new tour of Australia and New Zealand had been planned, but on the advice of his doctors this was cancelled. He had gangrene in the right leg.

From now on, the queen took an even greater part in public affairs. She not only had to sustain a grievously sick husband, but she had to undertake more duties, piling them into an overcrowded programme.

During the night of 5 February, 1952, the king died.

A member of the royal household wrote later: "I never knew a woman could be so brave." Stunned by grief—for her husband, only a few hours before, had been laughing and happy—yet she rallied instantly. In the first hours of that grief she wrote letters to many, many people who had been near to him.

Her daughter was queen.

Now there was life to rebuild. She resolved not to collapse under her grief as Queen Victoria had done a century before: on the day following her husband's death she was playing with her grandchildren. And three months later she insisted on travelling to Fife to inspect the 1st Bn. Black Watch, *en route* to Korea. She was still of course in mourning, and like all royalty, in a heartbreaking, public, mourning, but she went straight through the arduous programme of farewell.

She moved to Clarence House in London. There she resides, spending only a part of the time in her Scottish Castle of Mey, the home she bought on an impulse while visiting friends near John o' Groats, in the early days of her widowhood. Even though she insists on taking a back seat, letting the spotlight fall, as it should, on her daughter, there are still so many engagements, so many tours, so many good causes to be helped, that she has little time to spend in her Scottish home.

Perhaps, with many of the cares of queenship over, she has a good life, surrounded by her loving family, her good friends. But whatever Queen Elizabeth the Queen Mother now gets from life, she has already repaid.

SIR BASIL SPENCE

There are two architects in this book (that is, if you count the Adam brothers as one). Both share not only the fact of being Scottish, but an approach to their work which is perhaps not general in the profession.

Robert Adam insisted, way back in the eighteenth century, that a house could only be designed if one took account of every fixture within it. In fact, as we know, his interest went beyond mere fixtures, he designed the furniture to go inside.

Basil Spence has the same approach. Not for him the plans of a building—with a more talented underling doing the perspectives for him—and then the fee. He takes an interest—*demands* to take interest—in everything that goes inside, whether it be Coventry Cathedral with its stained glass and its tapestry, or the furniture of Sussex University.

("If a student kicks the furniture I designed for it, he retires limping.")

But, of course, it is not for the man-sized chairs of Sussex that Basil Spence is best known, but for that great cathedral which has so splendidly and reverently replaced the one the Germans knocked down. Almost no building erected in Britain during the twentieth century has caused such a stir; and there are plenty of people to disagree with me that it is either splendid or reverent. It has been knowingly described as an *abattoir*, a super-cinema, a railway station, a factory. Though much of this criticism was made long before it was complete.

In 1951 they made the announcement: a little-known Scots architect would build a new cathedral in Coventry, raise it out of the bombed ruins of one that had stood there for six hundred years. The Coventry Cathedral Reconstruction Committee had offered a first prize of £2,000 for the best design. There had been two hundred and nineteen entries, and the announcement of the winner's name was made in August, 1951. The successful architect—still plain Mr. Spence—was out of his native Edinburgh seeing a client. It was some time before he learnt the good news.

From this day on his future was assured. Not that he had been anything but a good architect before then—he was already forty-four when he won the prize—for he had built lovingly and well a number of structures which included the Viceroy's house in New Delhi, and the hugely successful "Sea and Ships" exhibition for the Festival of Britain, on the south bank of the Thames. But not all good architects are rich; and Spence was not.

Nor would he be for a number of years. Perversely, his controversial designs for the cathedral frightened off a number of clients, before the real beauty of it earned him many more. Today they beat a path to his several doors, for his one small office has multiplied. The latest structure to start rising at Sir Basil's command is the—almost equally controversial—Knightsbridge Barracks for the Household Cavalry in London. It will ultimately loom two hundred and seventy feet above the town and cost £3 million. The architect's fee for this is the usual six per cent, or £180,000, which is an attractive sum of money. But Spence had been waiting ten years since his design was accepted, while various British governments froze and unfroze it. Until the building is complete, he and his associates do not receive anything like the full sum. Life for an architect, particularly on this scale, can be very, very frustrating. A year's work can be undone by the smudge of a ball-point pen in Westminster—and Spence's barrack ("I had to think a bit about getting that horse upstairs for mess parties——") is not the only project to have been thus interfered with.

But Basil Spence, the smiling Scot, is nobody's fool. He is unlikely to collapse like his Adam predecessor in the rubble of an Adelphi scheme.

His father, an Orcadian, was a member of the Indian Civil Service. He was accordingly born, in 1907, in Bombay. Old Mr. Spence's illness brought the family home to Edinburgh, but not before the boy had had a chance to assimilate the feel of India, to marvel at the Ajanta cave paintings on their island in Bombay harbour, at the Taj Mahal, the mountains. He even managed to win a few prizes in painting competitions for young people.

(His unusual knowledge of India made him critical, later, of Corbusier's Indian work: Chandigarh, and the town planning schemes in the Punjab, were too European.)

Back in Edinburgh, with painting still in mind, he attended George Watson's College by day, evening classes at night. Slowly his interest shifted from painting, through sculpture, to architecture. He got a scholarship to the Edinburgh School of Architecture—and now the road was clear. He also needed to travel, to see the work of other men in other lands, but this at first was not so easy.

He found, though, that his unusual talents earned him money in unusual ways: he had the rare ability of being able to draw at speed a really good perspective of a structure, seeing it clothed in its bricks and mortar and ferroconcrete as soon as he laid eyes on plan and elevation. He was soon doing these, for a consideration, on behalf of qualified architects.

To this day, when many other architects are unable or unwilling to produce accurate and graceful perspective drawings of their work, and hand the task over to others, Spence insists on doing his own.

Soon he could afford to travel, and it was in April, 1925, that his architectural journeying brought him to York, and its minster. Spellbound, the young man tiptoed into the south transept, stared up at the Five Sisters window.

It was a turning-point in his life. "I saw then," he wrote later, "that a cathedral was the highest expression of architecture. I resolved that one day, if I could, I must design a cathedral."

Twenty-five years were to go by before the announcement of a competition for the Coventry design. In the meantime there was work in the office of Sir Edwin Lutyens, designing part of the Viceroy's house in New Delhi. Like Robert Adam, he designed some of the furniture, in particular the Viceregal throne.

By the age of twenty-four—in 1931—he was in practice on his own, designing Scottish houses. Seven years later he was deeply involved in the Glasgow Exhibition which James Lithgow (on another page) had done much to arrange; he collaborated in the design, feeling his way with the new materials which were so altering exhibition architecture: glass, plasterboard, chromium.

The Second World War came, and his work had to stop while he fought in Europe. This, too, had a profound effect on him, for he noticed that all men at times of fear and danger turned to a religion they might not openly acknowledge at other times: in other words, a church, a cathedral, was not just a club for a few, half of them hypocrites—it fulfilled a real, perhaps unspoken, need.

War over, he worked on the "Britain Can Make It" Exhibition in 1946. There were British Industries Fairs at Olympia in London, and in 1950 his big "Sea and Ships" pavilion.

And now, though he had considerable fame, he was in danger of being cast in the permanent role of "the man who does all those exhibitions and things". It was from this that the Coventry competition rescued him. He sent for the leaflet setting out conditions, then paid his first visit to the town.

He was moved by the ruins of the old cathedral. Instantly, he knew that his own, new one would have to grow organically out of the old, would have to incorporate it.

He took a competition leaflet out of his pocket, made his first sketch of the new Coventry Cathedral on the back.

Back in Edinburgh, he got down to work. Somehow, it had become the most exciting, most worthwhile thing he had ever done. The ideas poured out of him—the great west window of clear glass, through which people would be able to look and see the whole way down the nave to the altar. And at the altar, where light must be reflected, made to shimmer, and where the echo of the great building's acoustic must be controlled, he sketched a tapestry. It would be one of the largest ever made: its theme would be "Christ the Redeemer".

His work, his drawings, went on for eight months; and if ever he questioned the wisdom of giving up all this time for what, after all, was only a competition, with the comparatively small prize of £2,000 at the other end—even assuming he won—he put it out of his mind. Gone were ephemeral exhibitions. Now he had an opportunity which comes to few men indeed. He would be designing, building, not for today and tomorrow, but for five hundred years. For a start.

And so his entry was submitted, and so, months later, he found out he had won. And so, Coventry Cathedral now stands proudly dominating its battered, rebuilt city.

So much for Coventry Cathedral: if you haven't seen it, try and do so. But you can take your time. If the nuclear holocaust is staved off, you can wait five hundred years.

But the cathedral, as far as we are concerned here, is but an introduction to the man, the man who is leaving his mark all over Britain, so that in years to come people will thumb their guide-books—possibly printed in Chinese—and ponder the work of this great man of the mid-twentieth century. They will look, perhaps, and wonder, just as we do when we survey the work of Sir Christopher Wren or Robert Adam.

For there will be many of these landmarks—and it may be hard for our descendants to see a unifying thread between them. Spence has always regarded himself as the servant of the man or body which commissions him: he is suspicious of people who try to put their own hallmark on everything. There is not the slightest reason why Coventry Cathedral, Glasgow Airport, the British Embassy in Rome, Thorne House in London, or the Knightsbridge Barracks should have anything in common at all—except that they should be as perfect structures for their role as Basil Spence has been able to design.

Architecture, in short, should be a background for life; not a foreground. A structure should be perfectly suited to its purpose, and at the same time aesthetically pleasing. Viewed from this Spence-ian standpoint, it would be monstrous if Coventry Cathedral and the Horse Guards Barracks should have anything obvious in common.

After all, nobody wants to get a horse up the spire.

Would the Cathedral look the same if he re-designed it today?

It would be considerably altered. (One wonders how the cathedral designers of six hundred years ago felt as, old and lame, they saw the walls go up.) Coventry would be simpler and broader. The windows would be narrower.

As proof of this, Sir Basil points to the Cathedral's Chapel of Unity. He designed it in 1958, seven years after the rest —and it is different. We may not agree as to how different it is, but we can take Spence's word for it that it would have looked very different had he drawn the plans back in 1951.

Probably it will be this ability to change and not mind, this reluctance to stamp work with a hall-mark, to say "Look—that's a *Spence* up there; the work has its own distinguishing marks, its characteristics, can't you see?" that will ensure it lasts. Ensures that the work of this neat, bearded Scotsman endures for all those foreign visitors with their oddly printed guide-books in the centuries to come.

BIBLIOGRAPHY

SAINT MARGARET
Keary, M. R.   *Great Scotswomen* (Maclehose) 1933

SIR WILLIAM WALLACE
Fergusson, J.   *Wallace* (Maclehose) 1938
Murison, A. F.   *Sir William Wallace (Famous Scots Series)* (Oliphant) 1898

KING ROBERT BRUCE
Barrow, G. W. S.   *Robert Bruce* (Eyre & Spottiswoode) 1965
Mackie, J. D.   *History of Scotland (Pelican Original)* (Penguin Books) 1964

MARY, QUEEN OF SCOTS
Morrison, N. B.   *Mary, Queen of Scots* (Studio Vista) 1960
Sitwell, E.   *The Queens and the Hive* (Macmillan) 1962
Linklater, E.   *Mary, Queen of Scots* (new edition, Dobson) 1952

JOHN NAPIER
Napier, M.   *Memoirs of John Napier of Merchiston* (Blackwood & Cadell) 1834
Knott, C. G., ed.   *Tercentenary Memorial Volume* (Longmans) 1915
Holmyard, E. J.   *British Scientists* (Dent) 1951

THE COUNTESS OF NITHSDALE
Buchan, J.   *A Book of Escapes and Hurried Journeys* (Nelson) 1937
Tayler, H.   *Lady Nithsdale and her Family* (Drummond) 1939

ROBERT ADAM
Sitwell, S.   *British Architects and Craftsmen* (Batsford) 1948
Swarbrick, J.   *Robert Adam and his Brothers* (Batsford) 1915
Milne, J. Lees-   *The Age of Adam* (Batsford) 1947

JAMES WATT
Smiles, S.   *Lives of the Engineers,* 5 vols. (Murray) 1874
Hart, I. B.   *James Watt* (Weidenfeld & Nicholson) 1963
Dickinson, H. W., and Vowles, H.   *James Watt and the Industrial Revolution* (British Council: Longmans) 1948

SIR HENRY RAEBURN
Orpen, Sir W., ed.   *The Outline of Art* (revised edition, Newnes) 1961

THOMAS TELFORD
Smiles, S.   *Lives of the Engineers,* 5 vols. (Murray) 1874
Meynell, L.   *Thomas Telford* (Bodley Head) 1957

SIR WALTER SCOTT
Pearson, H.   *Walter Scott* (Methuen) 1954
Davie, D.   *The Heyday of Sir Walter Scott* (Routledge) 1961
Lockhart, J. G.   *Life of Sir Walter Scott (Everyman series)* (Dent) 1957

LORD BYRON
Marchand, L. A.   *Byron: a Biography* (Murray) 1958
Read, Sir H.   *Byron (Writers and their Works series)* (British Council: Longmans) 1956

SIR JAMES YOUNG SIMPSON

Gordon, H. L.   *Sir James Young Simpson and Chloroform* (Unwin) 1897

Simpson, E. B.   *Sir James Young Simpson* (Oliphant) 1896

DAVID LIVINGSTONE

Livingstone, D.   *Livingstone's Private Journals* (Chatto & Windus) 1960

WILLIAM MCGONAGALL

McGonagall, W.   *Poetic Gems selected from the Works of William McGonagall, Poet and Tragedian* (David Winter & Son, Dundee) 1890

ANDREW CARNEGIE

Carnegie, A.   *Autobiography* (Constable) 1920

MARY SLESSOR

Keary, M. R.   *Great Scotswomen* (Maclehose) 1933

O'Brien, B.   *She had a Magic: Mary Slessor* (Cape) 1958

ROBERT LOUIS STEVENSON

Furnas, J. C.   *Voyage to Windward: the Life of Robert Louis Stevenson* (Faber) 1952

Elwin, M.   *The Strange Case of Robert Louis Stevenson* (Macdonald) 1950

KEIR HARDIE

Cockburn, J.   *The Hungry Heart* (Jarrolds) 1956

Fyfe, H. H.   *Keir Hardie (Great Lives series)* (Duckworth) 1935

SIR JAMES BARRIE

Green, R. L.   *J. M. Barrie (Bodley Head Monographs)* (Bodley Head) 1960

SIR HARRY LAUDER

Lauder, Sir H.   *Roamin' in the Gloamin'* (Hutchinson) 1928

MARY GARDEN

Garden, M., and Biancolli, L.   *Mary Garden's Story* (Joseph) 1952

Lockspeiser, E.   *Debussy, His Life and Mind* (Cassell) 1965

LORD TWEEDSMUIR (JOHN BUCHAN)

Buchan, J.   *Memory Hold the Door* (Hodder & Stoughton) 1940

Buchan, S. C.   *John Buchan, by his Wife and Friends* (Hodder & Stoughton) 1947

SIR ALEXANDER FLEMING

Maurois, A.   *The Life of Sir Alexander Fleming,* translated Hopkins (Cape) 1959

SIR JAMES LITHGOW

Reid, J. M.   *James Lithgow, Master of Work* (Hutchinson) 1964

JOHN LOGIE BAIRD

Moseley, S. A.   *John Baird* (Odhams) 1952

LORD REITH

Reith, J. C. W.   *Into the Wind* (Hodder & Stoughton) 1949

Reith, J. C. W.   *Wearing Spurs* (Hutchinson) 1966

HAROLD MACMILLAN

Macmillan, H.   *Winds of Change, 1914-1939* (Macmillan) 1966

Hughes, E.   *Portrait of a Politician* (Allen & Unwin) 1962

INDEX